T0392097

A Moral Theory of Liveliness

A Moral Theory of Liveliness

A Secular Interpretation of African Life Force

KIRK LOUGHEED

OXFORD
UNIVERSITY PRESS

Oxford University Press is a department of the University of Oxford.
It furthers the University's objective of excellence in research, scholarship,
and education by publishing worldwide. Oxford is a registered trade mark of
Oxford University Press in the UK and in certain other countries.

Published in the United States of America by Oxford University Press
198 Madison Avenue, New York, NY 10016, United States of America.

© Kirk Lougheed 2025

All rights reserved. No part of this publication may be reproduced, stored in a retrieval system, transmitted, used for text and data mining, or used for training artificial intelligence, in any form or by any means, without the prior permission in writing of Oxford University Press, or as expressly permitted by law, by license or under terms agreed with the appropriate reprographics rights organization. Inquiries concerning reproduction outside the scope of the above should be sent to the Rights Department, Oxford University Press, at the address above.

You must not circulate this work in any other form
and you must impose this same condition on any acquirer.

CIP data is on file at the Library of Congress

ISBN 9780197781982

DOI: 10.1093/9780197782019.001.0001

Printed by Marquis Book Printing, Canada

The manufacturer's authorized representative in the EU for product safety is
Oxford University Press España S.A., Parque Empresarial San Fernando de Henares,
Avenida de Castilla, 2 – 28830 Madrid (www.oup.es/en).

To the memory of my mother,
Diane Rose Lougheed (1954–2023)

Contents

Preface	ix
Chapter Summaries	xi
1. African Ethics, Life Force, and the Motivation for this Book	1

PART I. SETTING THE STAGE: THE AFRICAN CONCEPTION OF LIFE FORCE

2. The Legacy of Placide Tempels' *Bantu Philosophy*	17
3. Contemporary Accounts of Life Force and Moral Theory	36

PART II. LIVELINESS AS A MORAL THEORY

4. Liveliness as Secular Life Force	61
5. Liveliness as a Moral Theory	71
6. Further Implications of Liveliness as a Moral Theory	93

PART III. LIVELINESS AND ALTERNATIVE AFRICAN MORAL THEORIES

7. Liveliness and Normative Personhood	121
8. Liveliness and Harmonious Relationships	138

PART IV. LIVELINESS, METAETHICS, AND MEANING

9. The Metaethical Grounds of Life Force	165
10. The Metaethical Grounds of Liveliness	185

viii CONTENTS

11. Liveliness and Meaning in Life 204
12. Conclusion 216

Bibliography 221
Index 235

Preface

This book marks roughly the last five or so years of my thinking about the African philosophical tradition. Though normative theories based on ideas from the African tradition like personhood and harmony had been systematically developed in monographs, I noticed that life force, or vitalism, lacked similar treatments. Though work on vitalism appears in books on African religious ethics, I did not think there was a systematic treatment of it such that it could be clearly compared to other African normative theories, in addition to some of the main Anglo-American ones. Furthermore, there has been no systematic treatment of the concept of liveliness, the naturalistic version of life force. This book therefore marks the first extended treatment of liveliness as a normative theory which is based on African life force. Though primarily intended to be a secular theory and therefore palatable to philosophers around the globe, I believe that much of what I say in this book also applies to the more metaphysically thick notion of life force.

There are many people to thank for helping to bring the book into existence. I received feedback on some of the manuscript from Ada Agada, Aribiah Attoe, Brian Ballard, Rebecca Chan, Joshua Maffuccio, Bernard Matolino, Thaddeus Metz, Tony Oyowe, Michael Robinson, and John Roman. Parts of this project were presented at the Fifth International Conference on Philosophy and Meaning in Life (June 2023), the Canadian Society for the Study of Practical Ethics (May 2023), and the California Ethics Workshop (November 2023), among other, less formal work-in-progress groups at the University of Pretoria, Toronto Metropolitan University, and LCC International University. I am grateful to the audience members at these sessions, and I apologize to anyone I missed. I would also like to thank the following journals and their editorial teams for providing permissions for the following papers to be included in various degrees in the book:

- (2024). African Liveliness as a Secular Moral Theory: Problems and Prospects. *The Monist* 107(3): 225–236.
- (forthcoming) Unfriendly Cases for Metz's Modal Relational Moral Theory. *Social Theory & Practice.*

X PREFACE

- (2024). Liveliness as a Theory of Meaning in Life. *Journal of the American Philosophical Association* 10(4): 797–813.
- (2022). Molefe on the Value of Community for Personhood. *South African Journal of Philosophy* 41(1): 28–36.

There are three philosopher friends I would like to especially thank. Brian Ballard and his family facilitated an informal writing-retreat for me in sunny California, which provided me with a block of time to review the entire manuscript. Liz Jackson (and her husband, Alex, and son, Asher) have been a source of encouragement, especially for dealing with the challenges that come with the profession. Finally, in early 2024 Thaddeus Metz hosted me in Johannesburg, where I was able to meet and converse with colleagues I had only known via email up to that point. This book was written during a personally challenging time in my life, and I do not think these individuals realize how helpful they were in getting me to think of other things, including the writing of this book.

LCC International University is also owed thanks for providing me with the time to work on this project, including significant release from teaching. This was also made possible by a research grant from the Council for Christian Colleges & Universities. I would also like to thank my editor at Oxford University Press, Peter Ohlin, for providing the opportunity to publish this book and to give African philosophy a global platform. Thanks also to Alex Rouch for her efforts in the production process, and especially to Rick Delaney for masterful work copyediting. Thanks are also owed to two anonymous referees. Finally, thanks to my research assistant, Viktoryia Dobkina, for help with the bibliography and for compiling the index.

This book is dedicated to the memory of my mother, Diane Rose Lougheed (1954–2023), who exhibited liveliness in many different ways, but especially in the care of her family.

Kirk Lougheed
Assistant Professor of Philosophy and Research Associate in Philosophy
LCC International University/University of Pretoria

Chapter Summaries

Chapter 1: African Ethics, Life Force, and the Motivation for This Book serves to introduce the reader to the main themes of the project, in addition to the contours of the book. The first issue I address is what counts as African philosophy. I argue that whether an idea counts as African is a matter of degree. Ideas that have been salient in Africa for an extended period of time, more so than in other places, should count as African. This means that whether an idea is African is a matter of degree, in addition to implying that an idea need not be exclusive to the continent in order to count as African. After outlining some challenges for this definition, I suggest simply taking African philosophy to refer to ideas salient in the writings of contemporary indigenous African philosophers. I then briefly explain that the normative conception of personhood and accounts that focus on harmonious relationships are the two streams that have dominated contemporary African moral philosophy, thereby providing some of the motivation for an alternative in this book. I observe that a comprehensive development of life force as a secular theory has not yet been attempted. I submit that the theory I spell out in this book should be treated as a serious rival not only to other African moral theories but also to other moral theories on a global stage, including those that have dominated Western thought. I conclude that my primary objective is to construct the strongest possible account of liveliness as a moral theory, not to argue that such a theory is in fact true. The description offered in this book will necessarily include reasons to think the theory is true, but this is incidental to my main goal of offering the strongest and most plausible description of it.

Part I: Setting the Stage: The African Conception of Life Force

Chapter 2: The Legacy of Placide Tempels' Bantu Philosophy introduces the reader to the work of Placide Tempels, who was the first European to identify life force, in his work *Bantu Philosophy*. He surmised that Bantu peoples believed that literally everything was imbued with imperceptible energy and

xii CHAPTER SUMMARIES

that the goal of life is to increase that force. However, the legacy of Tempels on African philosophy is fraught. On the one hand, he was sanctioned by his church for attributing a deeper and coherent set of beliefs to an African people than many at that time typically thought them capable of forming. On the other hand, though his work was initially received positively by some scholars, as time wore on, numerous African thinkers began to question it. Tempels' work was an instance of ethnophilosophy, and a poor one at that, given the numerous overgeneralizations. Ethnophilosophy is misguided in taking folk beliefs and culture to represent a system worthy of philosophical study, while simultaneously lacking conceptual clarity and argumentative rigour. It is no surprise, then, that Tempels' work is hardly as sophisticated as what one finds in the Western or Anglo-American philosophical canon. Underlying these criticisms is the view that philosophy ought to be universal, which means it should be detached from culture. In this chapter, I appeal to the work of Edwin Etieyibo in an attempt to show that the debate between particularists and universalists is at least partially misguided. Ideas do not arise out of nowhere in a vacuum. They are necessarily tied to a culture, at least to some degree. However, this does not mean that an idea or concept that necessarily arises can potentially be universal. In some sense, this book is an attempt to see whether ideas about life force are universalizable, at least when it comes to formulating a normative theory. I therefore endorse a moderate view between the particularists and universalists. However, I conclude by emphasizing that the reader need not accept my methodological approach to African philosophy in order to benefit from the book. In the next chapter I outline contemporary descriptions of life force primarily from African exponents and therefore I do not rely on Tempels' work in my theorizing about life force. Finally, regardless of the legitimacy of the origin of the theory I present, it can be evaluated in its own right by way of comparison with other African and global normative ethical theories.

Chapter 3: Contemporary Accounts of Life Force and Moral Theory summarizes the contemporary literature on life force as found mostly in the writings of indigenous Africans. There is widespread agreement about the main features of life force, at least as it is described among its academic exponents. These features include life force as the most important value in life; the interconnectedness of everything that exists; the African chain of being; and other ideas about life, death, epistemology, and how to control force. I suggest that, although one rarely finds in this literature explicit normative principles based on life force, it is relatively easy to identify a number of them. After my description of life force, I therefore point to theories of moral status and right action that can be straightforwardly identified based on life force. One such theory of right action says, roughly, that an action is right inasmuch as it promotes and protects the life force in oneself and others, and wrong when it degrades it. I conclude the chapter by observing that though there is a thread of thought on life force that can be traced in the continental European tradition, in addition to versions of animism found in other indigenous cultures, my focus will be on accounts of life force as found in the contemporary African literature.

Part II: Liveliness as a Moral Theory

Chapter 4: Liveliness as Secular Life Force explains the secular conception of life force called liveliness that I will use for the rest of the book. Liveliness is a force, not a substance, and is associated with health, creativity, reproduction, courage, etc. A lack or decrease of liveliness is represented by disease, weakness, destruction, etc. I argue that these features of liveliness and its lack so strongly accord with most of our intuitions that I do not need to offer a more complete metaphysical picture of liveliness. However, I gesture at possible connections between work in African metaphysics and panpsychism for those who desire a more complete metaphysical framework for liveliness. This chapter therefore explains the transition from life force to liveliness in order to exclusively focus on liveliness as a moral theory.

Chapter 5: Liveliness as a Moral Theory develops an entirely secular and naturalistic moral theory based on life force, which I call liveliness. One version of liveliness is teleological in saying that the goal of morality is to increase liveliness. Alternatively, a deontological version of liveliness says that a person has a dignity that must be respected either in virtue of possessing liveliness or having the capacity for it. I then test these different versions against various widespread and important African and global moral intuitions. Thaddeus Metz believes that liveliness is susceptible to problems associated with welfarism, that it cannot explain why plural voting is wrong, that it does not motivate reconciliatory justice well, that it cannot make clear why certain types of racial segregation are inappropriate, and finally, that it does not show why lying is wrong in itself. I demonstrate that while such worries might apply to teleological versions of liveliness, contra Metz, they do not apply with equal force to deontological versions. Deontological liveliness

xiv CHAPTER SUMMARIES

can explain almost all of the African moral intuitions, and it can explain all of the global intuitions. Though I try to leave open different versions of liveliness, my preferred approach for the rest of the book is to work with deontological versions of it. The normative theory of liveliness has therefore passed one significant test in being able to account for important African and global intuitions.

Chapter 6: Further Implications of Liveliness as a Moral Theory continues to develop the moral theory of liveliness by critically comparing it to a well-known normative theory from the Anglo-American tradition before turning to address some objections. Specifically, I examine how a prominent version of consequentialism in the form of utilitarianism addresses difficult counterexamples. I begin by briefly explaining the basic idea behind utilitarianism. I then turn to examine some of the classic counterexamples to utilitarianism that involve sacrificing an innocent person to save a group of people. I argue that both teleological liveliness and deontological liveliness have an easier time issuing the correct verdict in these cases. I then turn to explore the possibility of developing liveliness as a two-stage utilitarian theory, and then as a hybrid theory that incorporates both teleological and deontological elements. I then respond to two objections to appealing to liveliness as a moral theory, first in that it entails welfarism and second that it is overly anthropocentric. To conclude, I explore the strengths and weaknesses of an account of dignity or human rights grounded in the capacity for liveliness. This chapter completes my exploration of the ways that liveliness can be developed as a moral theory.

Part III: Liveliness and Alternative African Moral Theories

Chapter 7: Liveliness and Normative Personhood explores how liveliness fares when compared to the influential normative African theory based on personhood. I begin by explaining the influential Menkiti–Gyekye debate on African normative personhood. For Ifeanyi Menkiti, the community is what matters, not the individual. Kwame Gyekye gives equal moral worth to the community and the individual. Menkiti wants to say that humans are by nature social, leaving no room for individual rights. Gyekye, on the other hand, affirms that humans are social, but also that they are rational and autonomous by nature, and he thereby makes room for individual rights. Motsamai

Molefe argues that community is not essential for developing personhood. However, I suggest that this leads to an unpalatable dilemma that cannot be avoided for personhood. At this juncture the astute reader will have observed that it ultimately does not matter how one interprets the Menkiti–Gyekye debate nor does it matter on which version of personhood they settle. If the community is essential for personhood, then counterintuitive trade-offs between the individual and the community follow. If it is not essential for personhood, then at best the role of community in personhood can be said to be unclear. While I do not take this discussion to constitute a decisive blow to proponents of personhood, it bodes well for deontological liveliness (all else being equal), because it is not subject to the same worry. That deontological liveliness posits that people are valuable inasmuch as they are lively or have the capacity for liveliness explains why individuals do not need to forfeit opportunities to increase their liveliness for the sake of the community (provided those pursuits are respectful).

Chapter 8: Liveliness and Harmonious Relationships examines how liveliness compares to the strain in African ethics focused on harmonious relationships. Teleological harmony represents the most common approach to African normative ethics, at least among its academic exponents. These views emphasize harmonious relationships as the end that must be sought above all else. A significant problem with these views is that they fail to account for human rights. They cannot justify acting in self-defence or in the defence of others, when doing so would create more disharmony. They also cannot always justify creating disharmony based on a person's past wrong actions. Thaddeus Metz's moral relational theory nicely avoids these objections by instead placing value on a person's capacity for harmonious relationships, or friendliness. Deontological liveliness also avoids the worries associated with teleological liveliness. However, after outlining Metz's theory in more detail, I suggest that it faces some difficult counterexamples in the existence of possible scenarios where it seems to issue the intuitively wrong moral verdict. After analyzing these cases in more detail, the bad news for the moral theory of liveliness is that this chapter does not provide sufficient reasons for holding it superior to Metz's moral relational theory. However, the good news is that the chapter does not show the converse, either, offering little reason to think Metz's theory should be preferred to liveliness. I submit that this in itself adds to the case that liveliness ought to be considered as a contender for the best African moral theory on offer.

xvi CHAPTER SUMMARIES

Part IV: Liveliness, Metaethics, and Meaning

Chapter 9: The Metaethical Grounds of Life Force begins by explaining that there is a dearth of literature on metaethics in contemporary African philosophy. What one can find are attempts to move from claims about metaphysics to normativity. Though I believe that in general nothing normative follows from metaphysics, this is not true with respect to the existence of God. If God exists, this will have a significant impact on normativity. This leads me to explore the extent to which, if at all, life force is compatible with Divine Command Theory. I argue that if Robert Adams' wide conception of what counts as a divine command is correct, then life force can indeed be grounded by Divine Command Theory. However, the Euthyphro Dilemma is a serious challenge to it, and claiming that life force itself is the ethical grounds does not successfully avoid this challenge. I conclude by exploring Abraham's Dilemma, and suggest it may be easier for life force to navigate than Divine Command Theory. My work in this chapter is exploratory and should be taken as an invitation for philosophers who might defend life force to think more carefully about the metaethical architecture it requires to succeed.

Chapter 10: The Metaethical Grounds of Liveliness explores possible realist metaethical grounds for liveliness. The ideal observer theory could supply such grounds if the judgements of the observer turned out to support liveliness. However, I suggest that epistemic challenges levelled against Divine Command Theory apply with more force to the ideal observer, and so I do not endorse it. Instead, I suggest that the most promising metaethical theory for liveliness is ethical intuitionism. I outline a version of it as located in the work of Michael Huemer, who holds that ethical claims can be directly apprehended. This is a type of non-inferential knowledge that does not need evidence in order to be justified. I claim that this theory can be used to ground liveliness because at least some of the truth claims of liveliness are known by intuition. Even if this is incorrect, it can still support liveliness provided moral judgements supporting liveliness ultimately rest upon ethical intuitions. I further argue that this account is consistent with metaphysical naturalism and the fact that it is a theory about moral knowledge should not be trivialized as insignificant. Though I focus on using available theories in the Anglo-American tradition, it is highly likely that there are resources in the African tradition that can be appealed to in order to establish unique African metaethical theories. This is all the more reason to believe that this discussion is just the beginning for African metaethical ethics.

Chapter 11: Liveliness and Meaning in Life develops a secular theory of meaning in life that says that a life is more meaningful the more it promotes liveliness in others and in oneself. Thaddeus Metz believes that this theory has difficulty accommodating two sets of intuitions. Metz claims that a liveliness theory of meaning cannot explain why pursuing knowledge because it is intrinsically valuable can confer meaning on a life, nor can it explain a similar claim regarding the value of progress. I argue that a solution to this problem can be found in other parts of Metz's own work. Elsewhere he suggests that African theories of meaning should also consider existential needs beyond just the social and biological. Pursuing knowledge or progress for its own sake is an existential need that can contribute to a person's self-realization and thereby can confer meaning on their life. But an accomplishment that merits admiration and esteem plausibly increases a person's liveliness. So, liveliness can explain how pursuing knowledge and progress can confer meaning on a person's life once such pursuits are recognized as an existential need. Finally, I conclude that, contra Metz, it is reasonable to think that the knowledge that would increase one's liveliness is constitutive of it. This is because the sort of knowledge that is valuable will be closely connected to a person's self-realization. My conclusions here are tentative, and more work remains to be done exploring the potential differences with respect to meaning between traditional life force and secular liveliness. As it stands, I have shown that there are reasonable responses to Metz's objections to the liveliness theory of meaning in life and as such it merits consideration among both African theories of meaning and globally better-known alternatives.

Chapter 12: Conclusion wraps up the book by summarizing my main conclusions. I also suggest that possible next steps include not only adding the theory of liveliness to the list of long-standing Anglo-American moral theories, but also to include it in even larger comparative evaluations. By this I mean it should be considered as a moral theory alongside moral theories from other regions of the global south such as Latin American, in addition to those found in Eastern thought. Given the extremely small probability of any single philosopher mastering a truly global philosophical canon, this project must become a group effort. Philosophy as conducted in the Western world has recently taken its first steps towards becoming a truly global discipline. While this is commendable, much work remains to be done. My hope is that this book will serve as an invitation to a global moral philosophy in particular, and a global philosophy in general.

1

African Ethics, Life Force, and the Motivation for this Book

1.1 Introduction

The main purpose of this book is to develop a normative moral theory based on what is known in African philosophy as 'life force' or 'vital force' or 'vitality'. This is a kind of imperceptible divine energy imbued in literally everything, including both animate and inanimate objects (e.g., Mbiti 1975, Magesa 1997 Bujo 1997, Kasenene 1994). This concept is typically grounded in the robust ontology of the monotheistic religion known as African Traditional Religion (see Lougheed, Molefe, and Metz 2024; Mbiti 1975; Metz and Molefe 2021; Wiredu 1998). I seek to decouple the key ethical insights to be found in life force from its religious ontology, and thereby to develop a secular theory that is consistent with metaphysical naturalism. For the sake of clarity and ease, I will call the secular version of life force, *liveliness*.[1] It is my hope that the theory I develop in this book, which is really a family of theories, will be considered as a legitimate competitor to the African moral theories that focus on normative personhood (e.g., Menkiti 1984, 2004; Molefe 2019; Ikuenobe 2006) or harmonious relationships (Metz 2022a, Tutu 1999). More ambitiously, in the future I would like to see this theory taken seriously as a global competitor to better known normative ethical theories found in the Anglo-American philosophical tradition such as consequentialism, deontology, and virtue theory.

The title of this book is somewhat misleading, because I will not be developing one unique moral theory of liveliness. Instead, I take myself to be exploring the best possible moral theories that can arise from liveliness. This includes theories of moral value and of right action that can be classified as teleological or deontological (see Part II). Where relevant, I distinguish

---

[1] As far as I can tell, Thaddeus Metz was the first person to use 'liveliness' to explicitly distinguish it as a secular theory (2012, 25).

A Moral Theory of Liveliness. Kirk Lougheed, Oxford University Press. © Kirk Lougheed 2025.
DOI: 10.1093/9780197782019.003.0001

between these theories, but in other places I refer to a singular moral theory of liveliness for simplicity and ease of prose. I believe that pluralizing the title of this book risks creating even more confusion.

The secondary purpose of this book is to explore relevant topics in metaethics and meaning, themes that have not been explored to the same extent as normative theories in contemporary African philosophy. I hope to show that there are plausible moral realist grounds for the normative theory of liveliness, in addition to a credible objectivist theory of meaning in life grounded in liveliness. In doing so, I aim to spur more work on these topics in the African literature.

While this book will be of interest to ethicists who are already familiar with the African philosophical tradition, it is also designed to be accessible to those who are unfamiliar with it. Part of the reason for this is that so far as I am aware, this work constitutes one of the most detailed attempts at systematically developing life force qua moral theory, moving beyond the mere description of life force that other philosophers and theologians (not to mention social scientists) have tended to offer of it to date. The majority of this book will therefore be intelligible to those unfamiliar with the African moral tradition. My survey of the concept of life force in Part I, my subsequent development of it as a secular theory in Part II, and my comparison of it to other African theories in Part III, presupposes no serious background in African philosophy.

I will say more about this below, but it is worth acknowledging from the outset that readers familiar with the work of Thaddeus Metz, including his *A Relational Moral Theory: African Ethics in and beyond the Continent* (2022), will notice some structural similarities between his book and this one. This similarity is indeed intentional, and I readily acknowledge that Metz's work in African philosophy, especially his methodology, has been influential in my own thinking. I believe that the structure of *A Relational Moral Theory*, including the topics and the order in which they are covered, is an excellent way to develop a normative moral theory and demonstrate its application.[2] Furthermore, in 'Chapter 5: Vital Force' of *A Relational Moral Theory*, Metz offers one of the first systematic explanations of a secular ethic based on life force, ultimately concluding that "[a]lthough an appeal to liveliness as the ground of a moral theory deserves much more attention than it has received

---

[2] One noticeable difference is that I will not attempt to apply my theory to the same vast array of topics in applied ethics, though I hope to do so in future projects.

from moral philosophers, professional ethicists, and related thinkers around the world [. . .] it is vulnerable to serious counterexamples" (Metz 2022a, 84–85). Thus, this book partly serves as an answer to Metz's call that philosophers give more attention to life force in ethics. While I urge readers to evaluate this book on its own merits, it will come as no surprise if those already dissatisfied with Metz's approach cannot tolerate mine.[3] I hope that everyone else, familiar or unfamiliar with African philosophy, will in some way benefit from this work.

1.2 What Makes an Idea African?

Though my own view is that questions about what constitutes African philosophy are less interesting than doing philosophy itself, a project of this kind cannot escape them. I say this because certain readers will inevitably wonder whether this book is a genuine work of African philosophy, while others may perhaps also wonder why the label matters at all. But there is heated debate about what can properly be called 'African'.

Metz uses the label 'African' to refer to an idea that is salient to large groups of indigenous black Africans in the sub-Sahara (see Metz 2022a, 7).[4] North Africa has a longstanding intellectual tradition that is clearly distinct from that found below the Sahara. That tradition is not my focus, nor does it appear to be what most contemporary thinkers have in mind when they use the label 'African'. Though philosophical thinking existed on the African continent for many centuries in the form of an oral tradition, professional philosophy in the narrow sense did not emerge on the continent until the 1960s. By this I mean that philosophy conducted by professional philosophers in universities did not appear until the 1960s. This coincided with the decline of (official) colonialism and the rise of literacy rates on the continent.

Since the 1960s, African philosophers south of the Sahara have tackled philosophical problems with appeal to ideas found in their cultures. It is unsurprising given the political instability throughout much of the continent that so much attention has been given to political and moral philosophy (e.g., Gyekye 1997; Wiredu 1980). Today, the discipline continues to expand, with

---

[3] Though Metz is widely regarded as a leading figure in the field of African philosophy, if not *the* leader, his methodological approach has received criticism, particularly from the influential African philosopher M.B. Ramose. See Ramose 2007.

[4] In other work I have followed Metz's approach. See Lougheed 2022a, 10–12.

more abstract topics in metaphysics, epistemology, and logic being given due consideration (see Metz 2021).

One of Metz's main contentions is that whether an idea is African is a matter of degree. For an idea or concept to be African, it does not *only* have to exist on the African continent or be *only* held by indigenous Africans (i.e., it does not have to be 'essential' to Africa). Instead, it merely needs to be an idea that is salient to a large group of indigenous Africans in ways that it is clearly not elsewhere. So, this does not exclude an idea that is properly African being believed outside of the continent (Metz 2022a, 8). To see this, consider an example from Metz:

> [B]aseball is American. Again, I suggest this claim is true, but not true 'essentially'. After all, the Cubans and Japanese are well known for playing baseball; it is of course true that not all Americans play it or even appreciate it; and there is nothing preventing Americans from giving up this sport entirely. Baseball is American insofar as it is salient there. (2022, 8)

One problem with the way Metz uses the term 'African' here is that it is simply unclear that there are ideas that have been particularly salient exclusively on the continent—at least not any more or less than in other places. Lucy Allais observes that Metz wants to use such ideas found in precolonized, small-scale African societies (forthcoming). However, he mistakenly assumes that there was widespread similarities in those societies such that it is possible to identify a common set of beliefs. Allais points out that:

> [T]here have of course been numerous large, centralized societies in Sub-Saharan Africa—of which the centralized, bureaucratized Ashanti theocratic monarchy, the medieval empires of Ghana, Mali, Songhai and others, the 800 year Benin kingdom, with its organized military, large cities, expansive trade are just a few examples, as well as being different from each other. (Allais, forthcoming)

Indeed, she quotes Oluefemi Taiwo, as suggesting that even communalism is not unique to Africa, given that in pre-industrial Europe many people lived in small villages where everyone knew one another:

> '[h]ow communalistic could the medieval Mali Empire have been? Once Islam became the principle of legitimacy when it came to governance, how

much communalism and how "traditional" could such polities be? The Ọyọ́ Empire was a multinational polity that had within its borders different national and ethnic groups. . . . 17th century Ọyọ́ with its hierarchies—including an aristocracy and monarchy that lived off the surplus labor of others—and a complex division of labor . . .?' (Taiwo 2016, 85 quoted in Allais forthcoming)

And finally:

'communalism's pedigree is not traced to geography or history; rather, it is to be sourced in the modes of production of material life. If this is so, communalism is distributed across cultures and peoples who are otherwise distinct and different in their cultural productions would share communalism insofar as their modes of production are the same or very similar. And this, indeed, is what we find in the literature. Communalism is widely diffused across the globe from Europe to Asia and the Americas at specific historical conjunctures' (Taiwo 2016, 92 quoted in Allais forthcoming).

In sum, if there were ideas held by a large number of indigenous Africans in the sub-Sahara, then the claim that whether a thing is African can come in degrees is plausible. The problem is that whether there are such beliefs, at least ones that are unique to Africa, can be called into question.

The simplest and best way to avoid having to adjudicate debates about whether this or that theory is genuinely African is to sufficiently narrow my claims. While Metz uses 'African' to refer to ideas salient to large groups of black peoples in the sub-Sahara, I will instead use it to refer to the body of work produced by professional African philosophers since (roughly) 1960. On this understanding of 'African', it is crystal clear that 'community' is an African concept; it is given far more emphasis than one finds in philosophical literature developed elsewhere. And notice that though the Africanness of Metz's own moral theory is repeatedly called into question, it would be much more difficult to do so if he made the more modest claim that his theory is African inasmuch as it interacts with and is inspired by the contemporary African philosophical literature.[5]

---

[5] Notice that even if my criticisms of Metz's use of 'African' fail, my theory would be considered African on his view.

6   A MORAL THEORY OF LIVELINESS

I therefore claim that the normative theory I develop in this book is genuinely African in that it focuses on ideas salient in the contemporary African philosophical literature. However, it is plausibly *less* African than other African theories for at least one important reason. In almost all cases, the initial instantiation of the ideas that inspire the theory I develop come from supernatural ontologies, with many descriptions implying the full-fledged ontology of African Traditional Religion. Since the theory I develop in this book is detached from the metaphysics of African Traditional Religion, it is plausibly less African than it would be otherwise.

It is also important for the reader to understand that this is not a sociological study. I am not claiming to accurately describe what large portions of Africans—pre- or post-independence—in fact believe about morality. My claim is instead more modest in that life force is a significant concept to contemporary African scholars (a claim easily demonstrated by numerous citations in Chapters 2 and 3). This is enough to make the label 'African' appropriate for the theory in some important sense.

Still, the reader may fairly wonder whether the degree to which my theory is genuinely African is strong enough to justify the label 'African'. But consider the following scenario: Imagine a world that is identical to ours in every single respect, inasmuch as possible, but in which contemporary African philosophy does not exist.[6] I submit that in such a world, the main ideas for this book would not exist. I would not know about life force, and as a result, there would be no basis for this book. This thought experiment is enough to demonstrate why it is fitting to label the theory I develop in this book 'African'.

If the reader still rejects the explanation in this section, they should simply take the theory in this book as 'African-inspired', since I am clearly inspired by the African intellectual tradition. If they refuse even this minimal association, it ultimately does not hinder my main aim. For such a reader should simply take the theory I develop here on its own terms without worrying about the label 'African' or the origin of the ideas.

---

[6] Modal sceptics will not like this example, but even if such a world is not metaphysically possible or we are not in a good position to know what such a world would be like, it is still epistemically possible.

1.3 Three Strands of African Ethics

Narrowing in on African ethics in particular, one may fairly wonder whether there is anything like a unifying ethical thought in the sub-Sahara. On the one hand, on the surface, one finds statements that seem to provide an affirmative answer. For example, the influential Congolese theologian Bénézet Bujo writes that:

> From the outset, we must state, together with most African scientists, that it is inappropriate to talk in the plural about ethics or religion in sub-Saharan Africa. Except for a few non-African researchers and scientists, most tend to agree on the unity of religion—and ethics—in Black Africa. (2005, 423)

This statement need not contradict the criticisms of homogenizing 'African' thought raised above, if understood as a statement about contemporary scholarship. Again, it is not necessary to make claims about what large numbers of black Africans believe about ethics. On the other hand, upon becoming more familiar with African ethical thought, one quickly discovers that there are three fairly obvious distinct interpretations of normativity, at least as found in the contemporary academic literature. These can be located in normative personhood, harmonious relationships, and life force. Does this mean Bujo, and the various other scholars of African morality, are wrong? It depends. That I have located three distinct strains (and that there are competing interpretations of how to work out the details of each) suggests that Bujo is seemingly insensitive to African morality. However, I think it is also fair to say that what he may be getting at is that even within these three different understandings of normativity there is widespread agreement between all three about the upmost importance of the community in morality.[7] In different ways, each of these three different strains emphasizes the role that community plays in morality and typically do so to a much larger degree than what is found in the moral tradition of the Anglo-American canon (with communism as a notable exception). So, in this very important sense, then, Bujo is clearly correct. The level of specificity versus

---

[7] Bujo is also making this point about the agreement one finds in African Traditional Religion. Others have made a similar point more recently (e.g., Metz and Molefe 2021).

8 A MORAL THEORY OF LIVELINESS

generality that one uses to discover whether there are more similarities or dissimilarities in the sub-Sahara will likely dictate the answers one will find. I will therefore often prefer to use the label 'African Communitarianism' or 'African Communitarian ethics' when referencing contemporary African moral thought in broad terms (i.e., at the level of generality). In the following subsections I briefly introduce each of the three understandings of normativity I have been able to identify in order to highlight the communitarian nature of each of them.

1.3.1 Normative Personhood

Normative personhood is by far the most widely discussed normative ethical theory in contemporary African ethics (see Chapter 7). On this view, the term 'personhood' does not refer to a biological human or the 'self'. Instead, it is a term used to make moral assessments about the character of the person. The basic goal of morality here is to develop one's character by exercising other-regarding virtues. Since other-regarding virtues can be exercised only in relation to others, the community plays a central role in morality on this view. When a person exhibits other-regarding vice, they are often labelled a 'non-person' or an 'animal'. This is to make a negative moral assessment of their character, not to imply that they lack a basic dignity or rights.

1.3.2 Harmonious Relationships

Another significant strand of African moral philosophy focuses on harmonious relationships; such relationships are thought to be the goal of morality (see Chapter 8). A community living in harmony is the final end that ought to be sought. Anything that leads to strife, discord, and disharmony ought to be avoided like the plague. While Metz's moral theory is fairly categorized within this approach, he locates value in a person's *capacity* for harmonious relationships, instead of in the relationships themselves. He argues that this view avoids serious problems with the more standard approach. For Metz, an individual exhibits harmony with another person if they identify with that person and express solidarity with them (see 7.4).

1.3.3 Life Force

As stated above, life force is the ethical idea most intimately connected with a religious framework in Africa, specifically the one found in African Traditional Religion. This view says that literally everything, both animate and inanimate objects, are imbued with an imperceptible energy known as life force (or vital force). In some sense, everything is alive. Life force also serves to ground the African chain of being or African hierarchy of being, with God having the most life force and all others' force dependent on God. Whatever protects and promotes life force in oneself and others is good, while whatever degrades it is bad (see Chapters 2 and 3).

1.4 Motivating the Project: Why Life Force?

At this stage, it is worth explaining in slightly more detail my motivation for writing this book. First, discussions of life force to date, including those offered by philosophers and theologians, tend to be descriptive. The reality is that much of the work on life force is sociological or anthropological in claiming to state what many indigenous Africans in fact believe about morality.[8] In his chapter dedicated to vital force, Metz says his goal "is to evaluate, more systematically than has been done up to now, the extent to which they [i.e., life force theories] are justified in the light of intuitions about right and wrong" (2022, 81). As far as I can tell, Metz is correct that his chapter offers the most systematic treatment to date of vital force as a moral theory. However, his analysis is still only ten pages or so, and contained in a book focussed on developing and defending an entirely different moral theory. So, as explained above, in the first instance my goal is to take up Metz's call that philosophers ought to pay more attention to life force by not only expanding but also by greatly adding to the ideas set forth in his chapter. Second, Metz concludes his chapter by levelling a series of objections to life force as a normative moral theory. Since I find these objections wholly unpersuasive, this serves as further motivation to develop the theory more fully, thereby demonstrating why the objections raised by Metz do not succeed. If life force

---

[8] As stated above, my aim is not necessarily to explore what is believed by large groups of indigenous Africans. I am instead focused on the post-independence philosophical (and religious) academic literature. However, that literature often takes itself to be identifying what large numbers of black Africans do in fact believe, but I do not evaluate this assumption.

10 A MORAL THEORY OF LIVELINESS

fails as a moral theory, it is not for the reasons identified by Metz. Third, and most important, I believe the theory I develop in this book deserves to be considered as a competitor to the current African moral theories on offer. More ambitiously, I hope it will be evaluated against other ethical theories on a global stage.

1.5 Global and African Desiderata for a Successful Moral Theory

As stated above, though I am influenced by the methodology Metz uses to develop his own theory, I believe he should limit his claims about what constitutes 'African' to the contemporary philosophical literature developed on the continent. The same is true for the desiderata he employs to assess the success of a moral theory. The criteria he uses are helpful, but again I want to limit their scope. Metz refers to the first set of criteria he adopts as a series of 'Global' moral intuitions suggesting that they tend to be accepted by both the African tradition and Western moral tradition of the last two hundred years or so. However, Allais observes that:

> It might be responded that while we cannot easily define the term 'Western', we know what we are referring to when we talk about it, or about 'Western' philosophy or 'Western' ideas. But this seems to me not just false, but also dangerously false, whether we are talking about the 2000 year philosophical tradition that is claimed as 'Western', or ideas that are now claimed by contemporary liberal democracies as their official ideology. What do we mean when we say that Tolstoy is a 'Western' writer (despite the contrast between the 'west' and the countries behind the iron curtain) and that Australia is a 'Western' country? Tolstoy comes from a region currently poised in opposition to supposedly 'Western' values, and Australia is geographically east of the geographical regions usually thought of as 'Western'. They have in common connections to European history, but if this makes something Western, then medieval Islamic philosophy is 'Western', which is highly problematic, since one of the main ways 'Western' is used is in contrast to the Islamic world. Modern Australia was shaped by European colonialism, but so was modern Africa, the obvious difference being the domination of white settlers in modern Australia, which supports Appiah's claim that when 'the west' is used in the sense that includes Australia, it is

not much more than a thinly veiled reference to whiteness (Appiah 2016).
(Allais, forthcoming)

Now, Allais continues to say that there may be no innocent way to employ the term 'Western' given that the last two hundred years to which Metz appeals contains the height of imperialism, colonialism, fascism, etc. (Allais, forthcoming). Here again, it would help Metz to avoid these concerns by simply narrowing his claim. Instead of using 'Western' to denote ideas salient in the West in the last two hundred years, I am going to use it to denote moral philosophy that focuses on Kantianism and deontology, consequentialism and utilitarianism, virtue theory as inspired by the ancient Greeks, and Judeo-Christian ethics primarily as located in natural law theory and Divine Command Theory. When I say 'Western ethics' and related terms, I am referring to these traditions. More frequently I will refer to these traditions as 'Anglo-American'. I therefore aim to avoid potential problems with using geographic labels to pick out traditions.

In this narrower use of 'African' and 'Western', I am going to borrow Metz's 'global' desiderata by which to assess a moral theory. He says that it is *pro tanto* immoral:

(a) to kill innocent people without their consent for money

(b) to have sex with someone against her will so as to feel pleasure or a sense of power

(c) to deceive a person, at least when not done in self- or other-defence

(d) to discriminate on a racial or gendered basis when allocating opportunities, at least when not redressing a previous comparable discrimination

(e) to express ethnic, sexual, or similar epithets towards others

(f) never to fight hunger, poverty, displacement, or the like suffered by those outside one's in-group, when one could do so at little cost to oneself

(g) never to prevent serious crimes done to others, when one could do so at little cost to oneself

(h) to torture an animal for the fun of it (Metz 2022a, 51).

While Metz believes that these certainly are not the only judgements that a successful moral theory needs to accommodate, I agree with him that they are a useful starting point by which to evaluate a moral theory.

12 A MORAL THEORY OF LIVELINESS

Additionally, a successful moral theory with a genuinely African pedigree needs to be able to accommodate desiderata for assessing the Africanness of the theory. Metz lists 'African' intuitions that tend to be less controversial in African ethics, when compared to Western ethics, including the idea that it is *pro tanto* immoral:

(i) to resolve political conflicts in the face of continued dissent, rather than seeking consensus

(j) to fail to do what is likely to make people's lives go better, if one is politically in charge

(k) to make retribution the fundamental aim of criminal justice, in contrast to seeking reconciliation

(l) to create wealth largely on a competitive basis, instead of a cooperative one

(m) to distribute wealth in a greatly unequal way and to fail to meet everyone's needs

(n) to avoid greeting people, especially elders, upon encountering them

(o) to remain isolated or to flout long-standing norms central to a people's self-conception, as opposed to partaking in customs

(p) to fail to marry and rear children, as opposed to creating a family (Metz 2022a, 53)

I will test the theory I construct in this book against both sets of these moral intuitions. With the exception of wanting to limit the scope of 'Western' and 'African', Metz's methodological approach is helpful here, and so it is unproductive for me to reinvent the wheel, so to speak. The global and African moral intuitions he lays out are indeed the ones that I believe any moral theory making serious claims to be attractive to both Western and African philosophical audiences must aim to accommodate.

1.6 A Metaethical Assumption

Part III of the book explores possible metaethical grounds of the normative theory, in addition to questions about meaning in life. Though I will explain the assumption there, it is worth stating up front that I will be assuming the truth of moral realism throughout this book. In plain terms, this means that I believe that ethical claims have a truth value that is *independent* of humans.

There may well be ways to make my ideas in this book consistent with anti-realism. However, I leave that project to any anti-realists who may be inclined to pursue it.

1.7 Truth versus Theory Construction

It may come as a surprise to the reader to learn that my goal is not to defend the moral theory I develop as true. Instead, my goal is to develop the best possible version of the theory. This includes defending it against objections, in addition to showing how it can accommodate both global and African moral intuitions. However, various places throughout this book will probably read as if I am defending the truth of the theory. This is somewhat unavoidable, as part of any good theory construction in philosophy involves offering reasons for the theory's truth (or at least showing why it is superior to other theories). It would also make for awkward prose to constantly include hedges as a reminder to the reader that I am not actually defending the truth of it. For the reader who is curious, what I do believe about the theory I develop in this book is that it ought to be taken as a serious competitor to other moral theories in the African philosophical tradition and around the globe. I believe that life force (both supernatural and, especially, the secular version) as moral theory is still in its infancy, at least with respect to its systematic development in a way that is palatable to professional philosophers. My hope is that others will add to this work, including offering not only fresh perspectives, but also novel criticisms, such that the truth or falsity of life force as a normative theory will begin to emerge more clearly. My primary aim in this book, then, is to construct a moral theory using life force, not to defend it as true. This is still very much the beginning of moral reasoning about life force, at least among professional philosophers.

1.8 Conclusion

The purpose of this book is to develop the best version of a secular moral theory of African life force. Whether an idea is genuinely African is a matter of degree. Though the theory I develop is fairly construed as less African than other moral theories, including one that embraces the supernatural ontology of African Traditional Religion, it is still rightfully African. This is because the ideas in this book would almost certainly not exist apart from the contemporary philosophical and religious academic traditions on the African continent. The different branches of African moral philosophy as located in personhood, harmony, and life force tend to be much more communally oriented than the theories that dominate in the Anglo-American moral tradition. Life force has received significantly less attention than the former two interpretations of African communitarianism, particularly with respect to its development as a normative moral theory. This book also partly serves as an answer to Metz's call that philosophers ought to give more attention to life force. It also follows Metz in affirming that a successful African moral theory ought to accommodate both global and African moral intuitions. Finally, the primary aim of this book is to construct the best possible version of a secular theory of life force on the assumption of moral realism, not to argue that such a theory is in fact true.

PART I
SETTING THE STAGE
The African Conception of Life Force

2

The Legacy of Placide Tempels'
Bantu Philosophy

2.1 Introduction

The purpose of this chapter is to highlight the work of Placide Tempels'
controversial book, *Bantu Philosophy* (1959), which is typically considered
the first place where life force was identified by a European. I begin by
summarizing the main claims in *Bantu Philosophy*, with special attention
given to the relevant moral implications (2.2). I then turn to examining the
wide-ranging reactions to Tempel's work (2.3), before shifting to a discussion
of the legitimacy of ethnophilosophy itself (2.4). I conclude by explaining
the methodological approach I will take to life force for the rest of the book,
including explaining that while Tempels' impact on African philosophy
cannot be ignored, I will instead rely on the contemporary philosophical
descriptions of what mostly African scholars have written on life force (2.5),
a task I take up in Chapter Three.

2.2 Placide Tempels' *Bantu Philosophy*

Placide Tempels (1906–1977) was a Belgian priest who worked as a missionary in the Congo from large parts of 1933 to 1962.[1] He produced a book
called *Bantu Philosophy*, which first appeared in English in 1959 but was
available earlier in Dutch/Flemish and French. The purported goal of this
work was to better understand the Bantu-speaking peoples of the Congo
in order to more successfully 'Christianize' them. As I will explain later,
Tempels' work is controversial not only because of his motivation and the
fact that he makes sweeping generalizations about *all* Bantu speakers, but

---

[1] For some unofficial biographical and bibliographic details of Tempels, see http://www.aequato
ria.be/tempels/index.htm.

A Moral Theory of Liveliness. Kirk Lougheed, Oxford University Press. © Kirk Lougheed 2025.
DOI: 10.1093/9780197782019.003.0002

18 A MORAL THEORY OF LIVELINESS

because he appears to take folk beliefs and local culture as the components of a philosophical system. On the other hand, some say that Tempels is rightly considered a father of African philosophy, because he recognized a deeper level of thought in Africans than had most of his European contemporaries. Before exploring some of the various reactions to *Bantu Philosophy*, it is important to be familiar with the content of the book itself.

Tempels begins the book by explaining that he believes that it is impossible to understand a peoples without understanding their ontology, and he therefore seeks to discover if the Bantu have a unifying metaphysical principle (1959, Ch. 1). He asserts that all of the behaviour of Bantu peoples can be explained by the value of vital force.[2] Tempels says that the frequent use of certain words provides clues about the most important values (1959, 30). Importantly, they reinforce the idea that the 'supreme value is life, force, to live strongly, or vital force' (Tempels 1959, 30). Tempels believes that practices which are opaque to Westerners can be explained by the desire to increase one's life force and avoid its diminution (1959, 30–31). This force can be controlled by words and appeals made to God, spirits, or ancestors, and such appeals are often for more strength or force (Tempels 1959, 31).

According to Tempels, God has the most force and is the source of all other force. Regarding the invisible world, the first ancestors possess great force, because they are considered the founders of the human race. Departed ancestors are only revered inasmuch as their progeny exhibit strong force. It is important to understand that for the Bantu, every single thing in the universe, including animals, vegetation, and minerals, possesses vital force (Tempels 1959, 31).

Human happiness results from possessing strong vital force, while misfortune is a degradation of force. In this way, '[e]very illness, wound or disappointment, all suffering, depression, or fatigue, every injustice and every failure: all these are held to be, and are spoken of by the Bantu as, a diminution of vital force' (Tempels 1959, 32). Sickness and death are caused by an external agent attempting to weaken a person's force. It is therefore essential to strengthen one's force through magic in order to be able to defend and protect it (Tempels 1959, 32).

---

[2] This term appears difficult to translate into English. It appears in the French translation as 'la force', 'vivre fort', and 'force vitale' (Tempels 1959, 30 n. 1). The introduction to the English translation of *Bantu Philosophy* notes that translating it into Dutch is equally difficult. This is hardly surprising, given that many African scholars observe that terms such as 'ubuntu' do not translate well into English.

THE LEGACY OF TEMPELS' *BANTU PHILOSOPHY* 19

With respect to ontology, Tempels explains that the Bantu believe all beings (i.e., literally everything that exists) share a vital force with one another (1959, 34). However, it is not right to think of vital force as distinct from the concept of being. Tempels says that force is a necessary component of being; there can be no being without force (Tempels 1959, 34). In other words, '[f]orce is the nature of being, force is being, being is force' (Tempels 1959, 34).

Though everything shares a force, things have different strengths of force. A thing's force is always capable of being increased or diminished (Tempels 1959, 36–38). An increase or decrease in life force should not be associated with strength, but instead with reinforcement or intensity (Tempels 1959, 38). All force is originally from God. The creation of life is ultimately within God's control, and a thing's life cannot come to an end by anyone other than God (though a person's force can be diminished by another person).

With respect to the interaction of forces, there is less emphasis on the idea that each thing is a distinct substance (Tempels 1959, 39–40). Instead:

> Transcending the mechanical, chemical and psychological interactions, they see a relationship of forces which we should call ontological. In the created force (a contingent being) the Bantu sees a causal action emanating from the very nature of that created force and influencing other forces. One force will reinforce or weaken another. This causality is in no way supernatural in the sense of going beyond the proper attributes of created nature. It is, on the contrary, a metaphysical causal action which flows out of the very nature of a created being. General knowledge of these activities belongs to the realm of natural knowledge and constitutes philosophy properly so called. The observation of the action of these forces in their specific and concrete applications would constitute Bantu natural science. (Tempels 1959, 40)

Tempels also identifies what he refers to as the 'hierarchy of forces'. God is above all forces, and it is God who is the source of all force and hence of all power and life (Tempels 1959, 41). After God, the 'first' or 'founding fathers' of various clans have the most force as given to them by God. These are followed by parents of the dead, the living dead, and living humans (Tempels 1959, 42). God has created humans, both living and dead, at the centre of the universe (Tempels 1959, 43–44). The living dead appear to have a diminished life force and only work to strengthen the force of those humans

20   A MORAL THEORY OF LIVELINESS

who already exist. The forces found in animals, plants, and minerals 'exist only, and by the will of God, to increase the vital force of men while they are on earth. Higher and lower forces, therefore, are thought of by the Bantu in relation to living human forces' (Tempels 1959, 44). Humans are capable of diminishing or reinforcing the force of other humans and can influence the force of lesser beings such as animals, plants, and minerals (Tempels 1959, 45–46).

Regarding epistemology, Tempels says that for the Bantu, it is 'ontological knowledge' that is important. This means that knowledge of forces and how they interact with one another are the most important (1959, 47). Since God necessarily knows how all forces interact with one another, God possesses all causal knowledge (Tempels 1959, 47).

According to the Bantu, humans have the strongest force such that:

> the 'muntu' should be able to grow ontologically, become greater, stronger; and equally that he should be able, as 'muntu', to diminish, lose his vital force and come to an end in the complete annihilation of his very essence, the paralysis of his vital force, which takes from him the power to be an active force, a vital cause. This state of the ultimate diminution of being is the fate of some of the dead. It is the condition into which those who have passed over fall if they have no means of renewal through those living on earth. (Tempels 1959, 66)

And:

> Just as Bantu ontology is opposed to the European concept of individuated things, existing in themselves, isolated from others, so Bantu psychology cannot conceive of man as an individual, as a force existing by itself and apart from its ontological relationships with other living beings and from its connection with animals or inanimate forces around it. (Tempels 1959, 68)

Regarding ethics, Tempels explains that for the Bantu, humans are not the final judges of their actions. Instead, each person must answer to God for how they have used their force since it ultimately comes from God (1959, 75). This is part of the reason why life ought to be respected. For the Bantu, all life is a gift from God, and other creatures were created to protect and promote the life force of humans (Tempels 1959, 78). What is good is whatever leads to a reinforcement of vital force. On the other hand, here are a series of important quotes regarding which acts are evil:

> Every act, every detail of behaviour, every attitude and every human custom which militates against vital force or against the increase of the hierarchy of the 'muntu' is bad. The destruction of life is a conspiracy against the Divine Plan; and the 'muntu' knows that such destruction is, above all else, ontological sacrilege: that it is for that reason immoral and therefore unjust. (Tempels 1959, 79)

> [T]he most degraded crime, the most cynical prostitution of the sacred laws of nature, is the voluntary and conscious crime of destruction by the 'buloji', or by sorcery. (Tempels 1959, 82)

> All enmity, hatred, envy, jealousy, evil speaking, even false praise or lying eulogy, are severely condemned by the Bantu. (Tempels 1959, 82)

> Every premeditated act directed towards the destruction of the life of others is called 'nsikani'; and true 'nsikani', that which wickedly brings harm upon the vital force of another, is the synonym of 'bufwisi' or of 'buloji'. Such a 'muloji' is held to be in the highest degree blameworthy by the Bantu. It is reprehensible in the sight of God, the giver and preserver of all life. Since the 'muloji' brings harm to the natural order, to natural law; and consequently to human law, the community has the right of defence against such an evil doer, who spreads destruction and death, who brings about the annihilation of being. (Tempels 1959, 82)

> The individual knows what his moral and legal obligations are and that they are to be honoured on pain of losing his vital force. He knows that to carry out his duty will enhance the quality of his being. (Tempels 1959, 88)

Human laws must be consistent with this ontological picture of which acts reinforce and diminish force.

This completes my summary of Tempels' *Bantu Philosophy*, where I have focused on those aspects that are the most relevant to understanding the notion that life force plays in ethics. As already mentioned, though Tempels'

22 A MORAL THEORY OF LIVELINESS

legacy looms large in contemporary African ethics, the nature of that legacy is far from uncontroversial.

2.3 Tempels' Legacy

The legacy of Tempel's work is complicated, to say the least. *Bantu Philosophy* is one of the most cited, if not the most cited, book in contemporary African philosophy.[3] As should be obvious from the above description to anyone who is familiar with contemporary African philosophy, Tempels' emphasis on life force was clearly accurate and touched on something important, even though his universal generalizations about all Bantu-speaking peoples are false. In spite of picking out the importance of life force, many philosophers on the African continent have hardly welcomed Tempels' claims, methodology, or motivation. The reasons for this are multifaceted, but before explaining them, I turn to providing additional context for Tempels and *Bantu Philosophy*.

2.3.1 The Context of *Bantu Philosophy*

Bantu Philosophy was read by European academics upon its publication. However, it also 'became an important book for students of African culture and philosophy in institutions of higher learning. In Africa, this was closely linked to the end of colonialism and the beginning of Africans' struggle for self-affirmation and legitimation' (Cornelli 2022, 8).

Mutombo Nkulu-N'Sengha reminds readers of the racist context in which Tempels produced *Bantu Philosophy*, writing that:

> Tempels, a contemporary of Joseph Kipling, Joseph Conrad, and General Dietrich Lothar von Trotha, came from a Western world well known for overlooking, intellectually and physically, the dignity and humanity of African people, even among Enlightenment philosophers. His was a Western world which, for centuries, had been shaped by the tradition of 'human zoo' exhibits, social Darwinism, racialist theories articulated by the German Society for Racial Hygiene, Houston Stewart Chamberlain, the

---

[3] I would not be surprised if it was *the* most cited work, but it is difficult to get clear numbers on its citations from Google Scholar, for example.

notorious Rassenpapst Hans Friedrich Karl Günther, Gobineau's ideology of the inequality of races, Kant's infamous lectures on Anthropology, Lévy-Bruhl's Primitive Mentality, Lombroso's criminology, Samuel G. Morton's phrenology, and by a plethora of anthropologists, historians, physicians, lawyers, philosophers and even theologians and Biblicists. Between 1810 and 1940, 35,000 human beings were exhibited to 1.5 billion visitors! (Nkulu-N'Sengha 2022, 111; see also Mosima 2022, 84)

Tempels admits to taking a dialogical approach in his missionary work with Bantu peoples only after years of not making the desired evangelistic gains in the Congo with respect to Christian conversion (Nkulu-N'Sengha 2022, 113). He also admits to arriving in Africa with the typical beliefs of white colonial superiority. It is noteworthy that upon the publication of *Bantu Philosophy*, the Catholic Church would not allow Tempels to return to the Congo for a number of years, and when he did, he was instructed not to write any treaties on philosophy or theology (Wijsen 2022, 2). His tacit 'acknowledgement of the full humanity of the Africans and their capability for rationality and sound morality' was clearly a problem to his European audience (Nkulu-N'Sengha 2022, 113). The ideas in *Bantu Philosophy* 'were seen as too extreme by both the colonial administrators and the church. This led his own Franciscan congregation to recall him from the missionary work he loved so much in the Congo [....] [H]is book was seen as neither a blueprint for a successful mission to civilize nor a desirable model of missionary attitude' (Matolino 2022, 67). Consider that:

> Bishop Jean-Felix de Hemptinne tried to control the circulation of 'Bantu Philosophy' and persuade Rome to condemn the book as heretical. He even insisted that Tempels be expelled from the country. All these attempts, however, failed and did not dissuade Tempels from proposing his work and, particularly, his ontology as a good way for white men to encounter Africans and understand them. (Mosima 2022, 87)

Bernard Matolino hypothesizes that the mixed reactions to Tempels' work can be explained partly by the fact that his 'project could be seen as having a dual intent: performing a rehabilitative philosophical exercise on the Muntu while at the same time maintaining the difference between the Muntu and the Westerner. This conflicting commitment has caused a mixed reception in the African academy to Tempels's project' (Matolino 2022, 66). Bernard

24 A MORAL THEORY OF LIVELINESS

Matolino also identifies Tempels as an important figure in the founding of the philosophical school called *ethnophilosophy* (see 2.4), further explaining that Tempels' aim is complicated because on the one hand he identified a distinct philosophy of the Muntu, while on the other he still thought they needed 'Western intervention' (Matolino 2022, 67).

Thus, on the one hand, there is a picture of a Tempels who is more enlightened than his European counterparts because he recognizes the shared humanity and rationality of African peoples. On the other hand, '[s]ome modern thinkers have seen his forays into Bantu philosophy as undermining the integrity of African thought. Others have gone as far as accusing him of complicity in the colonial mission's oppressive agenda' (Matolino 2022, 67). Perhaps the most apt characterization of Tempels with respect to his role in establishing contemporary African philosophy is that he 'is both hero and villain' (Mosima 2022, 84).

I close this subsection by highlighting what appears to be a little-known article by Willem Storm, 'Bantoe-Filosfie vs. Bantu Philosophy' (1993).[4] This article is important in observing potential translation issues which may well have affected and continue to affect the reception of *Bantu Philosophy*. In 1945 the version of *Bantoe-Filosofie* (i.e., the original version) appeared in a French translation as *La Philosophie Bantoue*, and it is this version which was used for the 1959 English translation known as *Bantu Philosophy*, which is the one that is still widely used by scholars today (Storm 1993, 67). Storm further observes that while the translator, Colin King, says in the Foreword that he showed the text to Tempels, the translation is not authorized. Furthermore, the level of Tempels' English-language proficiency is an open question. Importantly, Storm claims that '[o]ne does not have to know both Dutch and English to see at a first balance that the two versions differ [...T] he translators seemed to hold different views on African and Africans than Tempels and uses the translation to "correct" Tempels' (Storm 1993, 67–68).

Here are some of the main issues that Storm identifies when conducting a comparison between the original Dutch text and the 1959 English one that most academics use:

1) a large number of deviations from the meaning of the Dutch text;
2) in many cases the translator does not follow Tempels' paragraph ordering;

---

[4] Mungwini 2022, 54–55 brought this article to my attention.

THE LEGACY OF TEMPELS' *BANTU PHILOSOPHY* 25

3) some paragraphs are omitted, most footnotes are omitted;
4) the translator adds his own text and notes;
5) the original Foreword is not translated;
6) words like Baluba, Bantu, Zwarten are not translated strictly. Where the original gives 'Baluba', the translation is often 'Africans';
7) the Dutch word 'algemeen' means 'genera', but is often translated 'universal'. As far as I could find out Tempels does not use the word 'universeel', which is a term with stronger implications than 'algemeen'. Tempels is more reluctant to generalise and often uses the phrase 'and this probably also counts for other Blacks and Primitives'. (Storm 1993, 68–69)

Storm then identifies a number of mistranslations, none of which can be said to benefit the Bantu peoples.[5] Consider his claim that 'T14.3a (K36.2p) literally reads, "It is not at all certain that Bantu themselves will supply us with a complete philosophical terminology" and is translated as "We do not claim, of course, that the Bantu are capable of formulating a philosophical treatise, complete with an adequate vocabulary"' (Storm 1993, 69). Now, I do not read Dutch, nor am I a linguist or translator. But on the assumption that Storm has indeed identified some genuine translation problems with the 1959 version, it would be ideal to have an updated Dutch-to-English translation of *Bantu Philosophy*. This is especially so if, as Storm intimates, the mistranslations have negatively unnecessarily harmed Tempels' reputation in contemporary African thought. I leave this task to a linguist with the relevant skills and interest, and now turn to the reactions that *Bantu Philosophy* in its current English form has generated.

2.3.2 Positive Reactions to Tempels: A Father of African Philosophy?

In this subsection I highlight some of the more positive reactions to Tempels, beginning with Johannes Fabian, who suggests:

Tempels started out as a revolutionary of sorts. What he did in *Bantu Philosophy* was to challenge dominant ideas about the intellectual

---

[5] This implies it would also not benefit how the contemporary reader views Tempels' understanding of Africans.

capabilities of Africans, and, consequently, the methods of colonial administration and Christian mission, based on these dominant ideas. At this stage, he appears to us as a man who broke out of the sort of colonialism that has been aptly characterized as paternalism. (Johannes Fabian 1969, 170 quoted in Wijsen 2022, 1)

Frans Wijsen suggests that *Bantu Philosophy* 'was a breakthrough in philosophy and theology, which until that point had held that the Africans were primitives and could not think logically' (Wijsen 2022, 2). Some scholars have suggested that Tempels should be commended for speaking 'back to a Catholic church and academic establishment that had rejected the very idea of Africa having an intellectual life and heritage' (Cornelli 2022, 10). Additionally, Evaristi Magoti Cornelli writes that though '[i]t may not be known to many, but according to Chachage (1994), the book played a very significant role in the formation and articulation of negritude, a movement rooted in the Harlem Renaissance in the United States, which was popularized in Africa by Léopold Senghor (1906–2001), the first president of Senegal (1960–1980)' (2022, 10). Additionally, it is noteworthy that '[d]ominating the first two decades of independence were political philosophers such as Julius Nyerere (1922–1999), Kwame Nkrumah (1909–1972), Kenneth Kaunda (1924–2021) and Léopold Sédar Senghor (1906–2001). They accepted the broad outlines of *Bantu Philosophy*, particularly the thesis that Africans are rational and have a culture, religion and morals' (Cornelli 2022, 11). Finally, Cornelli makes the point that Tempels' work would have been directly in opposition to the racist attitudes of important philosophers such as Hume, Kant, and Hegel (Cornelli 2022, 14–16).

Martin Nkafu Nkemnkia says that he can 'affirm without hesitation that Tempels's work is a valid contribution towards dialogue between Western philosophy (Ontology) and African Thinking (Vitalogy)' (2022, 26). In the context of addressing Odera Oruka's criticisms of Tempels, Pius Mosima claims not only that:

African ethnophilosophy, as articulated in the work of Tempels, could be a valid and valuable source of African philosophical concepts best suited to crossfertilize world philosophies by promoting education and dialogue [... but i]n spite of the heavy criticisms by so-called professional philosophers, Tempels has succeeded in changing the conceptions of African peoples, as held by themselves and others, especially in his response to the sordid and corrupt views held by Europeans in terms of the African continent and her peoples. (Mosima 2022, 82, 100)

Finally, Nkulu-N'Sengha concludes that though Tempels should be credited for trying to bridge the 'us versus them' divide between Africa and the West, he did ultimately believe in the superiority of the West and Christianity (Nkulu-N'Sengha 2022, 123). Though Tempels' church and religious order reacted negatively to his work, it is fair to say that the more positive reactions to his work from scholars appear closer to the English publication in 1959, with more recent treatments of it being viewed with scepticism. I now turn to examining some of these negative reactions.

2.3.3 Negative Reactions to Tempels: An Inaccurate Colonizer?

Evaristi Magoti Cornelli outlines criticisms of Tempels found in prominent African thinkers during the colonial period, including those from Aimé Césaire (1913–2008) and Cheikh Anta Diop (1923–1986) (2022, 11). He explains that the former claims that Tempels merely sought to further the colonial agenda by helping to deal with political problems, while the latter was sceptical of ethnophilosophy in general, claiming that African philosophy should seek to re-establish its ancient roots with Egyptian thought (Cornelli 2022, 11).

A slightly different type of reaction to Tempels suggests that his failure is in itself what has served to canonize his work. For instance, Pascah Mungwini claims that *Bantu Philosophy* perhaps serves as an example of how *not* to do philosophy:

> It is true that, as many critics have proclaimed and continue to do so, the book is not a philosophical text. It is not a philosophy of the Bantu but of Tempels himself. In other words, the book is philosophical fiction created by the author for reasons other than philosophy. However, despite this, and contrary to expectation, Tempels's work has refused to go quietly. (2022, 54)

One reason some have been sceptical of Tempels is that his project compared African folk-philosophy to technical Western philosophy (e.g., Wirdeu 1980). This means that 'Tempels mistakenly thought that it was justifiable for traditional philosophy to be compared with modern philosophy. The results of this comparison led Tempels to commit to the idea that he had found a version of African philosophy that was comparable to modern Western philosophy built on Cartesian foundations' (Matolino 2022, 68–69). The problem with this project is that '[i]n his presentation of this primitive philosophy or thought system, Tempels was able to achieve an undesirable double: raising the Muntu to some thought system capable of its own standard of justification while at the same time lowering the Muntu to a different standard from the Westerner' (Matolino 2022, 70). Even if Tempels had good intentions, in identifying life force and a system of thought so entirely different from the West, he 'sank the African to the status of a second-rate thinker, whose categories of thought required special attention to be understood and, for the Muntu, who needed to be aided in getting rid of the most basic of his systems in favor of enlightened ways' (Matolino 2022, 75). Matolino believes that because of these issues, African philosophy has failed to be appropriately recognized by the Western tradition. Tempels' project is not part of the intellectual decolonization project (Matolino 2022, 75). Though Nkulu-N'Sengha does observe some positive items in relation to Tempels, he concludes that even though Tempels was critical of colonial abuses, he ultimately 'fully subscribed to the civilizing mission ideology and never doubted the superiority of Christianity, which he constantly referred to as "the true religion"' (Nkulu-N'Sengha 2022, 120). This can be labelled as a kind of 'benevolent colonialism.'

2.3.4 Why Tempels?

In sum, the debate about the legitimacy of Tempels has in general two opposing views. On the one hand, he has been viewed as a kind of father of African philosophy, setting a launching point for further discourse. On the other hand, he has been accused of only intending to further the colonial agenda, and engaging in a kind of inaccurate ethnophilosophy, prone to sweeping generalizations. Though I am mostly partial to the latter assessment of Tempels' work, this is not a conclusion I will argue for here. Instead, I point out that irrespective of how one ought to evaluate Tempels' work, he did identify life force, which is an important concept in African thought. Given that life force serves as the basis of the ideas in this book, it was necessary to explain where the idea came from in the English academic literature,

THE LEGACY OF TEMPELS' *BANTU PHILOSOPHY*   29

and this meant examining the work of Tempels. The body of literature on the legitimacy of *Bantu Philosophy* is itself significant, not to mention the even larger literature exploring life force and related ideas (whether directly or indirectly influenced by Tempels). In view of the fact that this book is about developing a secular moral theory based on life force, and not about evaluating the merits of Tempels, I have made no attempt at a comprehensive summary of that literature here, and instead aimed only to give the reader the broad contours of the debate.[6]

2.4 Ethnophilosophy

What perhaps lie at the heart of assessing Tempels' work are judgments about the legitimacy of *ethnophilosophy*. This is a school of philosophy that seeks to describe in philosophical terms the culture, beliefs, and practices found in the everyday life of a people group. It is not the result of systematic social scientific study, but instead is usually based on the observations that individual philosophers make about the culture around them. Mosima observes that though Paulin J. Houtondji is often credited with coining the term, it turns out that it appears in 'The Myth of Spontaneous Philosophy (1974), a PhD dissertation written by Kwame Nkrumah at the University of Pennsylvania' (Mosima 2022, 83).[7] The question that emerges here is whether *Bantu Philosophy* represents an early poor attempt at ethnophilosophy or if ethnophilosophy itself is fundamentally flawed as a philosophical methodology.[8] Though Tempels is widely rejected in African thought, the legitimacy of ethnophilosophy remains a matter of open debate. In the rest of this section, I highlight some of the main ideas in the debate over ethnophilosophy.

Matolino, a consistent critic of Tempels, says of ethnophilosophy that 'its nontechnical form has reduced African philosophy to a loose collection of folk beliefs, stories and myths' and that it is the job of professional philosophy to correct this work (Matolino 2022, 74). In taking *Bantu Philosophy* as a paradigmatic case of ethnophilosophy, Matolino says that he does not

---

[6] For more on the (de)merits of Tempels, see Ebo and George 2022; Kanu 2018; Matolino 2011; Ochieng-Odhiambo 2021; Okafor 1997; Okafor 1982; Owakah 2012.

[7] Mosima credits Osha 2011 with providing this information.

[8] Indeed, 'Hountondji (1996) and Towa (1971a,1971b) used the term ethnophilosophy to refer to leading thinkers inspired by Tempels' (Mosima 2022, 83).

30 A MORAL THEORY OF LIVELINESS

know of any philosopher who considers themselves a follower of Tempels and seeks to employ the same methodology (Matolino 2022, 74).

Peter Bodunrin locates the problem of ethnophilosophy in epistemic justification, claiming that it is problematic because it does 'not attempt to give a philosophical justification of the belief system or issues that arise in it' (1981, 72 in Mosima 2022, 83). Barry Hallen notes that the term 'ethnophilosophy' is used as a word of criticism (Hallen 2006 138 in Mosomia 2022, 90). Mosima writes that '[f]or Hountondji, ethnophilosophy is an ideological myth because it has to account for an imaginary unanimity to interpret a text that does not exist and has to be constantly reinvented' (Mosomia 2022, 93). A common theme throughout the criticisms of ethnophilosophy is that it lacks the argumentative rigour required of good philosophy.

Though known as one of the foremost critics of ethnophilosophy, it has been observed that Houtondji significantly weakens his stance towards it, saying that he 'clearly recognized, shortly after publishing [*African Philosophy: Myth and Reality*], that such studies were not only legitimate but absolutely necessary' (Hountondji 2018, 11 quoted in Mungwini 2022, 57). Mungwini explains that despite softening his stance towards ethnophilosophy, many scholars today still appeal to Hountondji's initial arguments against it (Mungwini 2022, 57).

On the more positive side of responses to ethnophilosophy, one finds the claim from Mungwini that an unwillingness to consider oral tradition is a kind of self-betrayal by African philosophers (2022, 58).[9] He claims that African self-apprehension 'may have been severely impacted by the negative perceptions created by the famous critique of ethnophilosophy which had the consequence of creating an impression that any work of that nature was false philosophy, anti-African and extroverted' (Mungwini 2022, 57). Mosima argues that 'ethnophilosophy must be understood as an attempt to render in discursive, cosmopolitan academic text the indigenous philosophizing of a particular culture—in this case an African culture' (Mosima 2022, 84).

As with the reaction to Tempels, I have made no attempt at a complete and comprehensive survey of the literature on the legitimacy of ethnophilosophy.[10] I also do not advocate for a position regarding ethnophilosophy. Instead, my point in this section was to highlight some of

---

[9] The legitimacy of utilizing oral tradition has been defended independently as *sage philosophy*, especially in the work of H. Odera Oruka (e.g., 1983, 1990a, 1990b).

[10] For more on the (il)legitimacy of ethnophilosophy, see: Agada 2019; Bell 1989; Hountondji 1996, 2018; Imafidon et. al. 2019; Kanu 2013; Mangena 2014; Mungwini 2014, 2019a; Oruka 1975.

the reasons for and against ethnophilosophy, noting that some of the evaluation of Tempels may well reduce to how one evaluates ethnophilosophy. However, my avoidance of taking a side in this dispute naturally gives rise to important questions about how I will proceed with the concept of life force for the rest of this book. I turn to these questions in the next section.

2.5 My Methodological Approach to Research on Life Force

Though in 1.2 I addressed my general methodological approach to African philosophy, at this stage it is pertinent to address my methodological approach to life force for the rest of the book. Consider that Mungwini writes that '[i]t is probably true that the story of African philosophy would not have been what it is today were it not for the amount of provocation that the little book by Tempels triggered' (2022, 51; see also Mosima 2022, 82). He also claims that despite many attempts, it is simply impossible to ignore Tempels' influence on contemporary (professional) African philosophy (Mungwini 2022, 52). In sum, Mungwini believes 'the text by Tempels will remain etched in the history of African philosophy and, for that reason, it is a text whose canonical status does not come from it being an exemplary text, but rather its influence stems from the amount of space and effort that has been devoted to refuting its philosophicality' (2022, 56).

As a Westerner originally trained in the Anglo-American philosophical tradition who now works in African philosophy, all of this has the potential to leave me in a rather awkward position. On the one hand, I want to mine the writing on life force to help create an explicit normative theory that is palatable to both African and Anglo-American philosophers. On the other hand, one might be left wondering how it's possible to avoid the pitfalls often associated with Tempels' work. Consider that though avoiding generalizations is easy enough, it is more difficult to understand which ideas ought to be gleaned from African cultures for philosophical purposes. Indeed, at the very heart of the debate about ethnophilosophy is the one between the universalists and particularists. The former group says that philosophy is universal such that it cannot be tied only to African ideas or culture. The latter group believes that philosophy cannot be separated from culture such that it is perfectly acceptable to intentionally draw on culture when conducting philosophy.

I suggest that a middle way is possible between the universalists and particularists. Why cannot observations about cultures, beliefs, and practices inform a philosophy that aims to be universal? Ideas do not appear out of thin air. In some sense, every idea is culturally grounded. This does not mean that such ideas are *never* universal. Ideas about life force arise in the context of various African societies. There is no denying that they are culturally rooted. But this does not mean that such ideas cannot possibly be universal. Indeed, exploring the extent to which such ideas can generate a plausible normative theory that applies across cultures is one way to test the extent to which the ideas are universal.[11] This book, then, serves as a kind of case study for the middle way I am proposing.

In his chapter 'Beyond Placide Tempels' *Bantu Philosophy* and in Defence of the Philosophical Viability of Ethnophilosophy', Edwin Etieyibo provides a helpful model for thinking about how to approach enthophilosophy, which turns out to be similar to my proposed middle path (2022). Etieyibo explains that '[a]s a trend in African philosophy, ethnophilosophy equates African philosophy with culture-bound systems of thought' (Etieyibo 2022, 89). He labels this kind of work *excavationist*, since it attempts 'to excavate elements of African cultural life and experiences and highlight the ways in which these can be said to constitute African philosophy' (Etieyibo 2022, 89). He further explains that:

> In general, the excavationism project is one that attempts to (a) build the edifice of African philosophy by articulating and systematizing the African cultural worldviews, (b) systematically retrieve and reconstruct African identity from the raw materials of African culture and (c) develop and construct African political ideologies and systems from the ground up, i.e. fundamental and native political systems of African peoples. (Etieyibo 2022, 89)

Critics of this approach tend to say that 'the raw materials of African culture are not genuine elements of philosophy and at best deficient cultural elements and paraphernalia' (Etieyibo 2022, 89). Etieyibo counters that ethnophilosophy is legitimate if it is simply either '(a) the study of indigenous philosophical systems or (b) culture as it exists, encountered or lived' (Etieyibo 2022, 89).

---

[11] This does not mean the test of universality is comparing ideas against the Anglo-American tradition. Testing universality in this way would involve utilizing philosophies from numerous traditions. This book is therefore just one step in that direction, but hardly a complete one.

The most extreme universalist view is that culture should play absolutely no role in philosophizing. This type of universalist says that philosophy must completely transcend culture. However, a more moderate view says that African culture should play a role in African philosophy:

> The point of this view is that given that philosophy is always about some particular culture and given that it is not possible to have an African philosophy that is not tied to African culture, African philosophers ought not to present African philosophy as if it transcends African culture. I will take this view as being consistent with the position of the excavationists/ethnophilosophers. (Etieyibo 2022, 92)

What Etieyibo calls the component stance is the idea that culture provides only *some* of the content for African philosophers (2022, 93). This is consistent with ethnophilosophy, at least broadly construed (Etieyibo 2022, 94–95).

Etieyibo's point is that the component approach will be palatable to universalists because they 'will not disagree with the claim that there is no philosophy that is not of *some* place (whether the place is one particular place or the world as a place), then the follow-up claim that context or culture provides *some* of the material for African philosophy will not be disagreeable to them' (2022, 96). The takeaway is that there is no philosophy that is placeless. This means that whether we think of philosophy:

> [A]s particular or universal, [philosophy,] as the [. . .] universalists have claimed, is always *philosophy of place*. If this claim is right and philosophy is not *placeless* and philosophers build their philosophical systems on the edifice of *some* place, the argument that one can extend from this then is that the place from which the philosophical enterprise springs from is one of culture and the elements that one draws on when one philosophizes from *that* place are cultural paraphernalia and imperatives. (Etieyibo 2022, 97)

Finally, Eiteyibo says:

> [e]ven if one thinks that the ideas, insights, arguments and conclusions of a philosopher who belongs to a particular epoch, culture or society are not tethered to such epoch, culture or society, she certainly does draw from the ideas and insights of such epoch, culture or society. The philosopher

may transcend his or her epoch, culture or society in generating ideas and proffering solutions to problems; such ideas and insights do not happen in a vacuum or come to him or her from some emptiness—they come to her from a particular place, and the place is her epoch, culture or society. (Etieyibo 2022, 97)

I suspect that Etieyibo could be doing his ideas a disservice by labelling them as a defense of ethnophilosophy. This is because his basic point is just that philosophy is never completely untethered from culture, even if it is universal. To deny that life force can be the object of study because it is too culturally rooted, amounts to a kind of reductio of this type of criticism of ethnophilosophy. If no ideas are entirely independent of culture, then there could be no philosophy, since all philosophy would be ethnophilosophy to some degree.

My approach to life force is that it is an important philosophical concept that ought to be studied closely, even if it is culturally grounded. Whether there are universal lessons from life force is an open question, which to some extent I hope to implicitly answer in the rest of this book. In the next chapter, I turn to outlining the understandings of life force found in the contemporary literature, mostly from contemporary African writers. It is unclear the degree to which, if at all, the contemporary exponents of life force would consider their work to be ethnophilosophy. Notice that even if they do, this does not commit me to an extreme form of either particularism or universalism for the reasons mentioned above; the fact that an idea is (necessarily) grounded in a culture does not mean that it cannot be universal.

Though I thought it important to address methodological issues given the nature and legacy of Tempels' work, I want to stress to the reader that they do not need to agree with my methodological approach in order to gain something from this book. In the next chapter I present contemporary work on life force, drawn almost entirely from contemporary African writers. This means that none of my claims in this book rely on the work of Tempels. Remember that my main goal is to develop a normative theory based on the relatively underexplored ideas of life force. It ultimately does not matter *where* this theory comes from if the reader is adamant that my approach is wrong. The theory can still be evaluated on its own terms. I will not address methodological concerns of these kinds during the rest of the book.

2.6 Conclusion

Placide Tempels was the first European to identify life force in his work *Bantu Philosophy*. He surmised that Bantu peoples believe that literally everything was imbued with an imperceptible energy known as life force, where the goal of life is to increase one's force. However, the legacy of Tempels on African philosophy is fraught. On the one hand, he was sanctioned by his church for attributing a deeper and more coherent set of beliefs to African peoples than the vast majority of his contemporary European colleagues were comfortable recognizing. On the other hand, though his work was initially received positively by some scholars, as time wore on numerous African thinkers began to question it. Tempels' work was an instance of ethnophilosophy, and a poor one at that, given that he makes numerous overgeneralizations. Ethnophilosophy is misguided in taking folk beliefs and culture to represent a system worthy of philosophical study, while simultaneously lacking conceptual clarity and argumentative rigour. It is no surprise, then, that Tempels' work is hardly as sophisticated as what one finds in the Western philosophical canon. Underlying these criticisms is the view that philosophy ought to be universal, which means it should be detached from culture. I appealed to the work of Etieyibo in an attempt to show that the debate between particularists and universalists is at least partially misguided. Ideas do not arise out of nowhere in a vacuum. They are necessarily tied to a culture, at least to some degree. However, this does not mean that an idea or concept that necessarily arises in a culture cannot be universal. In some sense, this book is an attempt to see whether ideas about life force are universalizable, at least when it comes to formulating a normative theory. I therefore endorse a moderate view between the particularists and universalists. However, I conclude by again emphasizing that the reader need not accept my methodological approach to African philosophy in order to benefit from the book. In the next chapter I outline contemporary descriptions of life force primarily from African exponents and therefore I do not rely on Tempels' work in my theorizing about life force. Finally, regardless of the origin of the theory I present, it can be evaluated in its own right by way of comparison with other African and global normative ethical theories.

3

Contemporary Accounts of Life Force and Moral Theory

3.1 Introduction

This chapter builds on the previous one by turning to survey what the contemporary literature says about life force, as found in the work of primarily (though not exclusively) contemporary African scholars. It thereby avoids any of the possibly pernicious effects of Tempels' work on life force. Though I do not claim to use every possible relevant source, I have made every effort to be as comprehensive as possible. I want it to be uncontestable that the characteristics I attribute to life force are found throughout the contemporary literature and as such I rely more heavily on quotes than is typical of most philosophy monographs. I believe that this chapter constitutes as thorough a description of life force as can be found in the contemporary literature to date. While this chapter is primarily descriptive, it serves the important purpose of bringing into focus a clear moral theory based on life force. This is a theory based on a wide-ranging supernatural ontology and thus helps explain my motivation for developing a secular theory in the next chapter. The description of life force offered in this chapter will explain such features as the African hierarchy of being, interconnectedness, the notions of visible and invisible, among many others (3.2). After this, I explain that normativity is implied in the descriptions of life force, including in the form of both theories of value and right action (3.3). I conclude by highlighting some alternative accounts of life force that I will not address in this book (3.4).

3.2 The Features of Life Force

This section contains an extensive summary of the main features of life force as found in the contemporary literature. Before proceeding, there are three important caveats to note. First, I have decided to organize this section in

A Moral Theory of Liveliness. Kirk Lougheed, Oxford University Press. © Kirk Lougheed 2025.
DOI: 10.1093/9780197782019.003.0003

terms of topic. It is inevitable that the categories I have chosen are somewhat arbitrary and artificial. However, I believe that the ambiguity this may create in certain places is far outweighed by the clarity it provides about many more ideas, particularly to the reader unfamiliar with life force. Second, notice that there is significant overlap between many of the ideas in this section and the ones found in the work of Tempels (2.2). This fact is further evidence for the claim that, despite its flaws, *Bantu Philosophy* constitutes an important foundational work in African philosophy. Third, there will also be some overlap in the various subsections here, because many of the same ideas appear in multiple sources on life force. But this is ultimately to the good, because it shows that there is widespread—though not universal—agreement about how to understand life force, at least among its academic exponents. I have therefore chosen to make explicit some of this widespread agreement, though at times this leads to some otherwise avoidable repetition.

3.2.1 Life Force as the Highest Value

There is virtually universal agreement among expositors of life force that for the peoples who affirm its existence, it is by far the most important value. For example, writing of the Igbo people, K. C. Anyanwu explains that the metaphysics of life force is what 'molds the lives of the Igbo people in their culture' (1984, 85). Everything in the universe is alive, and life itself is the highest value (Anyanwu 1984, 90). Interestingly, he also says that '[t]he word that features prominently in the African understanding of the ultimate reality is Life' (Anyanwu 1987a, 248). Its importance can also be found in sayings such as 'Life is First' and 'Life is greater than Wealth' (Anyanwu 1987a, 248). Deogratias Bikopo and Louis-Jacques van Bogaert add that 'the ontological base is the concept of energy, strength, and vital force. It is what gives beings their intrinsic value' (2010, 44).

Bert Hamminga confirms these ideas when he says that, at bottom, humans just are forces. He writes, '[v]ital power is what matters in life, we care for nothing else' (Hamminga 2005, 58). Pantaleon Iroegbu agrees, saying that '[l]ife is such an important value that it is rightly described as the ultimate *rasion de'etre* of all other activities of the human person. It is thus most valuable, indeed a *mega-value*' (2005, 447). He also refers to life as the 'ultimate value' and 'super-value' (Iroegbu 2005b, 449). Henry Sindima echoes similar language, when he writes that '[w]e are here saying that in

38 A MORAL THEORY OF LIVELINESS

African thought, the raison "d'Ctre" for all creation is life' (Sindima 1989, 546). Furthermore, '[t]o assert that life is the basic framework of living is to argue that life is the organizing logic in the African world' (Sindima 1989, 546). Bénézet Bujo says that 'life is the highest principle of ethical conduct' (2001, 3). Finally, George Ukagba explains that '[f]or the traditional African, the highest good, what Aquinas calles [sic] the *Sumum Bonum*, in other words, the highest value is life' (2005, 184).

Since it is the most important value, all obstacles to life must be removed (Uzukwu 1982, 194). Life or force is what animates a person and what gives them existence (Iroegbu 2005, 447). That one has life is not random, but it 'is regarded as the most precious gift of God' (Kasenene 1994, 140).[1] This is further confirmed when Vincent Mulago writes that '[e]verything created is a gift to people from the Creator to ensure their existence, to contribute to the enhancement and safeguarding of their life' (Mulago 1991, 125). So, part of what explains the importance of life force is that it comes from God.

3.2.2 Life Force and Interconnectedness

The metaphysics of life force also entails that everything is interconnected in virtue of possessing some degree of force which is all ultimately derived from God. For example, of the Igbo peoples Anyanwu writes that '[t]he same life-force that permeates the universe is also found in human persons and objects, and all the forces in the universe are constantly interacting and interpenetrating each other. In the Igbo universe of life-forces, nothing is lifeless or inert, and no life-force exists in isolation from others' (Anyanwu 1984, 90). That everything shares force provides the basis for what some have described as ontological unity (Anyanwu 1984, 90–91).[2] This unity is explicitly affirmed by Anyanwu when he writes that 'everything which exists is life-force, there are no forces in isolation. Rather, all forces are interrelated and are also in constant interaction' (Anyanwu 1987a, 249). Imafidon echoes this: '[t]he immediate implication of the theory of force as an African met-aphysical theory is the notion of the interconnectedness of all things based on a common essence such that beings within an African reality are onto-logically bonded and form a web of interacting relationship' (2014b, 144).

---

[1] See also Gbadegesin 1991, 40, 88.
[2] See also Behrens 2014, 55; Chemhuru 2014, 80; Kehinde 2014, 151, 152; Unah 2014, 109; Uzukwu 1982, 198; Weidtmann 2019, 108.

ACCOUNTS OF LIFE FORCE AND MORAL THEORY   39

Magesa confirms this when he writes that 'one cannot ensure the full enhancement of life *by* oneself. One's life force depends on the life forces of other persons and other beings, including those of the ancestors and, ultimately, God' (Magesa 1997, 52).[3]

Some go further than ontological unity or connectedness, saying that life force implies a kind of *sameness*. Anyanwu says that '[b]ecause everything is filled with force, the African concludes that all things are similar and share the same qualities in spite of apparent differences. And furthermore, in the universe of metamorphosis, things (forces) transform and transmute themselves' (1987a, 249).[4]

The life force between different things in the universe can be understood as impacting the force in others. For example, '[t]hey know that between them [i.e., humans] and the cosmos there is a vital flux making up the solidarity of creation as a whole and ultimately connecting them to the supreme being, God, the source of all life' (Bujo 2005, 426).[5] Hamminga also explains that '[t]here is no way to study forces in isolation. Nature as a whole operates on nature as a whole. This implies that it makes no sense whatsoever to do controlled experiments in order to acquire knowledge of forces' (2005, 72).

The interconnectedness in question here is not just between other humans or non-human animals, but 'we understand a relationship in being and life of each person with descendants, family, brothers, and sisters in the clan, with ancestors, and with God who is the ultimate source of all life' (Mulago 1991, 120). This means that 'vital union is the bond joining together, vertically and horizontally, beings living and dead; it is the life-giving principle in all. It is the result of communion, a participation in the one reality, the one vital principal that unites various beings' (Mulago 1991, 120). In general this interconnectedness cannot be broken, though it can be in some instances. This means that '[f]or Africans, beings always retain their intimate ontic relationship to one another, and the idea of distinct beings which happen to be alongside one another but completely independent is quite foreign to their thought' (Mulago 1991, 123). This understanding of unity and interconnectedness is not just about ontology but informs and orders sociopolitical structures and religious institutions in traditional society (Sindima

---

[3] See also Magesa 1997, 91, 154, 285.
[4] See also Mulago 1991, 124.
[5] See also Bujo 2001, 56.

1989, 538). The implications are far-reaching such that 'the social, religious or moral fibre is grounded in and guided by the concept of *bondedness* of *life*' (Sindima 1989, 538).

3.2.3 The Visible and the Invisible

Another salient feature of life force is that it applies to a very large ontological realm. The Abrahamic faiths often distinguish between the physical world (or natural or material world) and the spiritual world (or supernatural or immaterial world). Though these two worlds can interact with each other, Westerners typically understand them as distinct realms. In the African tradition, though a distinction is usually drawn between the visible and invisible, the occupants of each are considered very much a part of the same realm (e.g., Gbadegesin 1991, 85). For example, the living dead are recently deceased relatives who remain very much a part of the community. They are merely invisible. It is not as if they exist in a faraway or totally different spiritual world (e.g., Bujo 2001, 10; Bujo 2001, 85; Ehiakhamen 2014, 98; Imafidon 2014a, 38; Mulago 1991, 119).

Anyanwu explains that the Igbo do 'not make a clear-cut distinction [. . .] between the visible and invisible worlds but regard all as a field of aesthetic continuum. The world is centred on the self and is inseparable from it. As a result, the self fuses life into the world so that the soul or spirit of man becomes the soul or spirit of the world' (Anyanwu 1984, 89). The aesthetic continuum here is a reference to shared force that exists across all entities. C. N. Ubah writes that the 'Otanchara-Otanzu [of the Igbo] religion consists of a wide range of beliefs and practices relating to invisible forces which are thought to determine the lot of men on earth. Life is held to exist in two planes: the tangible world of the living and the immaterial world of the spirits' (Ubah 1982, 91). Elvis Imafidon says, '[t]he beings or entities existing in these two realms of existence are lively and active in varying degrees because they are vitalized, animated, or energized by an ontological principle or essence or *force*, given them by the Supreme Being' (2014a, 38). Finally, though life force is presumably not subject to empirical scrutiny, Magesa suggests that it is 'more concentrated in some parts [of the body] than in others' (1997, 162). This explains the importance of certain parts such as blood and hair in various rituals (i.e., they are thought to contain more life force than other parts).

3.2.4 The Hierarchy of Being

The existence of life force also helps to explain what is known as the 'African hierarchy of being' or 'African chain of being'. In this sense, life itself is hierarchical (Anyanwu 1984, 91).[6] God has the most life force. All force is derived from God, which explains why God is responsible for the creation of all life (Anyanwu 1984, 92–95).[7] Anyanwu explains that 'LIFE is the only ultimate reality though it manifests itself in diverse forms, and LIFE is God (Chi *wu ndu)*. Ancestors, divinities, personal *chi,* etc. are not ultimate realities but, at best, penultimate ones, since their power and existence are dependent on the ultimate reality, namely, God or *Chukwu*' (Anyanwu 1984, 94). Bénézet Bujo affirms this when he writes that '[t]he African conception centers on life. Life articulates itself thanks to and through the community of the living, the dead, and the not-yet born, and it never forgets to refer to God, the actual foundation of this three-dimensional community' (Bujo 2005, 423). Finally, Laurenti Magesa explains that 'As a rule, the older the individuals, the more powerful their vital force; the greater the responsibility they hold in society, the more intense their mystical powers' (Magesa 1997, 51).

The highly communitarian nature of morality in the African tradition does not imply that God does not play a significant role in morality. For example, some describe God as the 'objective' grounds of life force (Anyanwu 1987a, 257–258). Bujo explains that '[i]n the traditional African conception, God is an unquestioned postulate, even though God is rarely mentioned' (Bujo 2005, 424). Life force 'is hierarchical, descending from God through the ancestors and elders to the individual' (Kasenene 1994, 140). God has placed humans at the centre of the visible universe (Uzukwu 1982, 194–195).[8] Departed ancestors exist to give their life force to living persons (Hamminga 2005, 58). However, departed ancestors and other spiritual entities have more force than humans, with humans having more force than anything else in the visible realm such as non-human animals and inanimate objects. Only stronger forces can act on weaker forces. A weaker force cannot causally impact a stronger force (Gbadegesin 1991, 112–113).

---

[6] See also Gbadegesin 1991, 88; Kehinde 2014, 151, 152, 156; Unah 2014, 109, 118; Uzukwu 1982; 195–196.

[7] See also Bujo 2005, 424, Bikopo and Van Bogaert 2010, 44–45; Hamminga 2005 63; Imafidon 2014b, 144; Kasenene 1998, 25; Mulago 1991, 124; Ubah 1982, 92.

[8] See also Dzobo 1992, 224; Magesa 1997, 51; Uzukwu 1982; 195, 203–208.

42 A MORAL THEORY OF LIVELINESS

In this tradition there is often reference to the 'not-yet-born' or 'to-be-born'. On the one hand, these are not fetuses that exist in the womb of a woman but just have yet to be born. On the other hand, they clearly have a referent. This is quite different from the Western tradition in which the 'not-yet-born' (i.e., prior to conception) do not, strictly speaking, have a referent. For example, anti-natalists speak of it being impermissible to bring new persons into existence. However, such persons do not exist until they are brought into existence and hence there is technically no referent for 'persons' until they actually exist. The yet-to-be-born in the African tradition appear to have a referent and thus refer to a being with ontological status. In this way they are a kind of life force that exists in the imperceptible realm in the same way as the living dead. Bujo indicates their importance when he writes that the ethical community includes 'the living, the dead, and the not-yet born. This community with its threefold dimension constitutes the anthropological foundation of ethics as a whole' (Bujo 2005, 424). Some of this discussion serves to explain why procreation is so important in this tradition. For '[a] prosperous progeny is indisputably one of the conditions ensuring the well-being of all. Thus, one cannot ignore the not-yet born; they already deserve to be called "persons" because, even before they take shape, they embody the living and the dead in such a way that they are the future and carry everybody's hopes' (Bujo 2005, 433).[9] However, it remains opaque to me what precisely such beings are, in addition to their place in the hierarchy.

3.2.5 Controlling Life Force and the Power of Spoken Words

Life force can to some extent be controlled; specifically, it can be strengthened or weakened based on the actions of other forces (i.e., other beings). When good or ill befalls a person, it is typically thought to be the result of forces acting on them. However, a consistent theme in the literature is that it can be very difficult to precisely discern which forces are acting, regardless of whether they are increasing or decreasing one's force (e.g., Bujo 2001, 46; Hamminga 2005, 65–71). Consider that 'in the world of forces, secret forces intervene in the course of events; and such interventions may be beyond conscious understanding' (Anyanwu 1987a, 249). Similarly, '[s]ince African thought recognizes the existence of "secret" (unknown) forces acting or

[9] See also Bujo 2001, 3–5.

ready to act in the universe, the knowledge of future events cannot be absolutely certain' (Anyanwu 1987a, 249). Even though deciphering how forces are at work in the world is difficult, and perhaps impossible in specific cases, it is typically thought that life force can be directed or guided at least to some degree. Thus, force is at least in some sense a typical cause, even if it is not subject to empirical scrutiny (see Anyanwu 1984, 91). Those with life force who possess intelligence can govern that force to some degree with the power of spoken word (Anyanwu 1984, 90).[10] Consider that:

> The Igbo are alive to the fact that word has a divine power because it is the principle of creativity, order and destruction. Word has consequences. It is a power that compels men and God to action; a power that transforms the world, men and things; a power that gives direction to life-force. For these reasons, the Igbo say that *Okwu wu ndu* (word is life). (Anyanwu 1984, 92)

Anyanwu goes so far as to describe words themselves as forces that act on other forces (Anyanwu 1987a, 254).[11] This means that '[w]ords are principles of creativity, order and destruction; and those who possess this power (a power which increases with age or experience) are admired and yet feared. Words have the power of controlling Life-Force; man, animal, natural phenomenon, and even God' (Anyanwu 1987a, 254).[12]

On the African view, forces never act randomly. An individual's life force is always strengthened or diminished ultimately by the intentional actions of other agents. It is therefore 'unthinkable that your vital power changed by a mere contingency. Even natural forces that change your vital power, like a torrential rain, are sent by people using power transmission procedures' (Hamminga 2005, 66).[13]

3.2.6 The Religious Nature of Life Force

In many ways, this description of life force could be just a description of African Traditional Religion itself. It would be impossible to give a description of African Traditional Religion without significant attention being given

---

[10] See also Hamminga 2005, 65; Jahn 1961, 112; Bujo 2005, 427.
[11] See also Gbadegesin 1991, 120.
[12] See also Mulago 1991, 124.
[13] See also Mulago 1991, 122–123.

44 A MORAL THEORY OF LIVELINESS

to the role of life force or vital energy. But that life force is inherently religious does not necessarily equate with what is meant by 'religious' in the West. For example, Anyanwu writes: '[t]o say that the Igbo live religiously does not mean that they spend all their days in prayer or that they do not exercise their power of thought. A person is not religious solely because he worships God, rather he is religious if he commits all the resources of his mind to and completely surrenders himself to the service of a cause in such a way that it controls his modes of thought, activities and behaviour' (Anyanwu 1984, 87). The normativity one finds based on life force is inherently religious and more in line with the Western notion because all life force stems from God. Peter Kasenene explains that 'African ethics is deeply religious, being influenced by a belief in an all-pervading Supreme Being who controls the universe and social relationships through a number of intermediaries' (1994, 140). He adds that '[a]ccording to African spirituality, there is no dichotomy between the sacred and the profane, the physical and spiritual, the religious and the moral' (Kasenene 1994, 142).

Bujo is perhaps the most obvious example of a contemporary African theorist who denies that ethics can be separated from religion. He writes that Western communitarianism 'deserves this name from the African viewpoint only in a *limited* sense, especially since it does not understand the dead as agents and pays no attention at all to the significance of the un-born' (Bujo 2001, 29). This implies that he would reject an ethic that did not give significant attention to ancestors, the living dead, the to-be-born, etc., thereby affirming the significance of a religious ontology. For Bujo the relevant moral community just is the community that includes these spiritual beings (e.g., Bujo 2001, 34).[14] Similar ideas can also be found in Kasenene, who writes that '[i]n African religions there is no separation between religion and ethics, between one's beliefs and one's actions towards others' (1994, 140).

3.2.7 Life Force and Death

Western monotheism tends to affirm the existence of an immaterial soul such that when a person's biological body dies, the soul detaches itself and joins the immaterial or spiritual realm. The soul represents the 'self' such

[14] See also Bujo 2001, 102.

that its existence over time is what constitutes personal identity. This is not death as understood by those in the African tradition who affirm the existence of life force. On this view, when a person's biological body dies, their force continues to exist, and they very much remain a part of the community. Consider these two quotes on death:

> Death is not the annihilation of life-force but the disappearance of the visible life in this world. Since individuals are inseparable from their families, lineages, and communities during their lives, the Igbo do not see why a separation should occur after death. Though the dead live diminished lives, they have more spirit-power because they live in the spirit-world, have deeper knowledge of life-force and continue to participate in the total life of the community. (Anyanwu 1984, 100)
>
> The concept of energy or vital force is central in African ontology; energy is being, and being is energy. The Supreme Being channels his energy through the clan's Chief to human and non-human living beings. Energy can wane and wax. Death comes when the resources in energy reach nil [...] What subsists after death is the 'self' that was hidden behind the body during life. The process of dying is not static; it goes through progressive stages of energy loss. To be dead means to have a diminished life because of a reduced level of energy. When the level of energy falls to zero, one is completely dead. (Bikopo and Van Bogaert 2010, 42, 45)

3.2.8 Life Force and Epistemology

Though not necessarily a consistent theme in the literature, there are references to the epistemological implications of life force, particularly in the work of Hamminga. For instance, some contend that 'knowing' is a communal activity, and that radically divergent opinions don't exist within the community. This implies that knowledge is a kind of 'togetherness' and that since '[t]ogetherness is our ultimate criterion of any action, the pursuit of knowledge [is] just one of them' (Hamminga 2005, 58). The action of knowledge acquisition 'serves the purpose of enhancing the vital energy, the procreation of the tribe. Together. What you do if you isolate, individualize yourself is worse than dying: you will never be a root' (Hamminga 2005, 59). Hamminga believes that it is not the individual who is the knower but rather the community. Since knowledge is a form of power, it necessarily

46 A MORAL THEORY OF LIVELINESS

comes from ancestors (Hamminga 2005, 59). Furthermore, '[t]he general rule always to agree with everybody holds most emphatically with respect to authorities. In the clan context, the elder's opinion is truth. All power, all truth comes up from the roots of the family tree, the dead ancestors, to the trunk, the elders, and passes up to parents and children, the branches, leaves and flowers' (Hamminga 2005, 61).

In this context, using arguments in order to convince members of the community is a weakness. It shows a 'lack of power and vitality. A good, forceful truth does not need arguments' (Hamminga 2005, 61). A person is typically thought to have a strong life force primarily because of age and wisdom, as opposed to possessing great physical strength. Wisdom here is not a reference to knowing many arguments. Instead, '[i]t consists of a wider and deeper understanding of the universe as possessed by those who have a deeper position in it. Wisdom is felt as a force' (Hamminga 2005, 61). Acquiring knowledge is just about understanding the nature of forces (Hamminga 2005, 63). Hamminga concludes that '[n]eedless to say, the community is a force, and *knowledge itself is a force, transmitted by the ancestors to the living*' (Hamminga 2005, 66).

Different epistemological ideas can be found in the work of Bujo, who believes that the palaver is an important source of moral knowledge. Indeed, it is through the palaver that knowledge from the ancestors is passed on. This process is supposed to respect the tradition passed down by ancestors while also offering relevant guidance in the present day. This knowledge is ultimately about strengthening the life of the community (Bujo 2001, 34–51). For example, it can inform the community when a practice either strengthens or degrades life force. This means that the palaver 'makes it possible to discern whether a different religion, or an individual who thinks differently, genuinely destroys the common good—for it is possible that in the last analysis, the same ideal is being maintained, viz., the bestowal and strengthening of life in fullness' (Bujo 2001, 163).

The above ideas are about the acquiring and transmission of knowledge. However, one also finds epistemological comments about structure. The existence of life force and the interconnectedness of everything that exists provide structure to the universe, making discoveries about it possible. Sindima explains that 'the notion of life provides the basic framework for both conceptualization and interpretation in the African world. Life orders the African world' (1989, 546).

3.3 Life Force as Moral Theory

Though it should be clear enough from the above description that life force grounds normativity, it is not often explicitly formulated as a normative theory. More carefully, descriptions do not typically match the precise formulations that can be found in globally better-known Anglo-American normative theories. However, one does still come across statements in the literature that clearly demonstrate that life force is indeed intended to constitute normative underpinning. The purpose of this section is to show how some of the above ideas can be developed into a normative moral theory. This involves demonstrating how it presents a theory of both right action and moral status. Specifically, I begin by highlighting some of the general normative statements of life force (3.3.1). I then turn to show how life force provides a theory of value, particularly regarding the moral worth of humans (3.3.2). I then explore how life force can generate a theory of right action (3.3.3).

3.3.1 Life Force and Normativity

As stated, it is rare to find explicit formulations of a normative principle based on life force that would match the depth and detail one finds in contemporary Anglo-American philosophy. Still, one does find a number of statements that can be plausibly interpreted as normative principles:

- Everything that contributes to maintaining, strengthening, and perfecting individual as well as communal life is good and right. (Bujo 2005, 428)[15]
- [A]ll people and activities that diminish life are in all cultures considered as evil, while those that promote it are regarded as good. (Iroegbu 2005b, 447)
- In ethical terms, any action which increases life or vital force is right, and whatever decreases it is wrong. (Kasenene 1994, 140)
- Human life, that is, human persons as the center of creation, is the criterion of good and evil. (Mulago 1991, 125)

---

[15] See also Bujo 2005, 431.

48   A MORAL THEORY OF LIVELINESS

- The absoluteness of maintaining excellent relations with all the personalities who come into vital contact with man in his world becomes evident when this relationship is upset by human offense—especially by offenses classified as abomination *(alu)*. The reaction of the Igbo in face of this danger brings out an important nuance in his perception of his universe: the objectives of life (its maintenance and augmentation) can only be achieved if equilibrium is maintained in the universe. Anything which endangers this equilibrium in a vital way is morally wrong, and could be morally abominable if it is *nso ala* (forbidden by the land, or touching the sacredness of the land) or *alu* (abomination). (Uzukwu 1982, 202)
- The individual person experiences vital force when she takes part in the process of reconstituting (re-viving) the community. (Weidtmann 2019, 109)
- While the idea of the vital force is not insignificant in ethics, the key to understanding this idea is supplied by one's membership in the community; and this means that vital force is a consequence and goal of ethical conduct rather than its basis—individuals live only thanks to the community. (Bujo 2001, 3)
- Whatever or whoever increases the life force is good and whatever or whoever decreases or destroys it is bad. A person is good in so far as he or she promotes, supports or protects his or her life force and the life-force of his or her neighbors [....] Wrong is anything that destroys or harms one's life-force or the life-force of others. (Kasenene 1998, 25, 39)
- [M]orality and ethics [i.e., right action] refers to thoughts, words, attitudes, and actual behavior that promote the force of life [....] when we speak of immortality and destruction, the reference is to those thoughts and attitude—and of course, people and other elements of creation—that act against the life force eventually destroy life itself. (Magesa 1997, 161)
- This maintains that there is an urge or dynamic creative energy in life, called *Se*, which works towards wholeness and healing, towards building up and not pulling down, towards creating and not destroying and towards synthesis and no conflict [....] Powerlessness or loss of vitality, unproductive living, and growthlessness become ultimate evils in our indigenous culture [....B]ehavior is right in humanistic morality not because it conforms to a code of conduct which has been laid-down,

but because it builds up instead of pulling down—in short, because it is syntropic. (Dzobo 1992, 227–228)

These quotes show that expositors of life force clearly imply that it has a normative dimension.

3.3.2 Life Force and Moral Status

The idea that humans have inalienable rights and inherent dignity, or possess a superlative final value and therefore must be respected, can also be found throughout some of the literature on life force. Here are some examples:

- [E]very human is from God and entitled to respect no matter his or her clan, ethnicity, or nation. (Bujo 2005, 431)
- The basic thrust of our argument is that no one has the right to deny another his or her natural right to exist and perform as a human being. For all have an equal right to live. No life is in itself superior to others. And before God, all lives are equally previous. Life is Life. Life A is equal to Life Z. Period. (Iroegbu 2005b, 446)[16]
- Human society is organised on the basis of vital force; life growth, life influence and life rank. This structure must be respected, and individuals are good in so far as they fulfill their duties to promote, support and protect the vital force within the community, according to their particular rank. (Kasenene 1994, 141)
- The African concept of person as well as the notion of community is grounded in the concept of life. To put it another way, the concepts of person and community arise out of the understanding of being bonded to natural life or the feeling of being in the network of life. From this it follows that the ethical imperative is not to treat the other or nature as a means, since the other is also part of the self. People belong to each other, being bonded in one common life. (Sindima 1989, 546)
- Human life is considered one of the greatest values because it has within itself the power of change, growth and development. This dynamic, creative energy in life works towards building up instead of pulling down, towards creating and not destroying. Life becomes meaningful and

---

[16] See also Iroegbu 2005, 447.

50 A MORAL THEORY OF LIVELINESS

worth living because of the dynamic creative energy that is lodged at the heart of human existence. (Dzobo 1992, 230)

From these ideas it is clear that life force provides a grounding for human value. Humans have a dignity, inalienable rights, and superlative final value in virtue of possessing life force, which is ultimately grounded in God. Precisely how God can serve as the ground of value will be explored in Chapter 8.

3.3.3 Life Force as a Moral Theory of Right Action

The above two sections also offer grounds for the development of a moral theory of right action. Though the majority of work on life force tends to focus on describing the qualities associated with life force a notable exception can be found in the work of Motsamai Molefe and Mutshidzi Maraganedzha (2023).[17] They focus on the normative aspects of life force and believe that it offers the potential for at least two different theories of right action.

The first is what they describe as a perfectionist normative theory. In African thought, personhood is a normative term denoting a person's character. Personhood can be developed only in the context of community because it requires exercising other-regarding virtues (see Chapter 6). Though personhood is usually developed in entirely secular terms, Molefe and Maraganedzha believe that an ethic based on personhood can be grounded in life force. They explain that '[a]t the heart of this approach to ethics is the expectation that the human agent has to develop her distinctive (spiritual) features to be characterized by virtue' (Molefe and Maraganedzha 2023, 362). The goal of morality on this view is to achieve a state of moral perfection, which comes with acquiring and developing other-regarding virtues. Molefe and Maraganedzha further explain that '[s]cholars of African thought tend to construe the excellence or perfection associated with the maturation of vitality, on the part of the agent, with relational virtues, such as generosity, kindness, respect, solidarity, and so on' (Molefe and Maraganedzha 2023, 363). These reflections lead them to posit the following principle of right action:

- An act is right insofar as it perfects the agent's spiritual nature; and, it is wrong if it fails to do so (Molefe and Maraganedzha 2023, 363)

---

[17] See also Molefe 2018.

ACCORDING TO THIS PRINCIPLE

According to this principle, the wrong of an action like murder can be explained by the fact that it does not contribute to the perfection of the wrongdoer and fails to relate positively with the victim in light of their own spiritual nature (Molefe and Maraganedzha 2023, 363).

Though Molefe and Maraganedzha are clear that they are just trying to demonstrate that there can be a moral theory based on life force and are not aiming to offer a defense of any such theory, I do not believe the perfectionist theory is a very promising candidate. The reasons for this are twofold. First, as will become clearer to the reader in Chapter 6, articulations of personhood in the literature are almost always entirely secular. It would take a lot more work to show that the virtues prescribed by personhood are identical to actions that increase life force. Of course, I do not deny that there will be some overlap here; my point is that perfect overlap cannot be assumed. Likewise, the appeal to personhood appears undermotivated, as it is so infrequently mentioned in conjunction with life force and any kind of supernatural ontology.[18] Second, though I believe normative personhood can be used to motivate a theory of right action, it is probably first and foremost a theory about moral value.[19] Again, more work would have to be done to justify the transition from a theory of moral value to one of right action.[20]

What Molefe and Maraganedzha refer to as a dignity-based normative theory, the second of their theories of right action, is more promising, or at least does not seem to face the same initial obstacles as the perfectionist theory. Instead of appealing to developing one's personhood, the dignity approach requires a focus on recognizing the value of life force. Pantaleon Iroegbu explains that '[b]ecause [life] is divine resemblance, it must be taken loftily and with highest respect. It must be seen for what it is: of high value' (Pantaleon Iroegbu 2005c, 448 quoted in Molefe and Maraganedzha 2023, 364). If life force grounds respect, then it implies strong negative duties of doing no harm and positive duties of empowering life. Accordingly, Molefe and Maraganedzha say a dignity-based theory of right action based on life force looks like this:

- An act is right insofar as it respects a person's spiritual nature, and [an] act is wrong insofar as it degrades this valuable human nature. (Molefe and Maraganedzha 2023, 364)

---

[18] Menkiti 1984 and Tempels 1959 are perhaps notable exceptions to the predominately secular approach to personhood.

[19] Indeed, an anonymous referee has pressed to make sure I am clear on this point.

[20] I take on some of this work in Chapter 6.

52 A MORAL THEORY OF LIVELINESS

According to this principle, murder is wrong because it degrades a person's spiritual nature. I believe that this principle is not only more plausible as a moral theory than the first of Molefe and Maraganedzha's theories discussed early in this section, but also more accurately describes what ensues from life force. If this principle from Molefe and Maraganedzha is a deontological one, there are also other principles of right action that could be derived from life force that are better construed as teleological:

- An action is right if and only if it strengthens, preserves, and protects the life force of oneself and one's community.
- An action is wrong if and only if it weakens and degrades the life force of oneself and one's community.
- An action is permissible inasmuch as it strengthens, preserves, and protects the life force of oneself and one's community.
- An action is impermissible inasmuch as it weakens and degrades the life force of oneself and one's community.[21]

These principles are distinct from the first perfectionist theory, because they do not focus on developing one's nature by way of personhood. Whether these principles could ultimately be construed as perfectionist is not relevant to my purposes. Now, there is much that could be explored here, especially given the dearth of moral theories that appeal to life force in the African tradition. For example, life force explains why all persons are valuable, but also why non-human animals and nature are owed respect. Since humans have the most force of anything in the visible realm, this could explain why they have a dignity while animals, rocks, and mountains do not. These principles could be tested against one another in order to determine which of them, if any, is superior. This could involve seeing how well they explain intuitions in various cases. Furthermore, they could be used to issue verdicts on a whole host of issues in applied ethics.

However, remember that my main purpose in this book is to explore a naturalized version of life force. I want to offer an ethic that is palatable to a global audience and therefore seek to avoid metaphysically controversial positions as much as possible. Indeed, in Parts II and III, I will put secular

---

[21] I have implied both self-regarding and other-regarding duties. However, there is debate about whether an individual should focus on increasing only the life force of others or if their own life force matters, too. When I formulate the secular version of the theory, I will address this issue in 5.2.1.

teleological and deontological principles of right action to the test. My point in this and the previous chapter has just been to show that normativity clearly follows from life force. There are clear implications for moral status, and there are multiple ways life force could be used to motivate a theory of right action. Since I believe I have demonstrated this to be the case, I am now ready to turn in Part II to developing a secular theory inspired by the life force. Before doing so, however, I conclude this chapter by briefly explaining why I am not appealing to alternative conceptions of life force.

3.4 Alternative Accounts of Life Force

In this section I explain that although I am aware of alternative accounts of life force, I will keep the focus of the book on the accounts of life force found in the contemporary African philosophical tradition. This section serves to highlight avenues for further research for those so inclined.

3.4.1 The Continental European Tradition

A potential objection or question arises from my choice of the particular descriptions of life force I have used in this chapter. Indeed, Ludwig Klages (e.g., 2013; see also Bishop 2018) and Henri Bergson (e.g., 1907) offer different accounts of life force or vitalism during the first half of the twentieth century, with the former coining the term *élan vital*. Indeed, it is *possible* that Tempels was influenced by Klages and Bergson. Furthermore, both Souleymane Bachir Diagne (2011) and Bruce Janz (2022) offer accounts of vitalism that may be consistent with those of the likes of Bergson and Deluze.[22] There are several reasons why I will not interact with these approaches. I aim to stay as close to the African tradition as possible, while recognizing that the boundaries of such cannot be precisely drawn. Notice that even if it is the case that Tempels was influenced by European thinkers, this does not make the concept of life force I am appealing to any less African. Indeed, it is partly for this very sort of concern that I am not relying on Tempels' explication of life force and instead turn to contemporary African

---

[22] I am grateful for anonymous referee for prompting me to consider these alternative approaches to life force.

54 A MORAL THEORY OF LIVELINESS

expositors in this chapter. I aim to rely primarily on the words of contemporary Africans, not Tempels. Though it might be observed that these accounts could still be useful to my construction of a secular theory of life force, I am doubtful that they could all be reasonably construed as naturalistic.[23] But even if my suspicions here are correct, it is still possible that the ideas found in these thinkers could be useful for my project. However, I am not suitably familiar with the continental philosophical tradition and French philosophy in particular to be able to effectively draw upon them. And even if I could, it would come at the risk of making the scope of this work unmanageable. I leave it to others who are more familiar with this tradition to draw relevant connections to my project.

3.4.2 Animism

The reader may also wonder why I have not mentioned any connections to varieties of life force found outside of the African continent. Indeed, if life force is a form of *animism*, then belief in it is widespread outside of Africa. Consider that Graham Oppy observes that many scholars identify themselves as animists, at least with respect to flora (2023, 209–211; e.g., Calvo 2016; Maher 2017). He further explains that the Wicca may be interpreted as animists (Oppy 2023; e.g., White 2022), as can some forms of paganism (Clifton and Harvey 2004; Davies 2011), Western Buddhism (Capper 2016), and apparently some versions of Christianity (Wallace 2019). Kathryn Rountree observes that different forms of animism can be found throughout various indigenous cultures, including that of the New Zealand Māori (e.g., Barnett 2017, Vicente 2020), the Norwegian Sámi (e.g., Kraft 2010, 2015), and the Yukaghirs and Eveny of Siberia (e.g., Willerslev 2007), among others (Oppy 2023, 342).

However, Mikel Burley observes that 'John Mbiti exhorted with reference to African religions in particular, for the term "animism" "to be abandoned once and for all" (Mbiti, 1969: 8)' (Burley 2023, 131). Part of the reason for Mbiti's suspicion of the term is that it can be defined in so many different ways, many of which turn out to be incompatible with descriptions of African life force, that the term is simply unhelpful. To take just one example,

---

[23] I am also doubtful whether all of the authors in question would accept the binary between naturalistic and supernaturalist that I am assuming exists.

consider that the Anglo-American philosopher of religion Evan Fales defines animism as 'to consist in a system of beliefs holding that denizens of the natural world—various plants, mineral formations and landmarks, other geological features such as rivers, celestial phenomena, and so on, as well as non-human animals—are invested with personal spirits' (2023, 179–180). But this definition is not consistent with the descriptions of life force found in this chapter. African life force is not always a personal spirit.

On the other hand, after surveying a number of different definitions of animism, Eric Steinhart proposes that they:

> point toward many different *theories of animation*. A theory of animation has three main parts: (1) It specifies the class of things that are animated. The definitions above list diverse things (beings, objects, mountains, rivers, trees, animals, weather, celestial bodies). It is far from clear what all these things have in common. If to be animated is simply to exist, then animism is trivial. (2) It specifies the class of things that do the animating. The definitions list diverse animators (spiritual force, animating power, life-force, souls, spirits, etc.). But the natures of these animators are obscure. (3) It specifies what it means to be animated. The definitions say that to be animated is to be alive, to be divine, to have a soul or spirit, to have personal qualities. But these are all very different. These definitions do not point to any clear theory of animation. (228)[24]

Now, if these really are the conditions which should be met by a concept in order to be considered as a theory of animism, then life force could indeed be one such theory. But labelling life force a version of animism seems to only risk creating unnecessary confusion.[25] The difficulty in even landing on a precise definition of animism may be reason enough in itself to avoid the term.

To complicate matters even more, animism can also be divided into what is known as the 'new animism' and the 'old animism'. The latter emerged with the work of Edward Burnett Tylor, especially in his two-volume *Primitive Culture* (1871, 1873). This work is now viewed as culturally insensitive, dealing with unnuanced accounts of 'folk' religion (Rosa 2023, 64). The

---

[24] Steinhart's own version of animism has similarities to atheistic paganism. See also Green 2019; Lupa 2021.
[25] See Rosa 2023 for a history of the term 'animism' in the academy.

56 A MORAL THEORY OF LIVELINESS

former attempts to be more culturally sensitive than the old animists, and importantly is often associated with an activist ecologist movement (see Bouissac 1989; Bird-David 1999; Harvey 2005; Ingold 2000).[26] New animism is more about 'the replacement of an emphasis on *believing* (e.g., in "Spiritual Beings") with the idea of *relating to beings* (of all kinds) in ways that involve "recognizing" them as fellow participants in a community that extends beyond the human sphere (Burley 2023, 137). As an additional complication, Rountree argues that the animism one finds in indigenous cultures is not the same as the new animism.

Having said all of this, I do not deny that there are important avenues for further research between other types of animism and life force. There are questions about the similarities and dissimilarities between all of the various views of animism and life force on offer. There are also questions about how resources from one view might be able to philosophically inform and enhance the prospect of other views. Likewise, socio-historical questions emerge about why different cultures have independently formed similar beliefs about animism (to the extent that they are similar and really were formed independently). Indeed, more pertinent to my research here is what kind of moral theory, if any, would emerge from other theories of animism? Would they be more or less plausible than what emerges from life force? I do not deny that any of these are important questions. But this work would simply take me too far afield not just within philosophy, but also well into other disciplines such as sociology, anthropology, and history, among many others. My focus in this book on the African philosophical tradition is not intended to deny that life force or related concepts exist elsewhere. But exploring all of the avenues presented here, in addition to the ones I have not even mentioned, would not only take me too far afield in terms of my own expertise, but it would also make the scope of this book entirely unmanageable.

3.5 Conclusion

The primary purpose of this chapter was to summarize the contemporary literature on life force in order to show what it implies about normativity. There is widespread agreement about the main features of life force, at least

---

[26] Nurit Bird-David is considered one of the leaders of 'new animism' (1993, 2017, 2018). The same is true of Graham Harvey (2006, 2010, 2013, 2017).

as it is described among its academic exponents. I suggested that though one rarely finds explicit normative principles based on life force, it is straightforward to identify them. I have therefore been able to identify theories of both moral status and of right action. My goal here has been to observe these normative principles, not to defend them. This chapter, in combination with the previous one, provides the backdrop for me to develop a completely naturalistic normative theory based on important ideas from life force. This is the task I take up in Part II.

PART II

LIVELINESS AS A MORAL THEORY

4
Liveliness as Secular Life Force

4.1 Introduction

With the significance of life force brought into view in Part I, I now turn to one of my main goals in this part of the book: developing an entirely secular and naturalistic moral theory based on life force. Since I want to bring insights from life force to bear on moral philosophy that will be taken seriously around the globe, it is a pragmatic choice to naturalize it. A naturalistic theory is more likely to be acceptable to professional philosophers everywhere in the world. This includes those working in African moral philosophy, as it tends to be dominated by secular normative theories. Of course, it is also my hope that much of my development and explication of the secular theory will also be consistent with ethical theories based on the more metaphysically robust supernatural metaphysics of life force.

In this chapter, I briefly explain the secular conception of life force called liveliness that I will use for the rest of the book (4.2), before turning to explain how it can work without the metaphysics of life force (4.3). I conclude by gesturing at possible connections between work in African metaphysics and panpsychism for those who desire a complete metaphysical framework for liveliness (4.4). This chapter explains the transition from life force to liveliness in order to exclusively focus on liveliness as a moral theory for the rest of Part II.

4.2 Naturalizing Life Force: Liveliness

In order to develop a secular moral theory based on life force, I draw inspiration from "Chapter Five: Vital Force" of Thaddeus Metz's *A Relational Moral Theory: African Ethics in and beyond the Continent* (2022). Though Metz ultimately rejects liveliness as the appropriate grounds for a moral theory, his chapter offers one of the most in-depth analyses of life force as a moral

---

A Moral Theory of Liveliness. Kirk Lougheed, Oxford University Press. © Kirk Lougheed 2025.
DOI: 10.1093/9780197782019.003.0004

62 A MORAL THEORY OF LIVELINESS

theory to date, and he is one of the only authors to explicitly attempt to naturalize it. Remember that in order to distinguish the supernatural from the natural, I will refer to the secular notion of life force as 'liveliness'. With Metz, I will 'work with a notion of vitality that: is construed in terms of force, not substance; is thought to be perishable, as opposed to eternal; comes in different degrees or kinds; and plausibly varies in value depending on the quantity or quality of it' (Metz 2022a, 80). As should be evident by Chapters 2 and 3, descriptions of life force:

> [T]end to say that human beings are good in some way for exhibiting a superlative degree of health, strength, growth, reproduction, creativity, complexity, vibrancy, activity, self-motion, courage, and confidence. Or they characterize undesirable states as reductions of vitality understood as disease, weakness, decay, barrenness, destruction, disintegration, lethargy, passivity, submission, insecurity, and depression. (Metz 2022a, 80)

Notice that such descriptions are at least on their face consistent with an entirely secular or naturalistic ethic. Furthermore, Metz says that he will 'presume that most readers will share the judgement that there is something strongly to be preferred about persons with more liveliness than less. They are better (more excellent) people, if not also better off (happier)' (Metz 2022a, 80).

I suspect that there are interesting connections between these claims and work in the social and cognitive sciences. For instance, there is likely work in psychology which would connect anxiety and depression to poor outcomes and a lack of flourishing. The opposite would likely be confirmed by those with qualities like vibrancy, creativity, and strength. Of course, such work will have to make normative assumptions about what constitutes flourishing or well-being in the first place, but my point is that it would probably confirm common intuitions about the value of liveliness, at least to some degree. Since I am not a social scientist, I will not attempt to draw out such connections here, and I leave it to others to make them in the future. The purpose of this book is theory construction, and it would take me too far afield to evaluate all of the relevant claims I make against social scientific findings. Instead, I am going to focus on defending the metaphysics (or lack thereof) of the shift to naturalism.

4.3 Liveliness without the Metaphysics of Life Force

One of the most significant challenges to my project would seek to stop it before it can even get started. This is motivated by the worry that it is unjustified to remove the rather bloated supernatural ontology of life force and naturalize it (Chapter 3). The normativity that is implied by life force is importantly connected to its metaphysics and cannot be separated from it. If this is right, then it is impossible to develop a plausible secular moral theory based on life force. Notice that this objection is not claiming that a naturalistic ethic cannot be successful. That is a stronger claim, and in even writing this book I am simply assuming that it is false. Instead, it is attempting to base a naturalistic ethic on ideas originally within a supernatural ontology that is supposed to be the problem.

One can see the beginnings of the worry clearly by reflecting on an analogy. Suppose one explicated a Christian ethic which says that humans are valuable because they are image bearers or reflections of the divine nature. Right actions are those that honour God, which tend to be those that embody self-sacrificial love. Though it is perhaps not prima facie impossible to describe a naturalistic version of such an ethic, one can immediately see why attempting to do so might prompt a healthy amount of scepticism. If God does not exist, then it is difficult to see how an ethic that appeals to God in order to ground moral value, explain which actions are right, etc., is supposed to work. An ethic based on life force implies the existence of God and an imperceptible metaphysical energy. How could an ethic be based on life force that denies its metaphysical foundation?[1]

Part of the problem comes into focus when reflecting on moral status. According to life force, everything possesses at least some force which comes from God. This is what explains value. Morality is about strengthening the force in oneself and in others. Humans are the most valuable of the visible world because they possess the most force. Delineating the moral community and how to make relevant trade-offs (e.g., between humans and animals) seems perfectly clear. Is not all of this, among other features, lost if we remove the substance of life force, and God, among other supernatural qualities? Why think that liveliness is valuable?

---

[1] Relatedly, many asking these questions will be concerned that such a theory cannot properly count as African, either.

64 A MORAL THEORY OF LIVELINESS

There are a number of ways to respond to this worry. To begin, consider Metz's description of the characteristics of liveliness. They are clearly similar to many of the features of life force I explicated in the previous chapter (Chapter 3). In other words, there is much (if not near perfect) overlap in the positive and negative traits associated with life force and liveliness. The description of the normativity implied by liveliness can be coherently stated in entirely naturalistic terms. Indeed, as with the example of naturalizing a Christian ethic, it is possible to describe actions that would honour God without any reference to God, particularly if one is inclined to interpret such actions as involving acts of generosity and sacrifice (e.g., predicate theology). According to perfect being theology, God has the maximal perfections, and this could imply that our conception of God is plausibly a function of what we take to be non-instrumentally valuable. Instead, I think part of the real worry here is one about the grounds of morality and so really about metaethics.

If life force coming from God is what grounds morality, then if you remove God, there are no grounds for morality. I here offer a promissory note and refer the reader to Part IV, where I take up the question of metaethics for life force and liveliness. I argue that there are plausible metaethical grounds for liveliness when one considers ethical intuitionism (or at least that liveliness fares no worse than life force with respect to metaethical grounding). The degree to which the reader believes I am successful in that part of the book will likely affect whether they think naturalizing life force succeeds.

Yet another question remains. One might reasonably ask why bother appealing to life force in the first place if my goal is to end up offering a secular theory. The reason is that I suspect there are important ethical insights to be gained from doing so; insights that would not arise (or would be more difficult to recognize) without an initial appeal to life force.[2] Whether I am right about this rests on what follows in the remainder of the book. The 'proof is in the pudding', so to speak. In order to know whether there are useful ethical insights to be gained from a secular moral theory based on life force, one has to do the work of developing and testing such a theory (or theories). If there is an argument for dismissing such a project out of hand, I cannot find it. Likewise, it is noteworthy that I am hardly alone in taking a secular approach to African ethics. Many influential indigenous African philosophers have adopted this approach in their work and write

---

[2] Consider how little the description of liveliness has in common with theories like deontology or consequentialism in the Anglo-American tradition. It is not obvious that a theory like liveliness would arise without inspiration from life force.

in a style that is palatable to a global audience (e.g., Gyekye 1997; Wiredu 1980; Molefe 2019). In sum, I hope that any worries about the coherence of naturalizing life force will be addressed in the development of the liveliness moral theories in Part II, and the subsequent evaluation against competing African theories in Part III, with more fundamental metaethical questions being addressed in Part IV.

4.4 Liveliness, Panpsychism, and Agada's *Mood*

Suppose an objector finds the above unsatisfying and insists that, contra Metz, any plausible version of liveliness must be thought of as *substance* instead of as force. The kind of metaphysical connection between things implied by life force must be maintained for any moral theory to be based on life force. Since there is no naturalistic alternative to life force, my project cannot even get off the ground. Though I believe this is mistaken for the reasons mentioned above, it is worth briefly examining a potential reply.

One way of conceiving of a naturalistic version of life force can be found in discussions of contemporary Anglo-American philosophy of mind. Specifically, it can be found in certain versions of panpsychism. The basic definition of panpsychism is that consciousness is somehow fundamental to everything that exists in the physical world. Versions of this theory can be found throughout the history of philosophy, and it is often motivated by the fact that it avoids problems with both dualism (e.g., how mind and matter are supposed to interact) and physicalism (e.g., that it cannot adequately explain consciousness) (Goff, Seager, and Allen-Hermanson 2022). Panpsychism 'literally means that everything has a mind' (Goff, Seager, and Allen-Hermanson 2022). If fundamental things are really at the micro-level, then everything that has parts will possess a mind. In the Anglo-American philosophy of mind, most panpsychists advocate for versions of *panexperientialism*, which is 'the view that *conscious experience* is fundamental and ubiquitous' (Goff, Seager, and Allen-Hermanson 2022).

Panprotopsychism is a related view which says that it is not consciousness per se that is fundamental but proto-consciousness, where the most fundamental parts of the universe can combine to '*transparently account* for the existence of consciousness, in the sense that one could in principle move a priori from knowing the relevant facts about protophenomenal properties to knowing the relevant facts about phenomenal properties' (Goff, Seager,

66 A MORAL THEORY OF LIVELINESS

and Allen-Hermanson 2022).[3] *Cosmopsychism* is the view that all facts depend on facts about consciousness at the cosmic level. This can be understood as implying that the facts about consciousness are constitutive of all cosmic-level facts or that they non-constitutive such that humans and minds are separate entities but are causally dependent on consciousness-involving micro-level facts (Chalmers 1995; Goff 2015, 2017). Indeed, a particularly unique version of cosmopsychism is found in the work of Philip Goff which says the universe is a kind of value-responding agent which explains laws of physics (2019; see also 2023).[4]

Now, this is only a terse summary of some ideas in panpsychism.[5] But my point is that there are ideas in panpsychism that perhaps express a kind of unifying substance that undergirds everything in the universe at the most fundamental level. This offers a potential naturalized version of life force. It is particularly noteworthy that Goff has posited that a kind of normativity or value is implied by cosmopsychism. I do not know whether the grounds for a full-fledged moral theory such as the one I am developing are present in any of these ideas, but they are certainly worth more consideration for those who are concerned with the metaphysical underpinnings of liveliness.

What is particularly interesting is that there appear to be independent ideas in the African tradition that support panpsychism or concepts similar to it. I briefly draw attention to the work of the Nigerian philosopher Ada Agada, particularly his book *Consolationism and Comparative African Philosophy: Beyond Universalism and Particularism* (2022a).[6] Agada argues that *mood*, something similar to consciousness, is 'the fundamental principle in the consolationist system' of philosophy that he defends (2022a, 62).

Agada believes that humans are melancholy beings and tend to seek meaning in everything, even where there is no apparent meaning (2022a, 62). Emotions dominate reasons such that we are fundamentally emotional beings. The purpose of human life is to strive for perfection, perfection that the universe must also strive for, but that neither will reach. He explains that:

> The immediate inspiration for the idea of a fundamental principle in which the material and immaterial, the emotional and the intellectual, the

---

[3] See also Chalmers 2015; Goff 2015, 2017.
[4] See also Nagasawa and Wager 2016.
[5] Indeed, at the time of writing the database philpapers.org contains 487 entries in its panpsychism category.
[6] See also Agada 2015, 2020a.

irrational and rational are simultaneously implicated, is the Idoma traditional view of *owo*, which is variously understood as a guardian spirit, the pure self, ubiquitous spirit, and mind or consciousness. (Agada 2022a 65)

Owo 'is a universal principle animating all things, present in every kind of being but only rising to the level of full consciousness in sentient beings like humans' (Agada 2022a, 65). *Mood* is a power in the universe that 'can neither be wholly mentalistic nor wholly material. *Mood* is a proto-mind given that it is an event rather than a strictly material or strictly immaterial phenomenon' (Agada 2022a, 66). Agada identifies *mood* as the fundamental concept that unifies the material and immaterial in the universe. He rejects physicalism and claims that '*Mood* is a proto-mind in terms of subsisting as an event, not by definition as something wholly immaterial. This primordial stuff is both partly physical and partly immaterial' (Agada 2022a, 68).

Agada claims that 'African traditional thought can be interpreted in panpsychist terms, more or less' (2022a, 73).[7] For Agada:

Proto-panpsychism is the framework for articulating the doctrine of *mood* as proto-mind; it endorses the complementary perspective and proposes that the fundamentality of *mood* implies that both consciousness and matter are ubiquitous in the universe and that the reason humans can observe and understand the world at all is to be found in the fact of fundamental similarity between humans and physical nature. (2022a, 73)

Humans are interconnected with everything else in the world and are able to know about the world because everything is made up of the same basic stuff (Agada 2022a, 73–74). Humans also ought to care about each other and non-human animals, flora and fauna, and minerals, because they are made up of the same basic stuff. Agada explains that:

Proto-panpsychism asserts that *mood* is an irreducible event-essence or quality distributed throughout the universe and constitutive things. It is at once the prototype of mind/advanced consciousness and body/matter,

---

[7] Indeed, he builds on the work of Gyekye's appeal to *sunsum* as the fundamental component of the universe. See Gyekye 1995, 1999. See also Agada 2022b.

68 A MORAL THEORY OF LIVELINESS

> with the minded quality of this prototype of universal being underlying its bodily or material quality. (2022a, 74)[8]

According to Agada, this is a 'watered down' version of panpsychism because it affirms 'the porosity of the mind-body boundary' (2022a, 74). Agada uses 'proto' to qualify mood, because he denies the basicality of neither the body nor the mind or consciousness (2022a, 74). It allows for interplay between both the mind and body, which makes it *complementary*. Accordingly, 'if proto-panpsychism is going to adequately account for the basic African complementaristic outlook, then the fundamental principle identified as *mood* should neither be wholly determined physically nor conditioned immaterially' (Agada 2022a, 75).[9] Agada denies that consciousness depends on anything physical, instead proposing 'that where there is no consciousness there can be no matter' (2022a, 75).

The reader will have noticed that one problem with appealing to Agada's conception of *mood* as a naturalistic alternative to life force is that it explicitly rejects naturalism. Agada consistently wants to blur the distinction between the immaterial and material, advocating for *mood* as the fundamental component of the universe that slips between the two. I believe it would be fair to construe this as consistent with a rejection of the categories of immaterial and material that one sometimes finds in African thought. However, that does not help my purposes, as I need a theory that is firmly naturalistic and hence makes no appeal to immaterial objects.[10] But the reason I appeal to Agada's theory here is because it offers a framework which could perhaps be made consistent with naturalism without creating an entirely new and foreign theory. Appealing to accounts like Agada's would also make the account of liveliness more genuinely African than it would be otherwise. If Agada is right that the African tradition is panpsychist, and if there are naturalistic panpsychist theories in the Anglo-American tradition, then it could be possible to merge views from these traditions such to create an African-inspired panpsychist theory that presents a concept that is a substance and also naturalistic.

---

[8] Agada claims that this is similar to Chalmers' panprotopsychism because it also posits that something precedes advanced consciousness.

[9] Interestingly, it is the failure to account for the complementarity between the material and immaterial that Agada identifies as Tempels' main failure (Agada 2022a, 75).

[10] It would probably be better to appeal to Wiredu's theory of mind in this regard. See Wiredu 1983.

Such a project would take me too far afield into metaphysics, and I want to stay focussed on moral philosophy. To those who would complete such a project, there are at least three important questions to address. First, the terms physicalist and naturalistic are slippery. Panpsychism is clearly intended as an alternative to physicalist descriptions of the universe. But is panpsychism consistent with naturalism? The answer to this question will depend on the details of the specific panpsychist theory under consideration. Second, if a plausible naturalistic and African-inspired theory can indeed be described, will the theory say anything about normativity? Positing a metaphysical substance does not in itself say anything about morality (see 9.2). Third, and related to the second, does a panpsychist framework offer the right kind of metaphysical connection between stuff to preserve the relevant notion of moral community that the objector fears is lost? Can it do so even if the connection based on life force is grounded in God? It would help any panpsychist theory or related theory here if there were normative implications that turn out to support the moral theories of liveliness I develop in the rest of Part II. For the reader concerned with what grounds the value of liveliness, I will address metaethics in Part IV. In what follows I will assume that liveliness can be coherently described in terms of force, not substance, and leave it to others more worried about this difference to develop these ideas further.

4.5 Conclusion

Metz's naturalized version of life force in liveliness says that it is a force, not substance. Characteristics of liveliness include health, creativity, reproduction, and courage, while a lack or decrease of liveliness is represented by disease, weakness, and destruction. Indeed, I believe these features of liveliness and its lack so strongly accord with most of our intuitions that I do not need to offer a more complete metaphysical picture of liveliness. Furthermore, if one is sceptical of my appeal to intuitions, I offer a more detailed explanation of this in Part IV. For the objector who is insistent that liveliness must also be construed in terms of force, I suggested that panpsychism *might* provide one possible model. It is further interesting that there appear to be analogues to panpsychism in African thought. However, the details of any such proposals must be scrutinized with particular care to show that they are consistent with naturalism, in addition to having the relevant normative implications.

70 A MORAL THEORY OF LIVELINESS

Though metaphysics and ethics are connected with each other and overlap in important ways, my primary concern in this book is moral philosophy. I will therefore not comment on the shift from understanding liveliness as a force to that of substance any further, and I simply assume that a coherent metaphysics of liveliness is possible inasmuch as it is necessary for the rest of my project. Metaphysical discussions will re-emerge when I address what grounds the normativity of life force and liveliness in Part IV.

5

Liveliness as a Moral Theory

5.1 Introduction

The first four chapters of this book have primarily been stage-setting. After explaining the motivation for the project, along with my methodological approach to the book in Chapter 1, in Part I, I turned in Chapter 2 to outlining the first academic explication of life force as found in the work of Placide Tempels. After that, in Chapter 3, I explained how life force is defined among contemporary academics, while also noting its clear normative implications. In Chapter 4, I began Part II by explaining the shift from life force to its secular counterpart in liveliness. With all of this background in place, I am now in a position to complete my main goal of the book: to develop the best possible secular moral theory based on life force, what I call *liveliness*.

It would be an interesting and worthwhile project to continue with the traditional conception of life force and explore how it could be further developed into a robust normative theory. However, as will become clear in Part III, though the African continent is highly religious, African ethics itself tends to be dominated by secular theories. I will not speculate as to why this is the case, but I believe that it is clear that African moral philosophy typically divorces normative commitments from supernatural ontologies.[1] I submit that contemporary African moral philosophy is decidedly secular and naturalistic.[2] I therefore suspect that part of the reason why life force lacks the development that other African normative theories have received (e.g., normative personhood or harmonious relationships) is that it comes with the rather full ontology associated with African Traditional Religion. My goal is to fill this gap in the literature by developing an entirely secular and naturalistic version of life force known as *liveliness*. This account avoids the metaphysical controversies associated with traditional understandings

---

[1] Of course, this is consistent with my discussion of Metz's apt observation that African normative ethics is typically grounded in ontology (9.2).

[2] For notable exceptions, see Magesa 1997; Murove 2007; Bujo 1997.

A Moral Theory of Liveliness. Kirk Lougheed, Oxford University Press. © Kirk Lougheed 2025.
DOI: 10.1093/9780197782019.003.0005

72 A MORAL THEORY OF LIVELINESS

of life force, though much of what I say will also be consistent with such understandings. Not only is explicating a theory of liveliness in entirely secular terms an inherently interesting project, but it also serves the pragmatic purposes of being more palatable to African moral philosophers, in addition to being more appealing to ethicists around the globe who also tend to work within a naturalistic tradition (e.g., contemporary Anglo-American ethics and Contemporary Confucianism).

I begin by explaining that there are numerous theories of moral value and right action that could be built on liveliness. I will focus on what can reasonably be called teleological and deontological theories (5.2). I then turn to examining the degree to which these theories, particularly the deontological version, can account for African moral intuitions (5.3) and global moral intuitions (5.4).

5.2 Liveliness as a Moral Theory

Recall that I am working with the basic description of life force as found in the work of Metz, particularly in "Chapter Five: Vital Force" of his *A Relational Moral Theory: African Ethics in and beyond the Continent* (2022) (4.2). With Metz, I will 'work with a notion of vitality that: is construed in terms of force, not substance; is thought to be perishable, as opposed to eternal; comes in different degrees or kinds; and plausibly varies in value depending on the quantity or quality of it' (Metz 2022a, 80). Recall also that descriptions of life force:

> [T]end to say that human beings are good in some way for exhibiting a superlative degree of health, strength, growth, reproduction, creativity, complexity, vibrancy, activity, self-motion, courage, and confidence. Or they characterize undesirable states as reductions of vitality understood as disease, weakness, decay, barrenness, destruction, disintegration, lethargy, passivity, submission, insecurity, and depression. (Metz 2022a, 80)

In the previous chapter (4), I explained why it is legitimate to naturalize life force. I suggested that determining whether the shift to liveliness succeeds will partly depend on the degree to which the normative theories I construct based on it are plausible (4.3). It is this task that I take up in the rest of this chapter, specifying more precise normative theories based on liveliness. I begin by offering a teleological theory, before developing a deontological one. Though my main focus is on developing theories of right action, I will also sometimes highlight what they imply about moral status. The reader should recall that my primary aim is to develop the *best version* of a normative theory based on liveliness (see 1.6). This means that though I will offer reasons to prefer the deontological version, I do not take such reasons to be definitive. If the reader believes the teleological version is superior, a strength of my project is that they are free to choose it. In 6.8, I develop a more detailed description of deontological liveliness that incorporates some aspects of the teleological version.

Finally, as stated in 1.1, the title of this book is somewhat deceiving, because I do not take myself to be offering *the* moral theory of liveliness. Still, I thought that calling the book *Moral Theories of Liveliness* risked creating undue confusion. For simplicity and ease of prose, in places where the differences are not important, I will use the singular tense and write of *the* moral theory of liveliness. However, in such places, this always refers to a family of related theories of moral value and right action, all based on liveliness.

5.2.1 Teleological Liveliness

I begin by exploring a teleological theory of right action based on liveliness. Teleological liveliness says that morality has a goal or end: that of liveliness. Right actions are therefore those that are characterized by pursuing the end of liveliness. In his explication of liveliness, Metz argues that one ought to care for the liveliness of others, as opposed to just focusing on one's own liveliness. Indeed, he goes so far as to suggest that "one should seek to advance liveliness either anywhere one can or perhaps only in others" (Metz 2022a, 81). His worry is that if right action involves only maximizing one's own liveliness, then it will justify actions that are intuitively immoral:

> For example, a prescription to do whatever it takes to promote one's own liveliness entails that one ought to commit murder if necessary to stay alive in the long run. Suppose that you need a new kidney to survive and that no one will give one to you. Then, to maximize your liveliness, you would need to kill another (let us presume, innocent) person so as to acquire his healthy kidney for a transplant. Or, if there is a single tiny lifeboat that seats

74 A MORAL THEORY OF LIVELINESS

only one person, and there are two of us who have so far survived the ship-wreck, then, if I lose the coin toss, I ought to rescue myself anyway, using force as necessary; for only thereby could I promote my own liveliness. (Metz 2022a, 81)

On this understanding of liveliness, there is a non-instrumental reason against killing an innocent person, which grounds a more impartial or other-regarding ethic than a prescription focussed on maximizing one's own live-liness (Metz 2022a, 82). Accordingly, 'one's basic duty is to act in ways that are expected to increase the liveliness of either anyone or only others besides oneself' (Metz 2022a, 82). This is clearly a teleological version of liveliness, where the goal or end of morality is to pursue the highest good, which is identified in liveliness (Metz 2022a, 83).

On the one hand, it makes sense to develop teleological liveliness only in terms of seeking to protect and promote the liveliness in others. For if I exclu-sively cared about my own liveliness, I may end up degrading the liveliness of those around me in order to increase my own liveliness. But on the other hand, it is puzzling that Metz's description so clearly separates an individual's liveliness from the liveliness of the other members of their community. He never considers in any detail the idea that increasing the liveliness of others could be a way for an individual to increase their own liveliness. This interconnectedness fits well with ideas in African Communitarianism more generally, which tend to say that a person cannot be thought of as properly flourishing unless all of the members of their community are flourishing, too. My point here is just that 'purely self-regarding' in the way Metz uses the term is incoherent on the African view inasmuch as an individual cannot genuinely care for themselves without also caring about the rest of their com-munity. An individual cannot pursue their own liveliness in isolation from the liveliness of the rest of their community.

While pursuing one's own liveliness in isolation from community is prob-lematic, the purely other-regarding description of the normativity of liveli-ness leads to a different set of counterintuitive results. Such a description fails to explain the fact that even though an individual is connected to their com-munity, they can still have legitimate goals that are distinct from the goals of other members of their community. Though some working in the African tra-dition embrace the idea that individual goals necessarily reduce to communal goals, I firmly reject this notion. Members of a community may share many of the same desires and goals, but it is implausible to think they are necessarily identical such that even when they appear to be different below the surface, their goals are really the same. For example, it is permissible for me to spend time and money on my education, which increases my own liveliness, even if doing so does not directly benefit my community (see Molefe 2019, 60).[3]

Of course, Metz or others may fairly respond that if an individual's liveliness is indeed so inextricably intertwined with their community's, they could not in fact spend resources on their education unless doing so demonstrably helps their community. In other words, if the view in question says that both one's own liveliness *and* the liveliness of others matter, then one cannot in fact pursue goals that do not align with one's community. If this is right, then the alternative description I offer reduces to Metz's view that right action should be construed in terms of concern only for the liveliness of others. This would mean that it suffers from the same problem in being unable to account for the fact that individuals can have different goals.[4] I do not intend to settle this matter here. My point in highlighting this tension is just that the proponent of teleological liveliness will have to grapple with this issue, particularly if they want to uphold the idea that individuals can in fact have different goals from the other members of their community.

In light of this discussion, a teleological theory of right action based on liveliness can be formulated along the following lines:

- An action is right inasmuch as it increases (or can reasonably be expected to increase) the life force in oneself and in others.
- An action is wrong inasmuch as it decreases (or can reasonably be expected to decrease) the life force in oneself and in others.

Teleological liveliness also says something about moral value. It implies that a thing is valuable to the degree to which it manifests liveliness:

- A being is valuable to the degree that it manifests liveliness.

Such a view could nicely accord with the intuition that humans are more valuable than animals and the natural world, since they exhibit a higher

---

[3] For more on the individual versus the community in African ethics, see 7.3.

[4] Another possible way out would be to distinguish between moral and non-moral goals. The former are other-regarding, while the latter can sometimes be self-regarding. If the moral does not always override the non-moral, then this is another possible way out. Thanks to Thaddeus Metz for this observation.

76 A MORAL THEORY OF LIVELINESS

degree of liveliness. However, it is difficult to see how this view implies that *all* humans share a high moral value, since not all humans exhibit a high degree of liveliness. Perhaps one could say that a human is valuable because it is the type of thing that can exhibit a high degree of liveliness. However, the most straightforward reading of teleological liveliness is that it is liveliness itself that is valuable. If an animal exhibited more actual liveliness than did a person (even if that person belongs to a class that usually exhibits more liveliness than animals), then the animal would be more valuable in that particular case.[5] More on this theme will come out during my evaluation of teleological liveliness against African intuitions (5.3) and global intuitions (5.4), in addition to its implications for dignity (6.10).

5.2.2 Deontological Liveliness

Though Metz rightly notes that teleological accounts of liveliness are the most common in the literature on life force, he observes that there is an attractive respect-based deontological version 'according to which we have a dignity inhering in our liveliness and wrong actions are those that degrade it' (Metz 2022a, 83). Notice that there are two different ways of formulating principles of deontological liveliness. Consider the following:

- An action is right inasmuch as it respects the dignity existing in oneself and in others' liveliness.
- An action is wrong inasmuch as it disrespects the dignity existing in oneself and in others' liveliness.

Metz rightly asserts that this approach can avoid the objection to teleological liveliness which says that it can justify killing an innocent person to save other innocent people (Metz 2022a, 83). Also notice that construing liveliness in deontological terms helps to avoid the apparent tension between individual versus communal interests. I am justified in pursuing my educational goals because I have inherent value based on my liveliness. Provided I am not degrading the liveliness of others, there is nothing wrong

---

[5] Notice that if I am right, then this would block the claim that humans who exhibit less force than animals are still more valuable because they have the *capacity* for higher amounts of life force.

with pursuing my own goals. This also points to the following theory of moral status:

- A being merits respect based on the degree to which it is lively.

Though this approach is clearly deontological, it still locates value most fundamentally in liveliness itself. Just as I mention above regarding teleological liveliness, certain worries arise when value is firmly located in liveliness in this way. For example, persons clearly exhibit varying degrees of liveliness. Even though it could be reasonably maintained that only large differences in liveliness matter morally, there are intuitively large differences between an adult who is healthy, has a fulfilling career, and has mutually loving relationships with family and friends, and an adult with a terminal illness who is on life support, has been placed in a medically induced coma, and has no chance of recovery. Now, on the one hand this consequence may well get the right result in certain cases. It is plausible that the healthy should receive moral consideration, say, when deciding who should get a scarce lifesaving vaccine, even if both individuals possess a dignity. Perhaps it is only when a person dies and is a mere corpse that they no longer possess dignity.[6] But on the other hand, this might imply that human dignity comes in degrees, which can be questioned. For example, if it is impermissible to kill someone because they have a dignity, it does not matter whether they are healthy or on life support. Thus, locating the dignity of persons in liveliness appears to imply that dignity comes in degrees, which leads to counterintuitive results at least in certain cases.

As I will explain later, for Metz, liveliness is neither the greatest nor the smallest value (8.3). Instead, he believes it is our *capacity* for communal relationships which is the highest value while recognizing that part of such relationships can involve increasing the liveliness of others (Metz 2022a, 89). He explains that 'action taken with the aim of improving others' liveliness is partially constitutive of the fundamental duty to treat individuals as having a moral standing because of their capacity to be party to communal relationships' (Metz 2022a, 89). What grounds the value of liveliness is that it 'is partially constitutive of the fundamental duty to treat individuals as having a moral standing because of their capacity to be party to communal

---

[6] This does not entail that there would not be impermissible ways of treating corpses.

78 A MORAL THEORY OF LIVELINESS

relationships' (Metz 2022a, 89). But why not think that the value of harmonious communal relationships is constitutive of treating people well because they have the *capacity* for liveliness? This is a modal property based on the *kind* of thing humans are, and not based on whether that modal property is exercised. The individual on life support has the capacity for liveliness in virtue of being the right kind of thing; namely, a human. It does not matter whether they are currently unable to exercise that capacity in the actual world. It just matters that they possess the relevant modal property. This leads to the following principle of moral value:

- A being is valuable if they have the *capacity* for liveliness.

If humans have the capacity for the highest amount of liveliness, this can be used to explain why they have a dignity while animals do not have a dignity. This means that:

- Humans have a dignity because they have the *capacity* for the highest amount of liveliness (of anything in the world).

Shifting to a theory of right action that focusses on the capacity for liveliness can be spelled out in the following principles:

- An action is right inasmuch as it respects individuals in virtue of their capacity to be lively.
- An action is wrong inasmuch as it degrades those with the capacity to be lively.

This does not attach importance to the actual strength of liveliness a person exhibits, and instead focusses on their capacity for liveliness. It is good to exercise and develop one's capacity for liveliness, but doing so is not necessary in order to matter morally. Even though with respect to many moral intuitions, these different versions of deontological liveliness will often issue the same verdicts, the former does a better job of explaining why humans, even terminally ill ones, are still more important than animals.

Metz ultimately rejects liveliness, concluding that 'it is unable to account for a variety of comparatively uncontroversial claims about ethics, including many that will appeal widely to Africans' (2022, 18; see also Metz 2012).

Though he phrases these claims in terms of teleological liveliness, he says that they 'usually apply with comparable force to the deontological one' (Metz 2022a, 83). However, I believe that this claim is too quick. In the next two sections, I argue that deontological liveliness does an excellent job of accounting for both African and global intuitions, including those intuitions where Metz denies that this is the case. The worries levelled by Metz against teleological liveliness do not apply with equal force to deontological liveliness. In applying liveliness to these different African moral intuitions and global moral intuitions, it will therefore become clear that deontological liveliness fares better than Metz supposes.

5.3 Liveliness and African Moral Intuitions

In this section I will focus on showing that deontological liveliness as a theory of right action can accommodate a wide variety of African moral intuitions, including the ones Metz says liveliness struggles to justify. I will also highlight places where results differ from teleological liveliness.

5.3.1 It Is *Pro Tanto* Immoral to Resolve Political Conflicts in the Face of Continued Dissent, Rather than Seeking Consensus

This is one African intuition that Metz believes liveliness cannot adequately defend. Consider that one defender of liveliness in Bujo has connected it to consensus-based decision-making in the political realm:

> His [i.e., Bujo's] central reasoning is that consensus amongst at least informed representatives, an ideal springing from traditional African chiefs having routinely consulted with popularly appointed elders before making a decision, is most likely to reveal the truth about how to promote liveliness. The 'palaver', as Bujo calls it, 'shows that norms can be and have to be found in a communal manner, hence free of domination and in dialogue'. (1997: 37) (2022, 85)

But Metz is sceptical of the idea that consensus-seeking among equals will in fact promote liveliness in the community, and do so better than

80 A MORAL THEORY OF LIVELINESS

alternatives. The first problem he identifies is the simple fact that it is incredibly unlikely that the insights gleaned from consensus will be better than those to be had from a supermajority of, say, 80% or 90%. Just consider that the time lost in attempting to establish a consensus could potentially decrease the liveliness of those waiting on the relevant political decisions (which could be important policies) (Metz 2022a, 85).

The second problem arises regarding what Metz calls 'plural voting'. According to Bujo, the 'palaver' requires the input of *all* members of the community (1997). However, notice that 'seeking consensus in such an egalitarian way would be wrong, if, as is plausible, giving the same number of votes to the uneducated as the educated would prevent liveliness relative to what would be obtained by giving the uneducated fewer votes than the educated' (Metz 2022a, 86). Thus, it appears at least possible that, contra Bujo, inegalitarian decision-making could produce more liveliness. Metz concludes that even according to deontological liveliness, 'while I [i.e., Metz] accept that there is something degrading about plural voting, it is hard to see why it would degrade people's *liveliness*' (2022, 86).

This may well be a problem for Bujo's understanding of life force, but I deny that it is a problem for the secular theory of liveliness in general. There is nothing in liveliness qua moral theory that suggests it *necessarily* prescribes egalitarianism.[7] It could be that plural voting respects individuals by increasing the overall liveliness of every community member, including of those who receive the least amount of voting power. This is one reason to reject Metz's intuition that plural voting is morally problematic. In other words, I think the proponent of liveliness can possibly 'bite the bullet' on this matter. Again, what this type of response would do is make the theory of liveliness less African (all else being equal) than other theories purporting to explain why plural voting is impermissible. This is so inasmuch as indigenous African cultures tend to favour consensus-based decision-making. However, none of this would show that liveliness as a moral theory more generally fails.

I believe that a better reply on behalf of proponents of liveliness comes in the form of focussing on respect. Metz is too quick here in claiming that plural voting would not degrade a person's liveliness. Suppose that inegalitarian decision-procedures would indeed tend to favour the least well-off

---

[7] Or more carefully, such a connection is not obvious, and an argument would have to be offered in order to show the connection.

and the least well-educated such that it is tempting to conclude liveliness cannot explain the problem with plural voting. What Metz does not figure into his analysis is the fact that an individual's self-esteem could very well be lowered by knowing that their vote was worth the least in their society, if anything at all. Knowing that one has the least say, particularly through no fault of one's own, can reasonably be thought of as degrading and disrespectful. If this is right, then the deontological approach to liveliness would prohibit plural voting. The end of increasing liveliness in the community is not justified if the means of doing so disrespects individuals either in virtue of their liveliness or their capacity for it.

5.3.2 It Is *Pro Tanto* Immoral to Fail to Do What Is Likely to Make People's Lives Go Better, if One Is Politically in Charge

This African intuition is straightforward to justify. If a person's life must be respected in virtue of liveliness or the capacity for liveliness, politicians must act in ways that respect this fact. This means enacting policies and laws that tend to promote the liveliness of each community member, including providing ways for people to exercise their liveliness. To do otherwise would be disrespectful of their constituents' dignity, which they possess in virtue of their liveliness or the capacity for it.

5.3.3 It Is *Pro Tanto* Immoral to Make Retribution the Fundamental Aim of Criminal Justice, in Contrast to Seeking Reconciliation

African theories of justice typically favour reconciliatory approaches, which tend to focus on a good outcome for both the wrongdoer and the victim, albeit in a way that disavows the wrong that was done (Metz 2022a, 2022b, 2022c). But according to Metz, though liveliness does not necessarily recommend retribution, it typically justifies approaches to justice that focus on deterrence, not reconciliation. He writes:

> Although it is clear that a prescription to promote liveliness in society would forbid punishing on grounds of retribution, it is unclear that it recommends seeking reconciliation between offenders and their victims

as the alternative. If the basic aim were to promote liveliness and hence to prevent other-regarding crime, such as murder, rape, and theft, then it appears that a state should often inflict severe penalties on individuals so as to deter them and others from committing it or lock people away so that they cannot re-offend. That is, vitality seems to justify deterrence and incapacitation, not so much reconciliation. (Metz 2022a, 86)

Furthermore, teleological liveliness cannot explain why the guilty ought to be punished. This is because '[i]mposing a penalty on one person so as to instil fear in others or using punishment to incapacitate differ substantially from imposing a penalty on a guilty person to prompt him to compensate his victims, to reform his character, and more generally to facilitate a mending of ties between him and his victims (Metz 2022a, 86).[8]

Contra Metz, I submit that it is false that teleological liveliness could not prescribe reconciliation. For reconciliation tends to prescribe that the wrongdoer ought to admit what they did, issue a public apology, and otherwise make amends with their victim. If the victim's liveliness has been degraded by the wrongdoer, this type of reconciliation could serve to restore their liveliness. Likewise, Metz himself defends a theory of reconciliation that includes constructive punishments where such punishments should compensate the victim, and ideally, reform the character of the wrongdoer (see Metz 2022b, 2022c). If his own approach to reconciliation is correct, then reconciliation could indeed serve to help prevent further wrongs.[9]

Deontological liveliness that grounds dignity or rights in virtue of each individual possessing liveliness or the capacity for it can also plausibly recommend reconciliation. It could be that reconciliation (including constructive punishment) is an important way of respecting victims. A wrongdoer who has to admit what they did, make an apology, and take on constructive punishment could do so out of respect for their victim. Failing to engage in reconciliation and instead focus on deterrence reasonably degrades the dignity of the wrongdoer, which still matters. If the wrongdoer does not pose a significant risk of harming others again, their dignity needs to be respected inasmuch as possible, something I submit that prison almost always fails to do. Coercion may be permissible in cases where someone refuses to take on a

---

[8] For Metz's objections to the retribution and deterrence theories of justice, see Metz 2022b, 2022c.
[9] I suppose it is in principle an empirical question whether deterrence would prevent more reduction to liveliness than the amount reconciliation might restore.

constructive punishment because they have forfeited some of their rights in virtue of their wrongdoing. But if they are genuinely remorseful and willing to engage in reconciliation, then deontological liveliness dictates they need to be given the opportunity to make amends. Metz is simply mistaken to suppose that neither teleological nor deontological liveliness can make sense of reconciliation.

Notice that on deontological liveliness, retribution is unjustified because it degrades the liveliness of the wrongdoer. A wrongdoer can have their liveliness degraded in self- or other defence, but the justice that comes after the act in question must respect their liveliness. This is consistent with allowing punishments that degrade liveliness only if they are directly connected to restoring the liveliness of the wronged party. Consequentialist approaches that favour deterrence are also unjustified on deontological liveliness. Deontological liveliness entails dignity (or inherent value or rights) such that a perpetrator cannot have their hand cut off for stealing even if doing so would prevent future crimes. The type of constructive punishments prescribed by Metz are meant to compensate victims (which restores their liveliness) and, ideally, reforms the character of the offender, which subsequently serves to restore and increase their liveliness.[10]

5.3.4 It Is *Pro Tanto* Immoral to Create Wealth Largely on a Competitive Basis, Instead of a Cooperative One, and to Distribute Wealth in a Greatly Unequal Way and to Fail to Meet Everyone's Needs

Metz believes that liveliness cannot explain why certain types of welfarism, something widely accepted in the African ethical tradition, are correct. To be more precise, there are three things that Africans tend to eschew (on the basis of welfarism) that liveliness struggles to explain (Metz 2022a, 85). These are the *pro tanto* wrongness of vast inequalities in wealth even in societies where everyone's basic needs are met and they pursue wealth primarily through competitive instead of cooperative means (even if the former strategy creates more wealth) (Metz 2022a, 70–71, 85).

---

[10] Having said that, if they are valuable in virtue of their capacity for liveliness, then there are ultimately limits to the punishments. For example, a torturer cannot be tortured. Notice too that such a punishment is not *constructive*.

84 A MORAL THEORY OF LIVELINESS

I believe that deontological liveliness can indeed go some way towards explaining the *pro tanto* wrongness of actions that violate the types of welfarism typically favoured on the African continent. First, consider vast inequalities in wealth. It could be that an extremely wealthy person ought to recognize the dignity inherent in other individuals based on their liveliness by sharing more of their wealth. This could mean helping others to achieve their goals, which respects their dignity and maybe also increases the liveliness of the individuals being assisted. Doing so also plausibly increases the liveliness of the wealthy person, too, even if everyone's basic needs are already met. Liveliness might not be able to show why there should be no inequalities, but it can go some way towards showing why the wealthy ought to share their resources above and beyond ensuring that everyone's basic needs are met.

Second, liveliness can also help explain why pursuing wealth primarily through competitive means is wrong. More carefully, it can make clear why it is wrong to pursue wealth through a thoroughgoing laissez-faire capitalism. Such an approach may not respect the inherent dignity of every individual, instead suggesting that they are mere 'competitors' that need to be defeated. Admittedly, liveliness may not be able to explain why a competitive approach with rules and regulations ensuring the basic protections for every individual is not to be preferred to purely cooperative ventures if the latter generates more wealth (and does so for everyone). In sum, though I admit liveliness cannot fully explain widespread African intuitions about welfarism, it can do so at least partly, and better than Metz suspects.

5.3.5 It Is *Pro Tanto* Immoral to Avoid Greeting People, Especially Elders, upon Encountering Them

It is straightforward to show that liveliness preserves this moral norm, though life force does so more easily. On life force, elders have more force than young people. They are morally more knowledgeable and closer to becoming the living dead or even departed ancestors. Thus, it is disrespectful not to greet them. On deontological liveliness, it may still be wrong to fail to greet people, because they have a dignity. However, it is more difficult to show why elders in particular should be greeted. The discussion in the next subsection on flouting long-standing norms is also relevant to explaining this moral intuition.

5.3.6 It Is *Pro Tanto* Immoral to Remain Isolated or to Flout Long-standing Norms Central to a People's Self-Conception, as Opposed to Partaking in Customs

Metz claims that liveliness cannot explain why it is wrong to flout long-standing customs (Metz 2022a, 85). However, the wrongness of rejecting long-standing cultural norms and practices can be explained to some degree by liveliness. Consider that to reject such norms is likely to create division and strife within one's community, thereby degrading the liveliness of community members. Liveliness can also explain why maintaining cultural norms must be balanced against respect for each person. For example, if homosexual behaviour were to violate cultural norms such that it would create division in a community, such division might have to be accepted as a consequence of recognizing the inherent dignity of each individual on the basis of their liveliness or the capacity for it.

5.3.7 It Is *Pro Tanto* Immoral to Fail to Marry and Rear Children, as Opposed to Creating a Family through Other Means

The most difficult African intuition for liveliness to explain is that it is immoral to fail to marry and procreate instead of creating a family through different means.[11] Life force easily explains this as increasing the literal force in the world, accomplished by bringing into existence new humans. Indeed, those yet-to-be-born also have a moral status. But without this metaphysical backdrop, it is more difficult to see how deontological liveliness could issue an obligation to marry and procreate. To fail to marry and procreate would not degrade the dignity of any humans who currently exist, so it is difficult to see how liveliness can accommodate this African intuition. However, life force aside, I submit that it is equally difficult for the other African normative theories to accommodate this intuition (see Part III). Perhaps the most that can be said is that procreating would be adding members to the community who could exercise their capacity for liveliness and contribute positively to the community. Still, it is difficult to see how such behaviour could be prescribed as *required* on liveliness.

---

[11] Indeed, elsewhere I have argued that any plausible African normative theory entails anti-natalism (Lougheed 2022b).

86 A MORAL THEORY OF LIVELINESS

5.3.8 Tentative Conclusions on Liveliness and African Intuitions

Deontological liveliness fares well with respect to its ability to explain and support key African intuitions. I argue that it can explain why it is *pro tanto* immoral to fail to make decisions by consensus (or at least why plural voting is immoral), to fail to make others' lives go better if one is a politician, and why it is wrong to seek retribution over reconciliation. I also believe that deontological liveliness can explain why it is wrong to flout long-standing norms, at least for no good reason. With respect to seeking wealth on a competitive basis and failing to distribute it in an equal way, liveliness can explain this intuition to some extent, though it does not outright prohibit any type of inequality. Finally, liveliness cannot adequately explain why it is wrong to fail to marry and procreate. Thus, deontological liveliness can explain and motivate almost all of the African moral intuitions that Metz believes a genuinely African theory ought to accommodate.

5.4 Liveliness and Global Moral Intuitions

In this section I examine the degree to which deontological liveliness is able to accommodate global moral intuitions. As with the previous section, there are some intuitions that Metz claims cannot be encapsulated by liveliness. Again, I disagree, and therefore argue that liveliness, particularly the deontological version, does a better job of explaining the intuitions than Metz supposes.

5.4.1 It Is *Pro Tanto* Immoral to Kill Innocent People without Their Consent for Money

It is straightforward to explain this global intuition according to deontological liveliness. Killing an innocent person for their money would be treating them as a mere means to an end. It would quite literally be taking all liveliness from them. It would be fundamentally disrespecting their dignity in virtue of the liveliness they possess or in virtue of their capacity for it. Worst of all, there is nothing that can be done to make amends once a person is dead, which gives credence to the intuition that murder is particularly egregious.

5.4.2 It Is *Pro Tanto* Immoral to Have Xex with Someone against His or Her Will so as to Feel Pleasure or a Sense of Power

It is straightforward to explain this global intuition according to deontological liveliness. Non-consensual sex uses someone as a mere means to an end. It fundamentally disrespects a person's dignity in virtue of their liveliness or their capacity for it. It is well known that such acts can cause the victim to feel a sense of powerlessness, often experiencing long-term anxiety, depression, and PTSD as a result.

5.4.3 It Is *Pro Tanto* Immoral to Deceive a Person, at Least When Not Done in Self- or Other-Defence

Metz believes that there are cases of lying that are intuitively impermissible even though liveliness cannot explain why they are wrong. Metz asks the reader to 'consider the case of a spouse who systematically cheats on her husband behind his back, and is so careful and conniving that he has no chance of finding out. It appears she would be enhancing the liveliness of her lover and herself, while not reducing that of her spouse' (Metz 2022a, 87–88). Even if it were stipulated that the deception could never be discovered such that the faithful spouse's liveliness is never threatened, it still seems wrong (Metz 2022a, 88). Finally, notice that if it is the discovery of the lie that degrades liveliness, then it is the *belief* that one has been deceived that causes degradation, not the lie itself. This makes it difficult for liveliness to explain why the lie itself is wrong, since it appears to be beliefs about deception that cause a degradation in liveliness (Metz 2022a, 88).

Yet again this objection is more serious to teleological liveliness than to deontological liveliness. For on deontological versions, lying to a person is disrespectful regardless of whether that person ever becomes aware of the deception. This suggests that something other than merely decreasing a person's liveliness is needed to explain why an undiscovered lie is still wrong. However, such an explanation is possible in terms of liveliness. A lie disrespects a person who possesses dignity (or inherent value or rights) in virtue of liveliness or simply in virtue of having the capacity for liveliness. Deontological liveliness can therefore explain why lying is wrong even if it is undetected and so may never *directly* decrease the liveliness of the person who is deceived. The lie is still fundamentally disrespectful. Metz also never

88 A MORAL THEORY OF LIVELINESS

considers that lying itself may well degrade the liveliness of the liar. If the cheater has a conscience, their liveliness will indeed be harmed by their deception. This would be a way for teleological liveliness to explain why lying is wrong. While the existence of psychopaths poses a problem for this explanation, their existence does not pose a unique problem to liveliness.

Finally, for those still unsatisfied with this response, a different way of analyzing this case is to say that right action and good character come apart. Thinking about liveliness in terms of good character might explain why cheating and deceiving one's spouse is never justified even if you do not get caught (and so it is not obvious that spouse's liveliness or capacity for it is diminished). According to liveliness, someone with a good character will not act in ways that are *likely* to degrade the liveliness in others, even if in some particular instances those actions would not turn out to be degrading. They should be developing their character such that they are always aiming to promote liveliness within the parameters of respecting others. I will not develop an analysis of liveliness as good character any further, but this is surely an area for further research.

5.4.4 It Is *Pro Tanto* Immoral to Discriminate on a Racial or Gendered Basis When Allocating Opportunities, at Least When Not Redressing a Previous Comparable Discrimination

Deontological liveliness dictates that, all else being equal, a person cannot discriminate on the basis of race or gender. Each individual has a dignity, and such discrimination would violate that dignity. However, Metz raises a related objection, arguing that a 'principle urging us to promote liveliness appears to permit racial and ethnic discrimination when it comes to romantic relationships, which is wrong by most contemporary philosophies' (2022, 86). Consider that there are ways a state could forbid interracial marriage without necessarily degrading anyone's liveliness. Metz asks the reader to:

> [I]magine that a racist state did not punish those who were to intermarry. Suppose it rather defined a valid marriage as one incapable of obtaining between members of different races and ethnicities. Mixed couples who have vowed to live together in romantic, long term relationships simply could not count as 'legally married'. Despite the absence of punitive or 'restrictive'

LIVELINESS AS A MORAL THEORY   89

law in H.L.A. Hart's (1961) influential terms, the state's segregationist 'facilitative' law would remain wrongful, indeed, a human rights violation. However, supposing the separated population groups had enough people within them for everyone to find a fertile spouse, it appears that no one's liveliness would be undermined. (2022, 86–87)

It might be reasonably objected that this lack of state recognition would actually be degrading to a person's liveliness. Indeed, that Metz cashes out liveliness here just with respect to fertility and procreation is puzzling. For he has sought to construe liveliness in secular terms, not as an imperceptible energy as understood by adherents of African Traditional Religion (see Chapter 3). It is reasonable to think that if an interracial couple is disrespected by the state in this way, it could cause them to feel depressed, anxious, and insecure.

However, Metz asks his reader to further suppose that the state enforced general race segregation such that romantic relationships across racial lines rarely, if ever, occurred, with most people holding that such relationships are immoral. In such a society, a person's liveliness would not be degraded by unfulfilled romantic desires, because they would not develop in the first place (Metz 2022a, 87). Now, the proponent of liveliness 'might plausibly suggest that "separate but equal is still unequal", meaning that such segregationist policies would likely result in lower self-esteem on the part of the race deemed inferior' (Metz 2022a, 87). But imagine that the racial segregation is not based on the idea that one race is superior but rather as a way of maintaining the races' unique cultures. Metz claims that in such a scenario it is difficult for liveliness to say why such segregation is wrong, even though it is in fact wrong (Metz 2022a, 87).

I submit that if each person has intrinsic value and should be treated with respect on the basis of their liveliness or on their capacity for liveliness, then this type of segregation may still be unjustified. For part of protecting a person's liveliness may include respecting something like Mill's harm principle (i.e., do not interfere with someone unless they pose an imminent threat to others). The type of paternalism and interference involved with the kind of racial segregation described by Metz, even if it is genuinely well intended, is probably still not permissible. My point is that it is reasonable to suppose that if persons were respected in virtue of possessing life force, such racial segregation would not be justified in the first place.

90 A MORAL THEORY OF LIVELINESS

More importantly, this objection also brings to the fore interesting questions about what precisely constitutes the relevant 'community' when examining ethical theories stemming from the African intellectual tradition. Some have criticized contemporary proposals of African Communitarianism or *ubuntu* as being infeasible in large, modern-day societies (e.g., Matolino and Kwindingwi 2013). Indeed, part of the criticism is that an ethic that is so intertwined with members of one's community is only workable in smaller villages or tribal contexts. It makes little sense in large, modern-day urban centres. I will not adjudicate this objection here as, even if it does apply to certain versions of African communitarianism, it does not touch deontological liveliness in any meaningful way. On deontological liveliness, all (or almost all) humans have the capacity for at least some degree of liveliness. The relevant moral community, then, includes *every* (or almost every) human. If every community member has dignity (or inherent value or rights), then it is impermissible to segregate individuals based on race, even if the motivation for doing so is genuinely benevolent.

5.4.5 It Is *Pro Tanto* Immoral to Express Ethnic, Sexual, or Similar Epithets towards Others

This global intuition can be accommodated by deontological liveliness. An individual's dignity is degraded if they are subject to epithets.

5.4.6 It Is *Pro Tanto* Immoral Never to Fight Hunger, Poverty, Displacement, or the Like Suffered by Those Outside One's In-group, When One Could Do So at Little Cost to Oneself

Deontological liveliness can also accommodate this global intuition. It is unclear that there can be people completely outside of one's 'in-group'. Though there is nothing in liveliness that prohibits valuing close relationships more than mere strangers, every person has a dignity on this view. One ought to act in ways that respects this dignity. This means acting in ways that are likely to increase the liveliness of others. Fighting hunger, poverty, and displacement at little costs to oneself is required by deontological liveliness.

5.4.7 It Is *Pro Tanto* Immoral Never to Prevent Serious Crimes Done to Others, When One Could Do So at Little Cost to Oneself

Preventing crimes when doing so costs one little is prescribed by deontological liveliness. On deontological liveliness one has a duty to promote and protect the liveliness of others. This is particularly so when one can protect the liveliness of others at little cost to oneself.

5.4.8 It Is *Pro Tanto* Immoral to Torture an Animal for the Fun of iit

Teleological liveliness can say that torturing animals for fun is wrong because they possess some liveliness, even if less than humans. Deontological liveliness may imply that animals are valuable because they possess the capacity to be lively, even though it is to a lesser extent than humans. Such differences may explain why humans have a dignity while animals do not. For more details about how to explain the value of animals according to liveliness, see 6.9.2.

5.4.9 Tentative Conclusions on Liveliness and African Intuitions

Deontological liveliness is able to accommodate every global intuition I am using to test it against, including that it is *pro tanto* immoral to deceive a person when not in self- or other defense, and that it is *pro tanto* immoral to discriminate along racial or gender lines.

5.5 Conclusion

In this chapter, I developed a moral theory of liveliness which is entirely secular and naturalistic. Specifically, I showed that there are ways of understanding liveliness as providing a theory of moral value, in addition to different theories of right action. After explaining deontological liveliness, which says that a person has a dignity either in virtue of possessing liveliness or the capacity for it, I went on to test it against African and global moral

92 A MORAL THEORY OF LIVELINESS

intuitions. Metz believes that liveliness is susceptible to problems associated with welfarism, that it fails to explain why plural voting is wrong, that it does not motivate reconciliatory justice well, that it cannot make clear why certain types of racial segregation are inappropriate, and finally, that it does not show why lying is wrong in itself. I demonstrated that while such worries might apply to teleological versions of liveliness, contra Metz, they do not apply with equal force to deontological versions. Deontological liveliness can explain almost all of the African moral intuitions, and it can explain all of the global intuitions. The normative theory of liveliness has therefore passed one important test. In the next chapter I will explore further implications of the moral theory of liveliness by comparing and contrasting it to utilitarianism.

6

Further Implications of Liveliness as a Moral Theory

6.1 Introduction

The purpose of this chapter is to continue to develop the moral theory of liveliness by critically comparing it to a well-known normative theory from the Anglo-American tradition in utilitarianism before turning to address some additional objections to it. I begin by briefly explaining the basic idea behind utilitarianism (6.2). I then examine some of the classic cases that serve as difficult counterexamples to utilitarianism (6.3), before exploring various ways a utilitarian might address them (6.4). After this, I explore how the different theories of liveliness deal with these cases. I begin explaining the verdicts that teleological liveliness issues on these cases (6.5). I then explore a theory of dignity based on deontological liveliness (6.6), which sets the stage for examining what deontological liveliness says about the cases (6.7). I argue that liveliness, especially its deontological formulation, fares much better than utilitarianism in addressing the difficult cases. After this, I turn to examining two further ways of developing liveliness, first as a two-stage utilitarian theory (6.8), and second as a more complete theory that includes both deontological and teleological elements (6.9). In the final section, I address two objections to appealing to liveliness as a moral theory: that it entails welfarism and that it is overly anthropocentric (6.10).

6.2 What Is Utilitarianism?

Utilitarianism represents a family of related views committed to the following three principles (Woodard 2019, 4). First, they are committed to *consequentialism*, which is the view that 'the rightness of actions, the justice of institutions, and the virtues and vices of agents [are] in terms of the goodness of outcomes' (Woodard 2019, 4). Second, utilitarians are committed to *welfarism*. This is

A Moral Theory of Liveliness. Kirk Lougheed, Oxford University Press. © Kirk Lougheed 2025.
DOI: 10.1093/9780197782019.003.0006

94 A MORAL THEORY OF LIVELINESS

the view that 'all well-being has noninstrumental value, and nothing else has noninstrumental value. This means that all well-being is good independently of its effects, and nothing else is. Though other things can be good or bad, their goodness or badness depends on their contribution to well-being' (Woodard 2019, 5). Since this does not explain how the value of an outcome is supposed to depend on well-being, utilitarians are also committed to a third principle, *sum-ranking*. This is the view that 'the value of an outcome is the sum of the goods (and bads) existing in that outcome' (Woodard 2019, 5–6).

There is room for a diversity of answers to the question of what constitutes well-being, the questions they address, and the relationship between rightness and good outcomes. (Woodard 20019, 6). For example, there are four basic versions of utilitarianism. *Act Utilitarianism* says that right actions are those that lead to the most well-being (Mulgan 2007, 115; e.g., Singer 1972). *Rule Utilitarianism* seeks to find the best set of rules that when followed produce the most well-being (e.g., Woodard 2008). *Motive Utilitarianism* says that the right actions are those motivated by trying to produce the most well-being. Finally, *Institutional Utilitarianism* says that utilitarianism is the right theory for political decisions, even if it is not so for private morality (Mulgan 2007, 127; e.g., Goodin 1995).

Since I will primarily analyze cases that show utilitarianism has counterintuitive results, here is one case to show why some find the theory attractive:

> The Rocks: Six innocent swimmers have become trapped on two rocks by the incoming tide. Five of the swimmers are on one rock, while the last swimmer is on the second rock. Each swimmer will drown unless they are rescued. You are the sole lifeguard on duty. You have time to get to one rock in your patrol-boat and save everyone on it. Because of the distance between the rocks, and the speed of the tide, you cannot get to both rocks in time. What should you do? (Mulgan 2007, 104)

It is intuitively obvious that all else being equal you should save the group of five swimmers. Utilitarianism provides a good explanation of these intuitions. This admittedly terse summary of utilitarianism is sufficient for my purposes in this chapter.

At this stage it is important to issue a disclaimer about the methodology of this chapter. Proponents of utilitarianism are unlikely to be pleased with this chapter, primarily because I had a difficult methodological choice to make when writing it. As far as I can tell, there are three main ways I could

FURTHER IMPLICATIONS OF LIVELINESS   95

have approached writing this chapter. The first is to deal with a relatively simplified or 'textbook' version of utilitarianism. The second is to address the work of a specific proponent of utilitarianism. The third is to attempt to systematically address all or almost all of the contemporary work on utilitarianism. For the sake of simplicity, I have mostly opted for the first approach. However, I have also tried to highlight for the readers additional places in the literature that are relevant. My main reason for taking this approach is that, even though I believe this chapter shows particular ways in which liveliness is preferrable to utilitarianism, I am mostly using it as a foil to help throw additional light on the details of liveliness.

6.3 The Difficult Cases

A number of cases have been raised against utilitarianism and are now considered seminal or classic counterexamples to the theory. I choose the following, as they are helpful in illuminating the distinctions I want to make:

> *The sheriff.* You are the sheriff in an isolated wild-west town. A murder has been committed. Most people believe that Bob is guilty, but you know he is innocent. Unless you hang Bob now, there will be a riot in town and several people will die. Utilitarianism says you must hang Bob, because the loss of his life is outweighed by the value of preventing the riot. (Mulgan 2007, 93)

> *The transplant.* You are a doctor at a hospital. You have five patients who will each die without an immediate transplant. One patient needs a new heart, two need a new lung, and two need a new kidney. Mary comes into a hospital for a routine checkup. By a remarkable coincidence, Mary is a suitable donor for all five patients. Utilitarianism says you should arrange for Mary to die unexpectedly on the operating table, as the loss of her life is outweighed by the lives of the five patients. (Mulgan 2007, 93–94)

Utilitarianism issues the wrong verdict in these cases. According to objectors, any plausible moral theory ought to be able to issue the correct verdict in these and related cases. The basic problem is that these cases 'are not at all interested in *how* happiness is produced, or in *whose* happiness is at stake. The general objection is that, as moral agents, we *should* care about these two things' (Mulgan 2007, 96). The intuitive wrongness of the actions in

96 A MORAL THEORY OF LIVELINESS

question is also explained by the nature of the special relationships in question. Given the nature of their work, sheriffs should never hang innocent people and doctors should never harm patients (Mulgan 2007, 96). Finally, it is also explained by the fact that utilitarianism fails to recognize the distinction between killing versus letting die.

6.4 Utilitarian Responses to the Cases

As stated above (6.2), utilitarianism represents a family of views and as such there are a wide variety of available responses to these cases.[1] The simplest response is to just 'bite the bullet'. Though our initial intuitions to these cases might suggest otherwise, utilitarianism does not in fact issue the wrong verdict. Stepping back and reflecting dispassionately shows that nothing is amiss in these cases (Mulgan 2007, 100–101). Another way to show this is to deny that the separateness of persons is metaphysically relevant to morality. For example:

> [S]ome utilitarians defend a *reductionist* account of personal identity. People are made up of experiences standing in various relations to one another. There is nothing to a person beyond those experiences. The boundaries between one life and another are not as morally significant as we think. If the boundary between people is not metaphysically significant, then there is no reason why I should be more concerned for my own future experiences than for anyone else's. If I value future experiences at all, I should value them all equally. This leads us to utilitarianism. (Mulgan 103; see also Parfit 1986)

A different approach is to deny that utilitarianism requires the wrong action in the cases in question. The sheriff does not need to murder the innocent person, nor should the doctor harvest the organs of an innocent person. One kind of argument along these lines is to suggest that since we cannot be sure of the consequences of the actions in question, but we are aware of the probabilities, they are impermissible on the grounds of maximizing expected utility. For example, a Rule Utilitarian could argue that the best

---

[1] Consider that Woodard 2019 is entirely motivated by dealing with objections to the theory, including to these types of difficult cases.

policies at promoting welfare in the long run are those that protect innocent individuals. Of course, it is still possible to ask about what the utilitarian should do in these cases *if* they could be epistemically certain of the relevant consequences, with some maintaining that any plausible ethical theory should not even make these cases possible (Mulgan 2007, 104–105). Likewise:

> [M]any are suspicious whether utilitarianism really can give the right answers, even in our original tales. It is not true that utilitarians should *always* focus on immediate or more certain consequences. Once the sheriff weighs up the values and probabilities involved, he may well conclude that, although hanging Bob is not *certain* to produce good results, it does have a higher *expected value*. (Mulgan 2007, 106)

Other responses involve challenging relevant assumptions about human happiness or altering the pertinent account of welfare. For example, the utilitarian might deny that tiny amounts of pleasure across many people could outweigh the suffering of one person (Mulgan 2007, 107). Finally, utilitarians could simply admit that these are indeed problematic cases for the theory while observing that no normative theory is able to completely avoid difficult cases. If all other normative theories have difficulty explaining certain cases, utilitarianism could still be the best theory on offer overall.

I will not attempt to evaluate these responses here. As I say above, I am dealing with a rather simplified version of utilitarianism, and I recognize that more sophisticated versions have been developed. Having said that, the Sheriff and the Transplant cases are such that any version of utilitarianism is going to have to address them. In the next two sections (6.5, 6.6), I examine how each of teleological liveliness and deontological liveliness addresses these cases, thereby illuminating further ways the theory can be expanded. I suggest that both issue the right verdict in these cases, but that deontological liveliness ultimately handles them better.

6.5 Teleological Liveliness and the Cases

Recall that teleological liveliness (5.2.1) can be identified with embracing the following principles:

98 A MORAL THEORY OF LIVELINESS

- An action is right inasmuch as it increases (or can reasonably be expected to increase) the life force in oneself and in others.
- An action is wrong inasmuch as it decreases (or can reasonably be expected to decrease) the life force in oneself and in others.

How do these principles suggest a person should respond in the Sheriff and the Transplant cases? Remember that I argued that a plausible version of teleological liveliness is going to value liveliness both in oneself and in others (5.2.1). Part of the reason for this was to avoid precisely these kinds of cases. The sheriff is supposed to be concerned with everyone's liveliness, including the person he would be sacrificing. The doctor is supposed to be concerned with the liveliness of the healthy patient, too. If everyone's liveliness is equally important, then it is wrong to snuff out someone's liveliness in order to promote the liveliness of others.

There are ways that an objector might push back against this response. It might be a plausible response when it comes to the Sheriff or Transplant case. Indeed, liveliness is the end that ought to direct all moral reasoning, and so diminishing a person's liveliness to the point of snuffing it out completely (i.e., death) is impermissible. But modifying the examples puts pressure on this type of explanation:

> *The sheriff.* You are the sheriff in an isolated wild-west town. A murder has been committed. Most people believe that Bob is guilty, but you know he is innocent. Unless you hang Bob now, there will be a riot in town and a thousand people will die. Utilitarianism says you must hang Bob, because the loss of his life is outweighed by the value of preventing the riot. (adapted from Mulgan 2007, 93)

> *The transplant.* You are a doctor at a hospital. You have a hundred patients who will each die without an immediate transplant. Suppose that advancements in medical science allow you to harvest everything you need to save the hundred patients from one healthy person. Utilitarianism says you should arrange for a healthy patient to die unexpectedly on the operating table, as the loss of their life is outweighed by the lives of the hundred patients. (adapted from Mulgan 2007, 93–94)

These examples put pressure on teleological liveliness, because it is less clear that an innocent person should not be sacrificed for the liveliness of many

FURTHER IMPLICATIONS OF LIVELINESS   99

people. On the assumption that death is the worst thing that can happen to a person (and perhaps also a very low quality of life that involves constant suffering), teleological liveliness could justify killing the innocent person in this case. In other words, it appears rather amenable to the type of utilitarian calculus that leads to these types of cases in the first place. Suppose one flourishing person represents ten units of liveliness. In *the Sheriff, there will be a loss of ten thousand units of liveliness unless ten units are sacrificed. Teleological liveliness seems to plainly dictate that the innocent person be sacrificed.

It might be objected that a person's liveliness can never be sacrificed for the sake of others' liveliness, especially if the sacrifice is non-consensual. But in the cases in question, the choice is a binary. There is going to be a loss of liveliness no matter which course of action is taken. If liveliness really is the end that ought to be pursued, and this value is what should dictate all decision-making, sacrificing the innocent person is probably required.

Now, I acknowledge that it is probably likely that intuitions vary more about the original cases than these extreme cases.[2] Still, I want to suggest that sacrificing the one innocent person is wrong. I want a moral theory that says it is (almost) always wrong to sacrifice an innocent person.[3] Though I do not definitively claim that teleological liveliness cannot adequately deal with these cases, I have suggested some reasons for thinking it struggles to do so. For those who are willing to 'bite the bullet' in these more extreme cases, teleological liveliness may remain attractive.

Lurking under the surface of this discussion is the extent to which, if at all, teleological liveliness is really just a dressed-up version of utilitarianism, with liveliness being the unit of measurement for utility. After all, recall that two key features of utilitarianism are consequentialism and welfarism. As I have described it here, teleological liveliness does seem to analyze the rightness of actions in terms of the outcomes, where those outcomes are assessed based on a conception of well-being as liveliness. I will return to this theme in 6.10.1.

---

[2] My point still stands even if this supposition is wrong.

[3] It might be objected that this contradicts claims I have made in Lougheed 2024 about the Christian Atonement. However, that sacrifice was *voluntary* and accomplished a particularly unique end. The sacrifice in question in these cases is not voluntary. Likewise, the Atonement need not be understood as a sacrifice in the relevant sense.

6.6 A Theory of Dignity Based on Liveliness

I believe that deontological liveliness has an easier time issuing the correct verdict regarding the cases in question, primarily because it is better suited to offer a compelling account of dignity. The purpose of this section is to gesture toward a theory of dignity based on liveliness. I use 'dignity' and 'human rights' interchangeably, because the latter tends to be eschewed in African ethics, though I suspect most ethicists in this tradition do not in fact deny the equivalent of rights. To begin, I briefly outline some of the main capacity accounts of dignity as located in both the Anglo-American and African traditions (6.6.1). I then speculate that a capacity approach to dignity based on liveliness has two main advantages in (i) being able to provide a coherent synthesis of the capacities mentioned in other accounts, and (ii) being able to explain why animals and the environment matter. Finally, to conclude I briefly consider an account of dignity that is based on the fact of liveliness, instead of the capacity for it, and speculate that this could be a place where life force fares better than liveliness (6.6.2).

As a disclaimer to the reader, I acknowledge that this subsection merely scratches the surface of what could easily be its own full-length chapter, and indeed a full-length book. When I began work on this book, I did not anticipate writing very much on dignity or human rights beyond merely noting some implications my view had for these values. I wanted to focus more exclusively on a normative theory of right action. However, after well into the writing of this book, I realized that there would simply be many gaps and unanswered questions if I did not say something more substantial about what liveliness implies for dignity or rights. Though I do not intend to answer all such questions in this section, I hope to minimally point towards a promising way of developing a mature theory of human rights or dignity based on liveliness. I hope that readers will think these tentative suggestions are plausible or, more modestly, that they at least offer a reasonable expansion of ideas that are consistent with the other claims I have developed thus far.

6.6.1 Extant Capacity Accounts

The most influential account of dignity in the Anglo-American philosophical tradition emerges from the philosophy of Immanuel Kant. For example, along Kantian lines, Alan Gewirth claims that '[a]ll humans have the human rights in full to the extent that they are inherently capable of exercising them. This inherent capacity pertains to each human so long as he is a rational agent in the minimal sense of having purposes he wants to fulfill and being able to control his behavior accordingly while knowing the particular circumstances of his action' (1982, 8). It is therefore something like the capacity to pursue rational ends that implies dignity or rights. Martha Nussbaum's well-known capacity theory is *'focused on choice or freedom*, holding that the crucial good societies should be promoting for their people is a set of opportunities or substantial freedoms, which people then may or may not exercise in action: the choice is theirs' (Nussbaum 2011, 18). Individuals have dignity in virtue of having the capacity to exercise various capabilities (Nussbaum 2011, 31). It is not actually achieving the relevant capabilities that can ground value for Nussbaum, since for her they are what societies should strive to offer their citizens, but often fail to provide. The ten central capabilities Nussbaum lists include the capacity for a life of a normal length, bodily health, bodily integrity, the ability to use one's imagination, among others (Nussbaum 2011, 33–34). It is reasonable to construe Nussbaum's account as a capacity approach given the language she frequently uses to describe the capabilities as *being able to* such and such. Sarah Clark Miller draws inspiration from the ethics of care literature to suggest that the capacity to care is a promising candidate for the grounds of human dignity. She explains that 'the distinctive capacity that humans have to perceive, understand, adopt, and advance another person's self-determined ends as their own' (Miller 2017, 115). Miller's account serves as an entry point to two African capacity accounts that share her approach in focusing on relational features of humanity and thus tend to eschew the more Kantian accounts.

There are two important African approaches to also ground the value of humans or dignity in certain capacities. Motsamai Molefe grounds the value of persons in their capacity for sympathy. This involves the 'capacity to connect, to be responsive to the needs of others and to emphasise the importance of social responsibility can best be accounted for by appeal to the primacy of sympathy' (Molefe 2020, 56–57). According to Thaddeus Metz, 'what gives us a dignity is our capacity to befriend others and to be befriended by them' (2022, 118). Given the communitarian emphasis in African ethics, it is unsurprising that, unlike many Anglo-American approaches, especially those that have been influence by Kant, the capacities mentioned here are relational.

6.6.2 The Capacity for Liveliness as the Grounds of Human Dignity

At times I have written that humans are valuable because they possess liveliness or have the capacity for liveliness. I now spell out some of the advantages of the latter approach with reference to the other capacity accounts just mentioned, before addressing some challenges it faces. A dignity grounded in liveliness says that humans are valuable inasmuch as they have the capacity for liveliness. Thus, having the capacity for growth, creativity, vibrancy, health, etc., is what makes an individual valuable, even if they do not in fact exercise that capacity.

I submit that a significant advantage of an account of dignity based on the capacity for liveliness is that it nicely synthesizes the other capacity accounts, which demonstrates the virtue of economy.[4] In other words, I believe that the capacities for autonomy, Nussbaum's capabilities, for caring, sympathy, and friendliness (or love), can be reasonably subsumed under liveliness. They can be explained as features of liveliness or as different ways of enacting liveliness. Consider that if a person lacked the capacity for autonomous agency or lacked the capacity for love, it is intuitively obvious that they would lack the capacity for liveliness or at least lack the capacity for it in important ways. For example, if someone's autonomy is constrained, their ability for creativity is probably hindered. Likewise, if they are unable to love, they will not be able to support and help others in ways that would increase their liveliness. Another virtue of this account is that it explains why animals are valuable without simultaneously holding that they are as valuable as humans. An animal has the capacity for some types of liveliness, as do even flora and fauna to a limited extent. So, they are valuable but not so valuable as to have a dignity and possess certain inalienable rights.

A persistent challenge to capacity accounts is their prima facie inability to accommodate humans who fail to have the relevant capacities. Certain humans simply lack the capacity for rationality or autonomy or love in any substantial way. Sometimes these are temporary states, but other times they are permanent. Indeed, some individuals are born with such severe deficits (e.g., the severely autistic) that it is difficult to show how these capacity accounts can include them. Of course, most of those proposing such capacity accounts want to preserve the intuition that such persons have a full dignity and/or all of the

---

[4] Thanks to Brian Ballard for drawing this to my attention.

FURTHER IMPLICATIONS OF LIVELINESS 103

human rights that everyone else enjoys. Furthermore, an approach which says that such persons have dignity or rights but to a lesser extent than everyone who possesses the relevant full capacities is problematic for a variety reasons. For example, certain entitlements of dignity or rights do not appear to come in degrees. Furthermore, this still results in the counterintuitive conclusion that certain animals are more valuable than certain disabled persons, since the former may have the capacities in question while the latter do not.

I do not intend to settle these matters here. Remember that I am trying to develop the normative implications of life force and liveliness to a greater extent than has been done previously. Such a project necessarily includes space for further development, and this is one of them. In particular, future work should explore the extent to which the successes and challenges of capacity accounts in the Anglo-American tradition (and elsewhere) apply with equal force to the capacity account based on liveliness. Furthermore, the success of the capacity account based on liveliness may not depend on the success of capacity accounts in the Anglo-American tradition. In order to help discover whether this is the case, it would be interesting to know whether there are resources unique to the African tradition that help address the usual challenges to capacity accounts. To conclude, consider a different approach to grounding dignity or rights in liveliness. Suppose that dignity is grounded in the fact of liveliness itself. This implies that any person who possesses any degree of liveliness has dignity and rights. Thus, any person who is alive, even if only in a vegetative state, possesses *some* degree of liveliness even if it is very limited. This account nicely solves the challenge to the capacity account based on the idea that it does not include certain disabled or terminally ill persons. Since they are alive, they have a dignity or rights. Notice that the same strategy is not available to the Anglo-American capacity accounts. For example, grounding rights in exercising autonomy or actually possessing interests would be of no help in including certain disabled persons.

However, the same problem regarding the status of the severely disabled humans and certain animals remains for this account. This is because it is plausible that certain animals will exhibit higher degrees of liveliness than, say, a terminally ill patient in a permanently vegetative state. This is a place where liveliness and life force may come apart in their plausibility. By my lights, there is no obvious way for liveliness to solve this challenge. However, life force has a built-in answer to it. Remember that according to most accounts of life force, God has placed humans at the centre of the visible world. This could be enough for showing that humans have a dignity and rights,

104 A MORAL THEORY OF LIVELINESS

quite apart from any values had by animals. It also points to the possibility of further interaction with accounts of human rights already on offer that appeal to God for their grounding. Again, all of this is tentative and primarily points to the need for further exploration.

6.7 Deontological Liveliness and the Cases

With the theory of dignity in view, I can turn to explaining how deontological liveliness assesses the above cases. Recall that deontological liveliness (5.2.2) says that:

- An action is right inasmuch as it respects individuals in virtue of their capacity to be lively.
- An action is wrong inasmuch as it degrades those with the capacity to be lively.

Deontological liveliness is more clearly able to issue the correct verdict regarding the cases in this chapter. It is impermissible to sacrifice an innocent person to save others, because they possess a dignity inhering in their capacity for liveliness. The fact of inalienable dignity does not change based on the number of people who would be saved in the cases in question. In all of them, it is wrong to kill the innocent person. It will almost never matter how the cases are modified. Of course, those of a more consequentialist bent will be unsatisfied with this approach. Again, my purpose is to explore varying accounts of the best versions of liveliness. Though I tend to favour deontological liveliness because it aligns better with my moral intuitions, others will prefer teleological liveliness. I now turn to explaining a worry that paves the way for a more robust account of deontological liveliness that incorporates both deontological and teleological elements to perhaps satisfy a broader scope of moral intuitions.

6.8 Agent or Patient: A Two-Stage Welfarism Approach to Liveliness?

Christopher Woodard issues a challenge to Metz's Moral Relational Theory (see 8.4) that may also be applicable to deontological liveliness, particularly

FURTHER IMPLICATIONS OF LIVELINESS   105

to the version I tend to favour, which locates dignity or value in the capacity for liveliness. Woodard presses Metz in the following way:

> Suppose that Agent has the capacity to act by her nature, but that throughout the whole of her life she lacks the ability to act, for contingent reasons. In contrast, Patient altogether lacks the capacity to act. Suppose, however, that Agent and Patient can both be benefited or harmed to the same extent, and that we face a choice between benefiting Patient or benefiting Agent by the same amount, but that we cannot benefit both. Metz's theory implies that we should favour Agent here, since she has the capacity to act, and so has a higher moral status than Patient. [. . .] [I]t seems to me to be an implication of Metz's view that we should favour Agent's interests in this case, because she possesses the capacity to act and so can be a subject in communal relationships. I have imagined that, for contingent reasons, Agent lacks the ability to actualise this capacity throughout her life — for the specific purpose of trying to isolate the moral importance of the capacity to act. Reporting my own intuitions: I cannot see why this capacity makes Agent's interests morally more important than Patient's [. . . .] My question is why we should accord greater status to any entity on account of a capacity to be a subject in communal relationships, which requires agency among other things. (Woodard, forthcoming)

Reinterpreted to apply to deontological liveliness, the worry is that if Agent never exercises their capacity for liveliness, it is difficult to see how they are any morally different than Patient. If Woodard's criticism holds, it puts pressure on deontological liveliness to shift back to teleological liveliness (or find an entirely different account of dignity). But then this means that it has to face any problems associated with teleological liveliness, including the worry that it cannot adequately account for rights or dignity. The Sheriff and Transplant cases rear their heads again.

Here are two possible responses to Woodard's worry. The first is to insist that if a person possesses any liveliness at all, then they matter morally. In other words, any and every person has a dignity simply in virtue of being alive. However, it is possible that this leads to counterintuitive trade-offs in the other direction. For example, one would have no reason to provide scarce lifesaving resources to a healthy twenty-year-old instead of someone who is older, suffering from multiple terminal illnesses, and guilty of crimes against humanity. The choice between them would necessarily be arbitrary. This in itself might be enough to insist that the capacity for liveliness is the best way to think about deontological liveliness. For on this version, more humans count morally, because there are more humans who possess the capacity for liveliness than who exercise the capacity or exercise it well.

The second response comes by way of a different formulation of liveliness that is inspired by Woodard's criticisms of Metz. His fascinating suggestion for Metz is that there are alternative teleological theories that might avoid some of the unpalatable consequences in view. For example, he says that '"indirect" theories such as collective consequentialism or rule consequentialism attempt to explain the idea that we can have reasons to perform or not to perform actions because of the kinds of actions they are' (Woodard, forthcoming). Though Woodard is discussing Metz's theory, his ideas can be applied to liveliness. For example, a welfarist rule consequentialist could endorse the idea that liveliness is the best (or one of the best) ways to promote well-being, thereby adopting a set of rules requiring the promotion of liveliness. It is not implausible to think that such an ethic would have rules against harvesting the organs of healthy individuals in order to save others.

One reason for not pursuing this line further is that the best version of liveliness as moral theory will ideally accommodate both African and global moral intuitions (see 5.3, 5.4). A two-stage consequentialist moral theory of liveliness may well capture many of the relevant moral intuitions. However, this approach would be a significant move away from the African tradition. Consider that Metz writes that '[o]ne will search in vain for any suggestion of two-level or indirect welfarism in the African philosophical literature' (Metz 2022a, 74 quoted in Woodard forthcoming). Thus, regardless of whether an 'indirect' theory can account for such intuitions, it is unlikely to be embraced in the African tradition.

6.9 A Hybrid Theory of Liveliness?

The above discussion leads me to wonder whether there is a hybrid moral theory of liveliness that gives weight to seeking the end of liveliness while respecting persons based on their capacity for liveliness. Consider the following two principles:

- An action is right inasmuch as (i) it increases (or can reasonably be expected to increase) the liveliness in oneself and in others and (ii) only

FURTHER IMPLICATIONS OF LIVELINESS   107

inasmuch as it also respects individuals in virtue of their capacity to be lively.

- An action is wrong inasmuch as (iii) it decreases (or can reasonably be expected to decrease) the liveliness in oneself and in others and (iv) inasmuch as it degrades those with the capacity to be lively.

I believe that this is still rightly construed fundamentally as a deontological theory because of the way it prioritizes deontological constraints. Consider that in the first positive formulation, that requirement (ii) acts as a constraint on (i). Likewise, (iv) acts as a similar constraint on (iii). The major difference between the hybrid theory and the original formulation of deontological liveliness is that the former explicitly aims at maximizing liveliness, just with a deontological constraint. I now want to work out some of the implications of this fuller deontological theory.

Recall the original Sheriff and Transplant cases. This updated deontological theory is easily able to explain why it is impermissible to kill an innocent person for the sake of saving more individuals. Though killing the innocent person to protect or save others plausibly increases the liveliness of a larger group of people, it does so at the expense of disrespecting an individual. Alternative ways of thinking about disrespect include the ideas that it would violate the innocent person's inalienable human rights or their inherent dignity. Though protecting and increasing liveliness is good, as is avoiding its decrease, it cannot come at the cost of disrespecting a person (or violating their rights). Of course, this theory also issues the correct verdict in the more extreme *Sheriff and *Transplant cases. In the vast majority of cases, no amount of increase of liveliness or prevention of a loss of liveliness in others can justify an action that comes at the expense of disrespecting an individual who has the capacity for liveliness.

At this point it might be asked how this description differs from the account of deontological liveliness mentioned in the previous chapter (5.2.2). Two observations are in order. First, though I have not said very much about moral motivation (nor do I intend to), what I have described here paints a fuller picture compared to the description in the previous chapter. This description makes clearer that pursuing the end of liveliness is recommended within certain parameters. Explicitly acknowledging the teleological motivation also helps to explain certain consequentialist intuitions about the cases discussed in this chapter, particularly the more extreme modified versions. Though I myself am not very tempted to admit that killing an innocent

108　A MORAL THEORY OF LIVELINESS

person to save hundreds or thousands of people is justified, this fuller deontological theory can explain the intuitions of those who are so tempted,
even though it does not ultimately vindicate them. It does so because it is the
case that liveliness is the end that ought to be pursued. Preserving the lives
of many people is good, all else being equal. It is just that in these particular
cases, not all else is equal, because an innocent person's life is the cost of the
liveliness of others.

This filled-out version of deontological liveliness also issues the correct
verdict in the Rocks case. It is right to save the group of five swimmers, letting the lone swimmer drown. The first item to note is that this case involves
the widely accepted distinction between killing and letting die. The lifeguard is not actively killing the lone swimmer. Though all else being equal,
it would be wrong for the lifeguard to fail to save the lone swimmer, there are
mitigating circumstances in this case. The lifeguard is forced to choose between whom to save and, as such, they should probably aim at maximizing as
much liveliness as possible, which means saving the group of five swimmers.
It is not disrespectful to the lone swimmer, because the lifeguard is forced
into a decision and a bad situation they did not cause. The act only becomes
disrespectful if the case is changed to one in which the lone swimmer is the
only one in need of rescue and the lifeguard does not help them.[5]

I conclude this section by revisiting the case of lying and deception
discussed in the previous chapter (5.4.3). Recall that I argued, contra Metz,
that it does not need to only be the belief that one was lied to that explains
why it is wrong according to liveliness (i.e., because the belief causes a
diminishment of liveliness). On deontological liveliness, lying is fundamentally wrong because it is disrespectful. This is so even if the person never
finds out they were deceived.

At first glance, deontological liveliness might not issue the correct verdict
in cases in which it is intuitively obvious that one ought to lie. It is well known
that Kant's moral philosophy suffers from this problem.[6] Consider the case

---

[5] It is not quite right to say I want a principle that it is *always* wrong to kill an innocent for the sake
of the greater good. For example, many (across cultures) have the intuition that it is permissible to
sacrifice an innocent in certain types of Trolley Cases in which a decision between one innocent and
more than one is forced. Examining these sorts of cases in detail would take me too far afield, though
I readily admit that it may prove difficult for liveliness to preserve the relevant moral intuitions. For
more, see Kamm 2015; Nozick 1974: 34–35. Thanks to Thaddeus Metz for pressing me on this point.

[6] The literature alone that Kant on lying has generated is evidence for this claim. For example, see
Bacin 2022; Mahon 2009; Sussman 2009.

FURTHER IMPLICATIONS OF LIVELINESS   109

of the Nazis at your front door who are looking for the Jewish family you are hiding in your basement. Not only is it permissible for you to lie and deceive the Nazis, but presumably you *ought* to lie in this case. Notice that it is easy for teleological liveliness to deal with this case. You ought to lie because doing so helps to protect and promote the liveliness of the Jewish family you are helping to hide. This liveliness outweighs any diminishment in your own liveliness over having to tell the lie.[7]

Recall that I explained that in the positive formulation of the hybrid theory of liveliness, the respect individuals have in virtue of their capacity is a constraint on the ways in which liveliness can be pursued as an end. This naturally leads one to wonder whether this is a problematic constraint in the case of lying to the Nazis. I cannot disrespect the Nazis by lying to them even though doing so promotes the liveliness of the Jewish family, just as I cannot harvest the organs of an innocent person even though doing so promotes the liveliness of five other people. But these cases are not analogous, because unlike in the Sheriff and Transplant cases, the Nazis are not innocent. The entitlements of fundamental respect (or dignity or rights) can be forfeited, at least to a degree.[8] The Nazis have forfeited their entitlement to respect. Since they are not deserving of respect, it is not impermissible to disrespect them by lying. This explains quite clearly how deontological liveliness issues the correct verdict in this case. Liveliness ought to be pursued provided no one's rights are trampled over. In this case, pursuing liveliness and respecting individuals both point to the requirement to lie to the Nazis.

The second observation is that even if one accepts that teleological liveliness plausibly entails that lying diminishes the liveliness of the liar, a more complete explanation of the wrongness would include something about the person being deceived. Again, hybrid liveliness is helpful here because on this view, a lie is disrespectful to the person being deceived (on the assumption they have done nothing to forfeit respect). This makes a fuller and more robust explanation as to why (all else being equal) a lie is wrong even if it is never discovered than the explanation that teleological liveliness can offer on its own.

One pertinent question is whether according to liveliness rights really can be forfeited in the relevant sense. For the Kantian, it makes sense to describe

---

[7] For more on lying, see Carson 2010.

[8] I add this last clause because it could still be wrong to, say, torture a Nazi as punishment after the war.

110 A MORAL THEORY OF LIVELINESS

the Nazi as having misused their freedom, which is the basis of their dignity. But can someone really misuse their liveliness? If not, then perhaps it is not possible for someone not to be owed fundamental respect in virtue of their capacity for liveliness. This would imply that a Nazi cannot be lied to or, worse still, that force cannot be used to resist them. To motivate this objection, further consider one common explanation of dignity located in the Judeo-Christian tradition, which says that every individual has a dignity because they are image bearers of God. *Imago dei* is not something that can be diminished or forfeited, no matter what evil acts a person commits. A person is still an image bearer of God, even if they perpetrate great evil. By analogy, a person who has the capacity for liveliness (i.e., the grounds for dignity) does not lose that capacity because they act in ways that undermine the liveliness of others.[9]

Though the capacity for liveliness and *imago dei* (and maybe immaterial souls) share similarities in being a property a person cannot willfully abandon, I believe this objection is ultimately not successful. *Imago dei* is not typically associated with a set of normative properties; people just have it. But liveliness is associated with a wide array of normative properties such that a person can indeed misuse their capacity for it. Even if there is nothing a Nazi could do to forfeit their dignity because they have the capacity for liveliness, this does not mean they cannot be lied to or resisted with force if they are degrading the liveliness of others. The resistance to them simply must be in proportion to and as a direct response of their degradation of the liveliness of others. This is consistent with admitting that the Nazi may well still have a dignity, which means that they cannot be treated in certain ways. For example, maybe this means that after the war it is impermissible to torture them or subject them to the same degrading treatment they perpetrated against Jewish prisoners in the death camps. But to acknowledge that people may, after all, have a dignity no matter what they do in no way entails that their degradation of others cannot be stopped.[10]

6.10 Two Additional Worries

Though I suspect that readers of this book are better situated than myself to step back and offer creative challenges to the moral theory of liveliness

---

[9] Thanks to Thaddeus Metz for prompting me to think through this objection.

[10] Though some within the Judeo-Christian tradition are pacifists, consider that the majority of those in the tradition are not and maintain that using force in self- or other defence is justified.

FURTHER IMPLICATIONS OF LIVELINESS   111

in all of the different possible versions I have presented, I want to close by addressing two potential objections. These are both obvious and serious objections and so it is important I address them before continuing. They are that liveliness (i) assumes welfarism and (ii) is unduly anthropocentric. I take each of these objections in turn, offering what I take to be the most plausible replies to be made on behalf of the proponent of liveliness. If the reader remains unconvinced, I hope that this exercise is at least helpful in continuing to shed more light on the theory.

6.10.1 Liveliness Entails Welfarism

One worry is that liveliness implies welfarism. Recall that this is the view that 'all well-being has noninstrumental value, and nothing else has noninstrumental value. This means that all well-being is good independently of its effects, and nothing else is. Though other things can be good or bad, their goodness or badness depends on their contribution to well-being' (Woodard 2019, 5). For further clarification, another definition claims that welfarism 'says that morality is all about individual welfare. It says that facts about the best interests of individuals are, in some sense, the building blocks of morality. Welfarists believe that the whole point of morality is to make individuals better off' (Keller 2009, 82–83).[11] If welfare is well-being, it is natural to ask what, specifically, constitutes well-being. Though it is typically identified with either subjective experiences (i.e., mental states), or desires, or with a set of objective goods that are good for everyone, welfarism as a general view can be neutral about what constitutes well-being (Keller 2009, 84). This means that:

> [W]e must understand it simply as the idea that morality is centrally concerned with the best interests of individuals. Welfarism identifies individual welfare, imprecisely, as the central concern of morality, or as the thing that morality is 'all about', but the exact form of that concern and the sense in which it is central to morality—the more precise sense in which morality is all about welfare—can be specified only in relation to certain

---

[11] Keller notes that many definitions of welfarism are not actually compatible with one another. He demonstrates this by comparing the definitions from Sumner (1996, 184), Moore and Crisp (1996, 598), Kagan (1998, 48), (Keller 2009, 86).

112 A MORAL THEORY OF LIVELINESS

> independent theoretical commitments, on which different welfarists can disagree. (Keller 2009, 87)

Keller points to three reasons why someone might reject welfarism. First, the moral good of a person should not be reduced to their welfare. What a person considers their welfare (i.e., interests) is perhaps too whimsical or contingent on social conditioning (Keller 2009, 89).[12] Second, we ought to care about something other than a person's good when evaluating her life morally. Perhaps our primary duties to persons are not to make them better off but to promote their autonomy or force them to accept the consequences of their action (Keller 2009, 90). Third, it might be the case that certain things do not really have interests but that we still have moral obligations to them. For example, perhaps we have direct duties to the environment or there is intrinsic value in works of art or cultural heritage (Keller 2009, 90). Of course, welfarists have responses to these worries, but it is not necessary for my purposes to wade into them here.[13]

With the basic idea of welfarism, one can see how liveliness might be identified as a version of welfarism. Liveliness just *is* well-being. It is the only thing that is of final and intrinsic value. All other things are only (dis) valuable given their relationship to liveliness. It is easiest to see this when thinking about teleological liveliness. The goal of morality on this view is to protect and promote liveliness. It is difficult to understand how else one could motivate this view except by assuming that liveliness is what is best for humans (i.e., it is the relevant form of well-being).

But deontological and hybrid liveliness could also be construed as welfarist. The set of rules implied by the respect for the capacity for liveliness garner their support from the fact that liveliness is what is best for people. In other words, '[t]he concept of welfare would be central to a deontological system, if the rules within that system were all constructed with individual welfare as a guiding value' (Keller 2009, 88).

I close this section by noting that this interpretation of liveliness is hardly uncontroversial. Suppose welfarism is about achieving one's interests while excellence is about self-realization. Liveliness nicely captures both interests and excellence at the same time. It should be in a person's interest to

---

[12] Keller points to Sen 1985, 21–22.

[13] Additionally, as a fourth reason, and at least at first glance, welfarism is incompatible with accounts of morality that rely on God. If God is morally valuable, this value cannot be explained as reducing to human interests or well-being.

maximize liveliness in themselves and others. However, aiming at liveliness is also to be aiming at the moral good. This means that it is probably fair to construe liveliness as a *perfectionist* theory.[14]

Of course, if one is already inclined to accept welfarism, then charging liveliness with welfarism is a feature of the theory, not a bug. But again, it is an open question whether liveliness should be construed as welfarist. Finally, though I will not argue for this claim, I believe the vast majority of African ethicists endorse welfarism, even if only implicitly (see Metz 2022a, 75). If this is right, then if liveliness entails welfarism it would just be one way in which the theory shows its African pedigree.[15]

6.10.2 Liveliness Is Overly Anthropocentric

The last objection I address says that liveliness is unduly anthropocentric. This is an objection that has been raised against many variations of African Communitarianism (e.g., Horsthemke 2015. Edwin Etieyibo describes the worry this way:

> [T]here is [an] ontological and existential divide between human and in-dividual organisms/nonhuman nature that is *sufficient* to lead us to the position that either (a) humans are the single and most important bearers of intrinsic value or (b) individual organisms/nonhuman nature pos-sess no intrinsic value. The ontological belief leads to the following eth-ical claim: We ought to promote 'anthrospherical egalitarianism' (simply, we should promote equally the intrinsic value of *only* humans) (Etieyibo 2017a, 149, quoted in Lougheed 2022b, 50–55).

Kai Horsthemke affirms this objection and believes that African commu-nitarianism is unduly anthropocentric such that it implies that animals are not intrinsically valuable. The relevant moral community is just other humans. Furthermore, Horsthemke holds that the hierarchy entailed by life force which places humans at the centre of the visible realm means that an-imals, plants, and minerals exist solely to protect and increase the life force

---

[14] Noteworthy is that when construed in this way it avoids challenges that hedonism faces (among other accounts) for simply having too narrow a conception of interests.

[15] For two general argumentative strategies to use in defense of welfarism, see Keller 2009, 90–92.

of humans (Horsthemke 2017, 97).[16] Since Horsthemke has life force in view when interpreting African ethics, this objection might turn out to be even more forceful when applied to liveliness. Since animals, flora, fauna, minerals, etc., have life force, they should be part of our moral concern even if they are not at the centre of the visible realm. We are still metaphysically connected to them. But as discussed in Chapter 4, significant work needs to be done in order to show that this metaphysical connection still exists on liveliness.

It would admittedly be a serious strike against any moral theory of value or right action if it could not account for basic and widespread intuitions about our duties to the environment and non-human animals. So, though my focus of this book is not animal or environmental ethics, it is important to gesture at possible replies. An initial observation is that, though I have said very little about animals and the environment, this does not mean that liveliness does not have anything to say about them. In what follows I briefly explore three possible replies to the anthropocentric objection.

First, it is plausible that some animals can exhibit certain levels of liveliness. For example, an elephant or a dolphin may exhibit more liveliness than dogs or cats, who in turn exhibit more liveliness than insects. I suggest that this kind of hierarchy aligns fairly well with many of our intuitions. We think humans are more valuable than elephants, but also tend to think that the latter deserve more of our moral consideration than, say, ants. One possible worry with this view is that it does not imply there is anything particularly unique about humans. For instance, it is difficult to say why only humans possess a dignity. Some ethicists are probably willing to 'bite the bullet' here and may even be inclined to see this as an attractive feature of liveliness. Though I leave this line open to further development, I am not inclined to pursue it, because I worry it could imply that a dolphin or an elephant that exhibits more liveliness than a human is more valuable than them. This is especially problematic when considering the value of infants or the severely disabled. On my view, there is something wrong with a moral theory that cannot explain why an infant or a severely disabled person is not more valuable than certain non-human animals. I leave it to others to develop a response along these lines that is able to simultaneously preserve the relevant intuitions about the value of humans.

---

[16] For more discussion, including replies, see my Lougheed 2022b, 50–57.

Second, deontological liveliness as I have construed it focusses on the *capacity* for liveliness. It is the capacity that grounds value, not whether the capacity is ever exercised. On the assumption that only large degrees of differences in the capacity for liveliness are morally relevant, it is possible to argue that humans have the highest level of capacity for liveliness. This high-level capacity for liveliness is what separates humans from the rest of the animal kingdom. One could then say that human infants have the *potential* for this capacity and that this separates them from animals. Furthermore, this provides a response to the anthropocentric objection, since it still explains why animals are valuable. Animals have the capacity for liveliness, just a lower degree of capacity for it than humans. The most serious worry for this response is what it says about severely disabled humans. Such humans may simply lack the capacity for liveliness to a very significant degree. Unlike babies, they have no potential to increase that capacity over time (see also 6.6.2).[17] Though I will not develop it here, one strategy is to say that severely disabled persons can somehow *borrow* the moral status of humans in virtue of being a member of the same species or sharing the same nature (e.g., Wielenberg 2021).

Third, borrowing a distinction from Metz, it could be that a person is valuable inasmuch as they have the capacity to be the *object* and/or *subject* of liveliness (2022; see also 8.4). Though severely disabled persons may not be able to be the subject of (very much) liveliness, they can still be the object of it. This means they can be related to in lively ways by other humans. Motivating this response further would involve showing how the liveliness between humans, even when one is the object, is particularly unique and valuable. Again, this type of response is consistent with the idea that non-human animals are valuable and worthy of our moral consideration.

Notice that these replies have said very little about duties to the environment. Briefly, consider that there are two primary ways to think about our duties to the environment on the hybrid theory of liveliness. The first is that liveliness entails that our duties to minerals, flora, fauna, etc., are *direct*. We have duties to respect these things in virtue of the fact that they possess some liveliness; however, they are not as valuable as humans or animals. There are

---

[17] If one argues that advances in medical technology make it impossible to say a severely disabled person could never increase their capacity for liveliness in a morally significant way, it is difficult to see why a similar appeal to technology could not also be made with respect to increasing the capacity that animals have for liveliness.

116 A MORAL THEORY OF LIVELINESS

two worries with this view. First, it does not make sense to think that flora or fauna have the *capacity* for liveliness. They just are alive. Second, one might argue that minerals do not possess liveliness in the relevant sense. What does it mean to say that a rock is lively? Regarding the first worry, perhaps it is possible to say that we have duties to flora and fauna because they are alive, while it is the capacity that matters when it comes to humans. With respect to the second worry, it seems easiest to simply acknowledge that the view does not apply to things like minerals.

I do not believe that either of these worries is insurmountable for the claim that liveliness entails we have direct duties to at least some parts of the environment. For those more sceptical, it is also possible to conceive of such duties as *indirect*. This means that we have duties to the environment inasmuch as they are connected to the liveliness of humans and non-human animals. Observe that on this view it is still the case that the widespread environmental destruction caused by humans is wrong. I believe an important key to any formulation of our duties to animals and the environment is to show that while they do indeed matter morally, they matter less than do babies and severely disabled persons.

6.11 Conclusion

This chapter completes Part II, which focussed on explicitly developing liveliness as a moral theory. Though I have explained that it offers a theory of moral value, I have focussed mostly on developing it as a theory of right action. In this chapter I also touched on its implications for a theory of dignity. My main goal in this chapter was to show that liveliness, especially deontological liveliness, is better able to avoid difficult cases that typically plague various versions of utilitarianism. I also responded to the worries that liveliness implies welfarism or that it is overly anthropocentric. All of this contributes to a cumulative case that lends support to my claim that liveliness is a plausible candidate for the best African moral theory on offer.

I conclude by noting that though I interacted with utilitarianism in this chapter, and while Kant has clearly exerted a substantial influence on African ethics (e.g., Fliksuch 2016; Okeja 2019), *much more* cross-cultural philosophical dialogue remains possible. This includes not only more interaction between African moral philosophy and Anglo-American moral philosophy, but also between other theories from the global south, including those found in Asia and South America and other regions. However, before taking this theory off the African continent, so to speak, it is important to see how it fares when compared to other major African normative theories. This is the task I take up in Part III. I will leave comparisons with globally better-known moral theories for a separate project, choosing to focus here on developing the best possible version of liveliness mostly as situated within the African tradition.

PART III
LIVELINESS AND ALTERNATIVE AFRICAN MORAL THEORIES

7
Liveliness and Normative Personhood

7.1 Introduction

The purpose of this chapter is to interact with one of the most influential African moral theories in the contemporary literature. When interpreted in terms of moral theory, African normative personhood presents both a theory about moral value and one of right action. Accordingly, what is valuable is having a high degree of personhood which is both exhibited and developed by exercising other-regarding virtues in the context of community (7.2). I argue that normative personhood faces an unpalatable dilemma about the role that community plays for it, a problem not faced by liveliness (7.3). In doing so, I add to the case that the liveliness moral theory deserves to be considered as a legitimate contender for the status of the best African moral theory.

7.2 Normative Personhood

As stated in 1.3.1, discussion of normative personhood dominates African philosophy. When understand as a moral theory, it says that the goal of morality is to develop personhood, which can be understood as character. As I will discuss later (7.3), it is typically understood that personhood can be developed only in the context of community. However, I begin by examining a debate between two important African philosophers on the nature of personhood as located in the work of Ifeanyi Menkiti (1984) and Kwame Gyekye. They offer different and competing accounts about how to best understand normative personhood.

It is important to acknowledge that not all interpretations of African personhood construe it is a moral theory. I claim that Menkiti and Gyekye *can* be interpreted this way, but not all do so. For instance, some think that personhood is better understood as a type of recognition by the community.

A Moral Theory of Liveliness. Kirk Lougheed, Oxford University Press. © Kirk Lougheed 2025.
DOI: 10.1093/9780197782019.003.0007

122 A MORAL THEORY OF LIVELINESS

The community dictates the norms for personhood such that personhood is contingent on the community. If the community ceases to recognize the concept of personhood, then personhood would no longer exist. It might have normative elements, but it is more a concept that is constituted by the community than a moral theory. Consider that in many traditional African societies participating in communal rituals such as male circumcision is an important part of the process of achieving personhood. But this is clearly different than a theory which says personhood is just about exercising other-regarding virtues (for more, see Oyowe 2022).

It is also worth briefly recognizing just how different talk of personhood as a normative concept will likely be to readers steeped in the Western or Anglo-American tradition, with the exception of those working on the debate about abortion. Such readers may instead associate the term 'person-hood' with debates about what biological features are necessary for full moral status (e.g., the debate about abortion), or which metaphysical features are essential for personal identity over time (e.g., psychological continuity) (see Gyekye 1997, 35–36). Instead, in the strain of the African moral tradition I am concerned with in this chapter, personhood is a normative term and is thus something that individuals can strive towards and earn. This means that 'personhood is something which has to be achieved, and is not given simply because one is born of human seed' (Menkiti 1984, 172). Personhood is a term used to designate moral success, and it comes in degrees. An individual can therefore be more or less of a person based on their moral success and failure. Indeed, a person who repeatedly fails in the moral realm is sometimes deemed a non-person or animal, though this is not intended to question their status as a human being possessing basic moral worth. It is noteworthy in that it presents a theory of value in addition to one of right action.

In what follows, I expound the theory of personhood as found in the work of Ifeanyi Menkiti (7.2.1) before turning to examine the work of Kwame Gyekye (7.2.2). I show that there are important unresolved interpretive questions about the Menkiti–Gyekye debate (7.2.3), before showing that there is an unpalatable dilemma for personhood regarding whether the individual takes precedent over the community or vice versa (7.3).[1] I conclude by demonstrating how liveliness deals with this dilemma (7.4).

---

[1] For other accounts of personhood, see Ikuenobe 2006 and Matolino 2014.

7.2.1 Menkiti on Personhood and Community

It is widely recognized that the most influential work in highlighting the uniqueness of the African notion of personhood is found in Ifeanyi Menkiti's (1940–2019) paper "Person and Community in Traditional Thought" (1984). The paper itself has been heavily cited and anthologized within African philosophy, with Menkiti's view receiving the label of *radical communitarianism*. As will be discussed below, this is because he appears to place the needs of the community always above those of the individual. The secondary literature on Menkiti's work is large, and instead of a comprehensive survey, I focus on providing a summary of Menkiti's own work.

The label of radical communitarianism is perhaps apt, given that Menkiti writes 'the reality of the communal world takes precedence over the reality of individual life histories, whatever these may be' (1984, 171). This is not just a metaphysical claim; it is an epistemological claim because, for Menkiti, a person can be known only within the context of their community (1984, 171). This includes a person's knowledge of themselves. Menkiti believes that '[w]ithout incorporation into this or that community, individuals are considered to be mere danglers to whom the description "person" does not fully apply' (Menkiti 1984, 172). He repeatedly emphasizes that individuals can develop their personhood (i.e., character) only in the context of community, in part because the very norms required for personhood are set by the community (Menkiti 1984, 172, 176). Notice that this explains the high place of respect given to elders in many African cultures; it takes a lot of time and work to develop personhood (Menkiti 2004, 325–326).

It is unsurprising the implications of Menkiti's views for the nature of human rights or dignity is often questioned. This is particularly so because it appears his view entails that individuals cannot have any rights that are not directly and closely tied to their community. Menkiti says that any time one finds ascriptions of rights, they are always ascribed to a person. He explains:

> That is so because the basis of such rights ascription has now been made dependent on a possession of a capacity for a moral sense, a capacity, which though it need not be realized, is nonetheless made most evident

by a concrete exercise of duties of justice towards others in the ongoing relationships of everyday life. (Menkiti 1984, 177)

Menkiti is not explicit on whether an individual could possess rights or a capacity for 'moral sense' outside of the context of community. A partial answer might be Menkiti's insistence that Westerners wrongly move from individuals to society instead of the way Africans tend to move from society to individuals (Menkiti 1984, 180). Menkiti explains that:

[I]t becomes quite clear why African societies tend to be organized around the requirements of duty while Western societies tend to be organized around the postulation of individual rights. In the African understanding, priority is given to the duties which individuals owe to the collectivity, and their rights, whatever these may be, are seen as secondary to the exercise of their duties. In the West, on the other hand, we find a construal of things in which certain specified rights of individuals are seen as antecedent to the organization of society; with the function of government viewed, consequently as being the protection and defense of these individual rights. (1984, 180)

In his most recent and final statement on personhood, Menkiti further clarifies his position on rights (2018). He says that '[a]n entity must first be morally situated before there can be a follow through regarding the bestowal of this or that moral right' (Menkiti 2018, 163). And finally:

It is admittedly the case that the ethics of human dignity is undetermined by the metaphysics of the person. But if we were to make a needed distinction between a nature and the person who has the nature, and then proceed to consider this to be part and parcel of the story of human dignity, we are surely in a better position to offer a more adequate account of the story of human dignity. (Menkiti 2018, 166)

Though Menkiti's position is not always entirely clear, I believe it is fair to interpret his view as implying that personhood does not exist outside of community and that no one has rights or dignity simply in virtue of being a biological human. Since such rights are attached to the community, it is easy to see why some have labelled Menkiti's version of communitarianism as radical.

7.2.2 Gyekye on Personhood and Community

Another influential account of personhood is found in the work of Kwame Gyekye (1939–2019), a founding elder of contemporary African philosophy. Indeed, Gyekye applied the label of 'radical' to Menkiti and sought instead to defend a *moderate communitarianism*. The debate over the nature of personhood that was sparked by Gyekye and Menkiti remains ongoing.

Though Gyekye first criticized Menkiti in his well-known chapter "Person and Community in African Thought" (1992), I am going to focus on his more detailed analysis found in his slightly more recent and classic work, *Tradition and Modernity: Philosophical Reflections on the African Experience* (1997). Near the beginning of this chapter, he writes that:

> It is possible for people to assume off-handedly that by emphasizing communal values, collective goods, and shared ends, a communitarian social arrangement necessarily conceives of the person as *wholly* constituted by social relationships. It might be thought that in doing so, such an arrangement tends to whittle away the moral autonomy of the person—making the being and life of the individual totally dependent on the activities, values, projects, practices, and ends of the community—and that, consequently, that arrangement diminishes his freedom and capability to choose or re-evaluate the shared values of the community. (Gyekye 1997, 37)

Gyekye cites Menkiti as one such scholar who holds this view. And this is the position that Gyekye ultimately rejects. He affirms that persons are communal by nature, needing the community to realize various possibilities and hence to reach their full potential (Gyekye 1997, 38). However, he denies that this is the *only* thing they are by nature. As such, he wants 'a moderate communitarianism, the model that acknowledges the intrinsic worth and dignity of the individual human person and recognizes individuality, individual responsibility and effort' (Gyekye 1997, 40). Yet each individual is in the end responsible for their own successes and failures and as such they must exert effort to succeed. Gyekye does not see the affirmation of communal values as entailing the rejection of individual values, concluding that 'the most satisfactory way to recognize the claims of both communality and

126   A MORAL THEORY OF LIVELINESS

individuality is to ascribe to them the status of an equal moral standing'
(Gyekye 1997, 41).

Part of what distinguishes Gyekye's account of personhood from Menkiti's
is the equal value that he assigns to both the individual and the community.[2] Though Gyekye does not deny that humans are social by nature, he
denies that they are exclusively social (1997, 47). Human nature includes
other components, such as rationality and moral sense, which explains how
individuals are able to make choices (Gyekye 1997, 53). This means that
though community is important, it is not the only thing involved in developing personhood. Gyekye asks us to consider the case of moral reformers
who appear to make perfectly legitimate moral judgments entirely apart
from their communities (Gyekye 1997, 53–54). Gyekye therefore wants to
preserve a degree of human autonomy that he believes is unavailable on
Menkiti's account. He therefore understands the self both as a "communal
being *and* as an autonomous, self-assertive being with a capacity for evaluation and choice" (1997, 59).

Gyekye believes that his moderate position is attractive because it
preserves human rights, a notion too often rejected by postcolonial African
socialists (1997, 62). None of this is intended to diminish the importance
of communal values, but instead it is to highlight that '[r]ights belong primarily and irreducibly to the individual. They are a means of expressing an
individual's talents, capacities, and identity, even though the expression, arguably can best be accomplished within a social framework' (Gyekye 1997,
62). Accordingly, Gyekye posits that persons are fundamentally both autonomous and communal. This naturally leads to questions about how to
resolve purported conflicts between the individual and the community.
Gyekye claims that in order to resolve such conflicts it needs to be established whether any resulting harm would be experienced just by the individual or also by their community. If only the individual would be harmed,
then the question involves rights that cannot be forfeited for the community. However, if the community would be harmed, then the individual rights
in question cannot be guaranteed (Gyekye 1997, 64–65). Gyekye may well
be appealing to something similar to Mill's harm principle to maintain this
distinction.

---

[2] For example, another person who holds the radical view and is perhaps at least part of the inspiration for Menkiti is the African historian and religious scholar John Mbiti. See Mbiti 1975.

7.2.3 Interpreting the Menkiti–Gyekye Debate

The debate about how to correctly interpret Menkiti and Gyekye on personhood, in addition to which of those interpretations are correct, continues to be carried on with great rigour in African philosophy. Part of the challenge is that I believe how one interprets these thinkers about the nature of personhood greatly impacts the philosophical plausibility of the account in question. In other words, the interpretive debate about personhood has significant philosophical implications and therefore cannot be ignored as a secondary issue which is not that important to philosophizing. In what follows (7.3), I am going to focus on an intervention into this debate from Motsamai Molefe (2019), in order to argue that there are problems for any of the main approaches to personhood. I choose Molefe's account because he believes personhood provides a theory of right action and of moral value such that it is straightforward to compared it to liveliness.

Molefe objects to Gyekye's criticism of Menkiti because he claims that Gyekye unwittingly switches from the metaphysical conception of personhood (i.e., personal identity) to the normative conception of personhood (2019, 27–28).[3] I agree. For example, contra Menkiti, in one place Gyekye claims that personhood has little to do with social initiations into adulthood. He also rejects as bizarre Menkiti's claim that personhood is something to be achieved over time (Gyekye 1997, 48–49). However, a few pages later, Gyekye claims that humans must try to achieve personhood and that this takes willpower and action on the part of individuals, which he says partly explains why he does not hold that personhood is entirely a function of the community (1997, 52). He writes that 'a moral conception of personhood is held in African thought: personhood is defined in terms of moral achievement' (Gyekye 1997, 52). What explains this apparent tension, if not outright contradiction, within the span of a handful of pages? The answer is that this seems a clear instance in which Gyekye mistakenly attributes a metaphysical or even biological account of personhood to Menkiti, who is clearly discussing the normative account of personhood. Indeed, this conflation may explain why some hold that Gyekye altogether misattributes the label of radical communitarianism to Menkiti (e.g., Eze and Metz 2016, 74). Notice that the plausibility of Menkiti's view is at stake here, which is a substantial philosophical issue, not a merely interpretive one.

---

[3] He notes too that this has also been observed by Matolino 2014, among others.

128　A MORAL THEORY OF LIVELINESS

Regarding Gyekye's later 1997 discussion of Menkiti, which is the focus of my explication above, Molefe claims that 'in the final analysis, it appears that Gyekye comes to endorse Menkiti's interpretation of the normative notion of personhood' (2019, 29). I disagree. Molefe is simply wrong that Gyekye (eventually) endorses Menkiti's understanding of personhood. Consider that in support of the idea that Gyekye does in the end agree with Menkiti, Molefe quotes the following: 'With all this said, however, this aspect of this account [i.e., Menkiti's] adumbrates a moral conception of personhood and is, on that score, interesting and relevant to the notion of personhood important for the communitarian framework' (Gyekye 1997, 64 quoted in Molefe 2019, 29). But Molefe is wrong about what this quote shows. For the sentence directly preceding the text just quoted from Gyekye is '[t]hus, Menkiti's analytic account of personhood in African thought is befogged with confusions, unclarities, and incoherences' (Gyekye 1997, 49).[4] Gyekye is only using Menkiti as a point of departure to discuss his own view of personhood. So, while I agree with Molefe that Gyekye conflates the metaphysical and normative conceptions of personhood, it remains clear that he never endorses Menkiti's position. Whether he would accept Menkiti's conception of personhood had he not made the conflation, in addition to whether Menkiti's view really is that radical, are separate questions. Yet no matter what one thinks of these interpretive issues surrounding the Menkiti–Gyekye debate, they have both offered (apparently) competing accounts of personhood that have generated a large secondary literature. Interpretive issues aside, they deserve credit for drawing our attention to such an important concept in African moral thought, and one quite different from much of the focus of the Anglo-American moral tradition.

7.3　Personhood and the Community versus the Individual

In this section I issue a challenge for personhood in the form of a dilemma. It may be surprising to readers more familiar with the Anglo-American tradition to discover that so many African philosophers deny the existence of basic human rights. Though it might be tempting to claim that this is an area where liveliness is superior to normative personhood, this is not the subject I will target, for two reasons. First, it seems possible to emphasize the

---

[4] My page numbering of Gyekye 1997 is different from Molefe's.

importance of community in ethical reasoning without denying individual rights. Gyekye's work is an example of this possibility.[5] Second, I suspect that much of the denial of rights by contemporary African philosophers is merely verbal. I submit that in many cases (though perhaps not in the case of Menkiti) African ethicists and Western ethicists would tend to agree on what basic entitlements are owed to each human simply in virtue of them being human. Consider the following: Certain forms of consequentialism aside, all (or most) African *and* Western ethicists would deny that it is permissible to harvest the organs from one healthy unconsenting individual in order to save the lives of four sick individuals.[6] This is so even though the African tradition typically emphasizes the value of community much more than what is found in the Anglo-American tradition. Instead, what I think this worry about rights does is really point to a serious tension that exists in normative personhood between the community and the individual.

7.3.1 Personhood and the Value of Community

In the African philosophical tradition, questions about the value of community are inseparably connected to debates about the normative conception of personhood. Here is why: It is often intimated that personhood can be achieved only in the context of community. A natural next question regards the precise nature of the relationship between community and personhood. Molefe suggests that there are two competing explanations of this relationship. The first says that community is intrinsically valuable, and the second claims that it is instrumentally valuable. In what follows, I explain why Molefe endorses the latter view. According to Molefe, many accounts of personhood hold that community is intrinsically valuable.[7] This equates personhood with positive social relationships. So positive social relationships are the end that ought to be pursued (Molefe 2019, 58–60). In this sense then, the normative conception of personhood collapses into community. This is because it is impossible to have personhood apart from the community. Molefe instead argues that community is only instrumentally valuable in that

---

[5] This is controversial. While Gyekye is adamant that his view includes individual rights, some argue that even moderate communitarianism precludes rights (e.g., 2014, Ch. 2).

[6] Thanks to Thaddeus Metz for discussion.

[7] Before continuing, it is worth observing that much of the literature in question is not sufficiently clear on the intrinsic/instrumental distinction. Molefe notes that this is observed by Metz (2013a). See also Molefe (2019, Ch. 3).

130   A MORAL THEORY OF LIVELINESS

it helps individuals to achieve personhood. Part of his reason for endorsing this view appears to be his rejection of the intrinsic account. The main argument he offers in this regard is that treating the community as the end itself that ought to be pursued will lead to unpalatable trade-offs between the individual and the community (Molefe 2019, 58–60). For example, if community is intrinsically valuable, then an individual may not be justified in spending her money on her education if it cannot be shown to directly benefit the community.[8] In other words, '[t]he point [. . .] is to recognise that the communal view exaggerates the role of social relationships. And, secondly, it misses the basic point that the focus of personhood is ultimately *personal development*' (Molefe 2019, 61). Thus, for Molefe, 'the goal of personhood is for the individual to achieve a sound character; and the social relationships serve as incubators where individuals carve out their personhood' (Molefe 2019, 61). Last, Molefe's 'perfectionist egoistic moral theory locates the good in what the agent achieves (moral perfection) and it posits relationships as the single most important instrument to achieve such an end' (2019, 62).

According to Molefe, social relationships are what help to bring about the development of personhood. This is because they tend to emphasize other-regarding virtues. And it is by exercising such virtues that one is able to enter into (positive) social relationships.[9] Such relationships are the way that individuals become persons. Molefe further explains that 'it is ultimately *the individual* that achieves personhood. In the light of the provisions made available by the community, the individual is expected to try, to exert herself, to fight temptations, to deal with limitations in her society, to make something out of herself morally speaking' (2019, 63).

7.3.2 The Dilemma for Personhood

In this subsection, I outline a dilemma for normative personhood. Though it comes through clearly in Molefe's analysis of personhood and as such that is the account I will refer to, I believe that any proponent of personhood must answer it. In other words, it is a problem for the personhood accounts I outlined above as located in the work of Menkiti and Gyekye. Before

---

[8] Metz has criticized what he calls self-realization views, which are similar to the ones advocated for by Molefe. See Metz (2007; 2013a; 2013b). Molefe (2019, 58–61) responds.

[9] See also Gyekye (1992), Wiredu (1992).

explaining the dilemma, however, I want to first note an important and rather glaring ambiguity in Molefe's analysis of personhood.

In one place Molefe writes that:

> I [Molefe] can *only* perfect myself as an individual by contributing to the well-being of others, in terms of exercising my other-regarding duties towards them. Essentially, it is in this exercise of other-regarding duties that I realise my true humanity and assist others to do the same. (Molefe 2019, 63; emphasis mine)

This quote implies that community is essential for the achievement of personhood because it is the *only* way it can be achieved. Yet elsewhere he writes that:

> The *best* way to pursue self-regarding duties of self-perfection is by investing in social relationships with others via other-regarding duties. In other words, the best way to realise one's true human nature is by being embedded in social relationships with others. All things being equal, on this view, self-regarding duties are not diametrically opposed to other-regarding duties. It is by relating positively with others that I realise my true self. (Molefe 2019, 64; emphasis mine)

This quote, on the other hand, suggests that Molefe holds that community is the best way to achieve personhood. But it does *not* follow from the fact that something is the best way that it is the only way. Hence, this quote suggests that community is not essential for personhood. As will become clear, this distinction is important.

Here is the dilemma I raise for normative personhood:

(1) With respect to personhood, either community is intrinsically valuable, or it is extrinsically valuable.[10]

Horn #1: Intrinsic value:

(2) If community is intrinsically valuable, then it is essential for achievement of personhood.

---

[10] Many authors, including Molefe, use 'instrumental' when they really mean 'extrinsic' (2019, 54). For more on these distinctions, see Korsgaard (1983).

132 A MORAL THEORY OF LIVELINESS

(3) If community is essential for personhood, then the distinction between intrinsic value and extrinsic value collapses into intrinsic value.

(4) If (3), then the problems raised by Molefe associated with intrinsic value remain (i.e., the unpalatable trade-offs between individual and community).

Horn #2: Extrinsic value:

(5) If community is extrinsically valuable, then it is not essential for achievement of personhood.

(6) If community is not essential to achieve personhood apart from the community, then, necessarily, community is not the only way to achieve personhood.

(7) If (6), then it is difficult to understand the emphasis that community is given in analyses of personhood in the first place.

7.3.3 Explanation of the Dilemma

With respect to Horn #1, (2) is true because in this dialectical context to say that community is intrinsically valuable is to say it is literally equivalent to personhood or at least largely constitutive of virtue. They are one and the same. Since it is impossible to have personhood without personhood, it is likewise impossible to have community without personhood. I will comment on (3) in the next section as it is relevant to the second horn, but needless to say the value of community is not extrinsically valuable on Horn #1. So, it follows that (4), the problems that Molefe associated with accounts of personhood that imply community is intrinsically valuable apply here. The main problem, of course, is the unpalatable trade-offs between individuals and the community.

Regarding Horn #2, (5) is true because in this dialectical context to say that community is extrinsically valuable is to imply that it is *not* identical with personhood. It is merely a tool which can be used to achieve personhood. The value of it is located outside of it; namely, in its ability to help an individual achieve personhood. (6) is more controversial and hence requires more explanation. It says that if (4) is true, then it is difficult to understand the emphasis on community that can be found in most analysis of personhood. But why is such an emphasis problematic? Well, with respect to an account like Molefe's, it leaves the reader puzzled why he goes to so much trouble to argue that community is only valuable in helping to achieve personhood, that it is not necessary for it, etc., when it turns out to be the only method of achieving personhood that he or any other philosopher working in the African tradition ever discusses. In what other contexts could one achieve personhood? Or what other methods could one use to develop their personhood? Another way of interpreting (7), then, is just that it makes an analysis like Molefe's entirely uninformative. Or, more carefully, it makes his analysis no more informative (or different) from those accounts of personhood which maintain that community is intrinsically valuable and hence essential for the achievement of personhood. In either case, personhood is only facilitated by community.

One possible strategy here would be for the proponent of personhood to concede that while community is not necessary for achieving personhood, it is the *best* way of achieving personhood. However, here is the challenge with such a strategy: the person employing it has to tell us why community is the best way to achieve personhood *without simultaneously implying that it is the only way*. The reason this strategy is challenging to effectively employ is because I suspect that as the reasons in favour of community are elucidated, it will turn out to be implied that it really is the only way to achieve personhood. If this is right, then such a strategy cannot be pursued (at least not in addressing Horn #2). But then, we can rightly ask: why place such an emphasis on personhood in the first place? This leads us right back to (7).

So, normative personhood either ultimately faces the unpalatable trade-offs between individuals and the community that face accounts which say community is essential for it (i.e., intrinsically valuable) or remains, at best, entirely uninformative. The only way to avoid this latter charge is by explaining why there is so much emphasis on community and to present alternative ways of achieving personhood. As it currently stands, neither (4) of Horn #1 nor (7) of Horn #2 are palatable options for proponents of personhood, and so a serious objection has been raised to normative personhood.

7.3.4 A Third Horn and Potential Ways Out?

There is an additional worry for normative personhood that could perhaps be used to generate a third horn and hence a trilemma. I will only briefly mention it here. If community is not intrinsically valuable, then it is not constituted by communal relations. Rather, it is the community that is caused to exist by such relations. But then, what is the nature of personhood

134 A MORAL THEORY OF LIVELINESS

here? What is *it* that is getting caused by such relations in the first place? Accordingly, it is difficult to see how proponents of personhood can give an account of personhood where community is not necessary for it. If they are able to give a description of personhood entirely apart from community, then even the extrinsic value of community can be called into question. In other words, if personhood can exist apart from the community, then why mention community at all in analysis of personhood? While my focus here is on the role and value of community with respect to personhood, this presents an additional problem for any proponent of personhood.[11]

Perhaps the most promising way to reply to this dilemma is for the proponent of personhood to maintain that it is possible to achieve personhood outside of the community, but in our particular world it happens to be the very best way of achieving it. This reply entails that it is only a contingent fact that community helps achieve personhood. But notice that this amounts to an incredibly strong empirical claim about the nature of the world. Why think that we are in a very good epistemic position to know its truth? Here someone might point to the other-regarding virtues that one needs to foster to become a person to show why this is the case. The claim is that one is best able to foster them in the context of community. However, I suspect that if one were to begin their case for why other-regarding virtues are best developed within the context of community, it would quickly become apparent that the claim is really that it is the *only* way. But then my response above or the dilemma itself comes back into play.

Moreover, to argue for this weaker claim means comparing how well the community contributes to personhood with various other ways of achieving personhood. For instance, in many ways solitary meditation in the Buddhist tradition could be thought to foster other-regarding virtues. On this view, pain and suffering are the result of striving. Part of the goal of meditation is to let go of such striving and in this way lose one's self (in some sense). This type of selflessness certainly fosters quite well at least some of the other-regarding virtues that proponents of personhood often have in mind. There are other examples. Suppose that one's consciousness could be uploaded to a hard drive. Free from all physical bodily needs, it might be much easier for one to develop other-regarding virtues in an online world. This could be accomplished even if there were no other human consciousnesses in the online world in question. An individual could acquire other-regarding

---

[11] Thanks to Thaddeus Metz for bringing this worry to my attention.

virtues by interacting with artificial intelligences. Thus, one could develop other-regarding virtues and hence personhood apart from community with other people. Of course, the easiest way to avoid these types of worries is to simply maintain that community with other people remains the only means by which personhood can be achieved. But as stated, this leads right back to the above tensions or the dilemma itself.

7.4 Liveliness and the Community versus the Individual

It would be a virtue of liveliness as a moral theory if it turns out that it is not subject to the above dilemma and related concerns. But remember that I have presented three different understandings of liveliness and they may not all issue the same responses to the questions posed to personhood in this chapter. In what follows, I therefore take each of them in turn in relation to the worries presented above. I suggest that teleological liveliness fares worse than deontological liveliness with respect to dealing with possible tensions between the community and the individual.

7.4.1 Teleological Liveliness on the Community versus the Individual

At first glance, teleological liveliness does not imply that the community is essential in order for a person to be lively. It may well be that many of the characteristics associated with liveliness are best exhibited in the context of community. However, nothing in the theory suggests that community is the only way to achieve liveliness. It could be that a solitary monk is able to develop their liveliness in significant ways. Though exhibiting certain other-regarding virtues is an important part of liveliness, such virtues are not the only way to achieve liveliness, nor are they the only indicators of liveliness. The goal of morality on teleological liveliness is to promote liveliness, and the community is therefore only valuable to the extent that it helps in this project. Teleological liveliness is not subject to the unpalatable trade-offs described in the dilemma above.

However, I believe that it would be premature to accept this response without further discussion. Recall the example about pursuing one's education instead of spending the tuition money directly on one's community

136 A MORAL THEORY OF LIVELINESS

(7.3.1). On teleological liveliness, if an individual reasonably believed that education would make them livelier, they are justified in pursuing it. Of course, on teleological liveliness there are additional questions to ask about the extent to which an individual ought to pursue their own liveliness if doing so does not also increase the liveliness of other members of their community. In 5.2.1, I suggested that teleological liveliness was best construed as entailing both self-regarding and other-regarding duties. Here is a place where more work is needed to show just how the individual and community are supposed to be balanced against each other on teleological liveliness. Though a trade-off involving sacrificing one's education is perhaps not a particularly extreme example, one can quickly see how more difficult trade-offs similar to those in the previous chapter can arise (see 6.3 and 6.5). The proponent of teleological liveliness needs to show why increasing the net total of liveliness at the expense of a particular individual's liveliness is impermissible (if they indeed are inclined to think it is impermissible, as I am so inclined).

7.4.2 Deontological Liveliness on the Community versus the Individual

Deontological liveliness much more clearly avoids the dilemma I set out for normative personhood compared to teleological liveliness. This is because liveliness is not an achievement on this view in quite the same way that normative personhood is considered an achievement. On deontological liveliness moral value is derived from the capacity for liveliness. All (or almost all) humans have the capacity for liveliness regardless of whether they are able to exercise it. There need not be any appeal to community on this analysis of value. The community will be valuable only inasmuch as it is respectful of individuals and enables them to be lively. If a person reasonably believes that pursuing their education will increase their liveliness, then they are free to pursue it, since doing so is not disrespectful to anyone else. Pursuing one's education may be a kind of self-respect such that an individual who chose to forgo some activity solely to increase the liveliness of others may well be disrespectful to themselves. This is especially so if forgoing the activity does not clearly lead to the increase of the liveliness of others. Finally, none of this is meant to imply that self-sacrifice is immoral. Rather, it implies that sacrificing one's own liveliness for the sake of increasing the liveliness in members of one's community is supererogatory.

7.5 Conclusion

I began by explaining the influential Menkiti–Gyekye debate on personhood. For Menkiti, the community is what matters, not the individual. Gyekye gives equal moral worth to the community and the individual. Menkiti wants to say that humans are by nature social, leaving no room for individual rights. Gyekye, on the other hand, affirms that humans are social, but also that they are rational and autonomous by nature, and he thereby makes room for individual rights. Molefe argues that community is not essential for developing personhood. But I suggested that this leads to an unpalatable dilemma. One thing that the astute reader will have observed is that with respect to the dilemma, it ultimately does not matter how one interprets the Menkiti–Gyekye debate, nor does it matter on which version of personhood they settled. If the community is essential for personhood, then counterintuitive trade-offs between the individual and the community follow. If it is not essential for personhood, then at best the role of community in personhood can be said to be unclear. While I do not take this discussion to constitute a decisive blow to proponents of personhood, it bodes well for liveliness (all else being equal). In particular, I showed that deontological liveliness is not subject to the same dilemma. That this theory posits that people are valuable inasmuch as they are lively or have the capacity for liveliness explains why individuals do not need to forfeit opportunities to increase their liveliness for the sake of the community (provided those pursuits are respectful). In the next chapter I examine the branch of African normative ethics that focuses on harmonious relationships. There I also argue that it faces difficulties that liveliness tends to avoid.

8

Liveliness and Harmonious Relationships

8.1 Introduction

While the normative conception of personhood tends to dominate the literature in African normative ethics, another important view can be found in those theories that focus on harmonious relationships. Such theories typically view the primary goal of morality to be to foster and engage in harmonious relationships within one's community. I begin by explaining teleological approaches to harmony in more detail (8.2). I then outline a serious problem for them, based primarily on the fact that they cannot adequately ground human rights (8.3). After outlining Thaddeus Metz's relational moral theory (8.4), I explain how both Metz's theory and deontological liveliness are able to avoid the objections to teleological harmony (8.5). I argue that Metz's moral relational theory struggles to issue the correct verdict in three difficult cases: the clitoridectomy of girls (8.6), religious offence (8.7), and romantic homosexual relationships (8.8). I conclude by examining the ways that focussing on flourishing and well-being might change the assessment of these cases (8.9), and what these theories have to say about the scope of the moral community, including severely disabled humans (8.10). This chapter continues to build the cumulative case that the liveliness moral theory deserves to be considered as a legitimate contender for the status of best African moral theory.

8.2 Teleological Approaches to Harmony

For just one indication of how important the notion of harmony is to African moral thought, consider that the slogan for the Centre for Leadership Ethics in Africa at the University of Fort Hare is 'Towards Social and Ecological Harmony'.[1] Harmony between individuals and all else, including nature (and,

---

[1] See Centre for Leadership Ethics in Africa | Towards Social and Ecological Harmony (wordpress. com).

A Moral Theory of Liveliness. Kirk Lougheed, Oxford University Press. © Kirk Lougheed 2025.
DOI: 10.1093/9780197782019.003.0008

according to some accounts, also the spiritual realm), is of the utmost importance in African ethics. I begin this section by explaining some key ideas found in the work of two important scholars who emphasize harmony in African thought: Mogobe B. Ramose and Peter J. Paris. The former is one of the most influential scholars working in African ethics, while the latter's *The Spirituality of African Peoples* is now considered a classic text in contemporary African thought. I then demonstrate that related ideas can be found in the work of many other African thinkers, before explaining how Metz interprets harmony.

8.2.1 Ramose and Paris on Harmony

Though both Ramose and Paris stress the importance of being in harmony with the spiritual realm, which includes God, spirits, ancestors, and the living dead, I submit that much of what they say can still plausibly be maintained by someone who is committed to an entirely secular ethic. Thus, in what follows I focus on harmony as applied to a secular and therefore entirely naturalistic ontology.

To begin, what, specifically, is harmony? Ramose explains that:

> The concept of harmony in African thought is comprehensive in the sense that it conceives of balance in terms of the totality of the relations that can be maintained between and among human beings, as well as between human beings and physical nature. The quest for harmony is thus the striving to maintain a comprehensive but specific relational condition among organisms and entities. It is the constant striving to strike, and then maintain, a balance between human beings and physical nature. (2015, 71)

And elsewhere he says that:

> The conclusions that Africans are persistently in search of harmony in all spheres of life is pertinently true of African thought. The concrete expression of African thought is the continual quest for consensus aimed to establish harmony (Ramose 2003b, 235).

Paris concurs with this assessment, writing that:

> [T]he African person is related to the family as part of a living organism is related to the whole. As the former cannot live apart from the latter, so

140 A MORAL THEORY OF LIVELINESS

the life of a person is wholly dependent on the family and its symbiotic functions of biological lineage, communal nurture, and moral formation. (1995, 101)

And he adds that:

[T]he preservation and promotion of community is the paramount goal of African peoples in all spheres of life [. . . . I]t [i.e., the preservation and promotion of community] is the determinative measure of value for all human activities [. . . .] In fact, the purpose of all the realms of life (spirit, history, nature) is to preserve and promote the well-being of the community. (Paris 1995, 130–131)

In different places Ramose also tells us that harmony is really a kind of balancing or 'restoration of equilibrium' (2001, 6). He also explains that a fundamental aspect of justice is based on the idea that it restores this equilibrium. This understanding of justice makes up a central feature in ubuntu philosophy of law (Ramose 2001, 4).[2] Another point of emphasis for Ramose regarding this kind of harmony as justice is *flexibility*. For example, regarding legal rules, he claims that since life is in constant 'flow and flux', legal rules can probably never be said to be permanent (Ramose 2001, 6). Ultimately, the flexibility is 'oriented towards balance and harmony in the relationship between human beings' (Ramose 2003a, 382).

In his understanding of harmony, Paris stresses the interdependence of humans with one another (and also with the natural and spiritual realms). He explains that an individual is part of a broader community and that she must assume responsibility for actions of those in the community, just as the community is also responsible for her actions (Paris 1995, 130). According to Paris, then, 'Africans never view wrongdoing strictly as an individual matter' (Paris 1995, 130). Additionally, he explains that because the harmony of the community is of the utmost importance, African morality is fundamentally practical. This is because ethical thought 'arises out of the problems of daily experience, and it is pursued for the purpose of discovering practical solutions for everyday problems. In short, African theology and ethics are practical sciences in the service of the community's well-being' (Paris

---

[2] See also Ramose 1999.

1995, 132).[3] These accounts emphasize harmony, and thus while they do not necessarily deny the importance of developing one's personhood, their primary focus does appear to differ significantly from accounts of personhood discussed in the previous chapter.

8.2.2 Other Teleological Approaches to Harmony

The ideas offered by Ramose and Paris are clearly teleological in suggesting that relational harmony is the end that ought to be pursued. It is worth observing just how common this approach is in the literature. I accomplish this by relying on 'Chapter Six: "Communal Relationship' of Metz's *A Relational Moral Theory*, which highlights many representative ideas. I will label these approaches 'teleological harmony'. To begin, consider the following quotes that further support the claim that teleological approaches to harmony can be found in the literature:

- [T]he highest good in African societies is the preservation of order and harmony within the community, on the one hand, and between the community and its spiritual protectors (the divinities and ancestors), on the other hand. . . . Harmony is the paramount goal within and among all the possible relationships within the cosmological order, and herein lies its ethical significance (as) the source and justification of all moral obligations. (Paris 1995, 43, 56 quoted in Metz 2022, 90)
- Harmony, friendliness, community are great goods. Social harmony is for us the summum bonum. (Tutu 1999: 35 quoted in Metz 2022, 90)
- We regard our living together not as an unfortunate mishap warranting endless competition among us but as a deliberate act of God to make us a community of brothers and sisters jointly involved in the quest for a composite answer to the varied problems of life. Hence in all we do we always place Man first and hence all our action is usually joint community oriented action rather than the individualism which is the hallmark of the capitalist approach. (Biko 2004, 46 quoted in Metz 2022, 92)
- In the moral universe of Ubuntu, humanity is conceived of as one large family that is bonded together by reciprocal ties of love and loyalty.

[3] For more on harmony, see Gbadegesin 1991; Mokgoro 1998; Murove 2007; Nkondo 2007.

142   A MORAL THEORY OF LIVELINESS

This is, of course, an ideal conception towards which we should forever strive.... The servant leader is the chief agent of striving towards harmony in community. (Khoza 2006, 58–9 quoted in Metz 2022, 92)

- At the heart of these [Shona and Zulu] proverbs lies a motif of an ethical reminder that one should always live and behave in a way that maximises harmonious existence at present as well as in the future. (Murove 2007, 181 quoted in Metz 2022, 92)

Metz observes that one can also find in the literature more detail on relationship concepts such as harmony and love:

- Every member is expected to consider him/herself an integral part of the whole and to play an appropriate role towards achieving the good of all. (Gbadegesin 1991, 65 quoted in Metz 2022, 92)
- Harmony is achieved through close and sympathetic social relations within the group. (Mokgoro 1998, 17 quoted in Metz 2022, 92)
- We say, 'A person is a person through other persons.' It is not, 'I think therefore I am.' It says rather: 'I am human because I belong. I participate, I share'. (Tutu 1999, 35 quoted in Metz 2022, 92)
- The fundamental meaning of community is the sharing of an overall way of life, inspired by the notion of the common good. (Gyekye 2004, 16 quoted in Metz 2022, 92)
- [T]he purpose of our life is community-service and community-belongingness. (Iroegbu 2005a, 442 quoted in Metz 2022, 93)
- If you asked ubuntu advocates and philosophers: What principles inform and organise your life?... the answers would express commitment to the good of the community in which their identities were formed, and a need to experience their lives as bound up in that of their community. (Nkondo 2007, 91 quoted in Metz 2022, 93)

8.2.3 Harmony as Identity and Solidarity

Metz understands the teleological approach to harmony in terms of *identity* and *solidarity*. Consider what Metz says about each of these notions. With respect to the cognition of identification, Metz explains that this involves thinking about oneself as part of a group. In order to achieve this, one must frequently take on the perspective of others. Thus, '[t]he key point is that cognitively identifying with others means not viewing them as separate from oneself, and instead considering them as members' (Metz 2022, 94). The emotion of identification with others entails feelings security and belonging in their presence. Such identification implies being embarrassed or proud at the action of others. Regarding the volition of identification, the key focus is joint activity, which means not only helping others to achieve their goals, but framing one's own goals within the group context. Metz writes that 'one participates in cooperative endeavours for reason beyond mere prudence' (2022, 95). This entails that an individual is motivated to help others reach their goals, independently of how well doing so enables her to reach her own. Metz believes that the opposite of identifying with others is creating division and holding to a 'us versus them'. Neither identification nor division is perhaps alienation (e.g., living as a hermit) (Metz, 2022, 95).

Expressing solidarity is at its core about acts of service (Metz 2022, 95). The cognition of solidarity implies having empathy for other people, and therefore 'knowing what moves [the other . . .] person and more generally what makes him tick, even if he does not fully recognize it' (Metz 2022, 96). This type of empathy and awareness of the other is crucial to building emotional solidarity. The volitional element of solidarity means taking action to improve the lives of others (Metz 2022, 96). Improving their lives will mean not solely helping a person achieve their goals, but also enabling them to become a better person. Solidarity is primarily motivated 'by the prior conditions of roughly empathetic cognition and sympathetic emotion' (Metz 2022, 96). The opposite of solidarity is 'ill will', which involves cruelty and doing what one can to degrade the quality of another's life. Neither solidarity nor ill will is indifference (Metz 2022, 97).

Metz believes that when evaluated separately, neither identification nor solidarity are effective explanations of morality. Consider that members of the South African Nationalist Party likely identified with one another in their promotion of apartheid. However, apartheid hardly promoted solidarity among everyone in South Africa. On the other hand, solidarity on its own appears to allow for intuitively impermissible forms of paternalism (Metz, 2022, 97–98).

All of this contributes to a theory of moral value, in addition to principles of right action. With respect to the former:

- A thing is valuable to the extent that it relates positively with others.
- A thing lacks value to the extent that it relates negatively with others or cannot relate to them at all.

144 A MORAL THEORY OF LIVELINESS

With respect to right action, the following principles emerge:

- An action is right inasmuch as it contributes positively to relational harmony.
- An action is wrong inasmuch as it contributes to relational disharmony.
- An action is permissible if it contributes positively to relational harmony.
- An action is impermissible if it contributes to relational disharmony.

8.3 Problems with Teleological Approaches to Harmony

Metz rightly observes that the main problem with teleological approaches to harmony is that they cannot adequately account for or ground human rights (2022, 91). Consider that such approaches to harmony appear to forbid any and all discordant actions, including those that are intuitively permissible such as acting in self- or other defence. But self- or other defence is justified even if it does not maximize harmony overall, in the long-run (Metz 2022, 101). Metz believes that '[s]ome non-teleological harmony-based or communal approach, which takes into account decisions others have made, is needed in order to account adequately for the permissibility of violence directed against aggressors to protect innocent lives' (2022, 102).

Reflect on the following case:

> A wife has become HIV positive because her husband had cheated on her behind her back and did not use protection when doing so, despite being aware of the risks. You have a single regimen of antiretroviral treatment, and must choose which of them to save. You give the treatment to the wife and not the husband. (She lives, and he dies.) (Metz 2022, 102)

According to Metz, decisions about allocating scarce resources in this case are rightly made based on the decisions that the patients have made. All else being equal, one ought to distribute scarce resources to those who need them through no fault of their own over those who need them because of previous wrong actions. It is unclear how teleological accounts of harmony can explain this position (Metz 2022, 102). Additionally, teleological approaches to harmony also cannot account for the transplant case (see 6.3). It is impermissible for a doctor to harvest the organs of one healthy innocent patient in order to save five sick people in need of new organs. This is so even if harvesting the organs of the healthy innocent patient is the best way to produce the most communal harmony in the long term. Innocent persons cannot be sacrificed in order to produce more harmony. Teleological approaches to harmony cannot explain why this is the case.

Finally, Metz believes that teleological approaches to harmony tend to be overly partial, in that '[t]hey do not readily admit that human persons generally have a moral status, that is, are owed moral treatment for their own sake' (Metz 2022, 103). Metz argues that some phrasings in the literature appear to imply that rightness and wrongness only occur in the context of mutually existing fellowship. This implies that when a stranger is encountered, I am not under any obligations to treat them in certain ways. In other words, only the 'in group' is morally relevant (Metz 2022, 103). I believe that Metz's objections to teleological approaches to harmony are successful. In the next section, I outline Metz's own theory, which is deontological in nature. This will enable me to show how Metz's own theory and deontological liveliness both successfully avoid the objections mentioned in this section.

8.4 Metz's Moral Relational Theory

Metz calls harmony (which he understands in terms of identification and solidarity) *friendliness*. Taking a clearly deontological approach, Metz claims that it is the *capacity* for friendliness that serves as the basis for human dignity, which, in turn, calls for honourific treatment. The deontological nature of this account clearly distinguishes it from the teleological approaches mentioned above. For Metz, the key is that '[i]instead of deeming relationships of identity and solidarity themselves to be a highest good to be promoted, I [Metz] take the *capacity* to be party to them to have a superlative non-instrumental value and to warrant *respectful* treatment' (Metz 2022, 104). This means that the 'view is not that communal relationship itself has a moral status, nor that only those who are in such a relationship have one, but rather that those who in principle could relate in that way have a moral status' (Metz 2022, 106).[4] There two different ways to possess the capacity for friendliness. First, a person may be a subject of friendliness which means she

---

[4] Metz observes that in light of this it is fair to characterize his theory as a modal view. See Samuel and Fayemi 2020.

has the capacity to identify with and exhibit solidarity with others. Second, a person can also be the object of friendliness, which means that it's possible for other humans to consider her as part of a 'we', and therefore act in ways to benefit it, etc. (Metz 2022, 107). The capacity to be either the subject or object of friendliness implies positive moral value. However, only those with capacity to be both the subject and object of friendliness possess dignity (Metz 2022, 107–108).

In light of this discussion, Metz's theory can be captured by the following principles:

- An act is right if and only if it respects individuals in virtue of their capacity to be party to harmonious ways of relating.
- An act is wrong insofar as it degrades those with the capability of relating communally as subjects or objects.
- An action is permissible if it treats beings as special in accordance with their ability to be friendly or to be befriended.
- An action is impermissible to the extent that it disrespects beings with the ability to be part of relationships of identity and solidarity. (Metz 2022, 110)

8.5 Deontology and Avoiding the Pitfalls of Teleological Approaches to Harmony

Metz's moral relational theory says that a person has dignity in virtue of their capacity for friendliness. This dignity is intact regardless of whether they ever exercise that capacity. This theory justifies the intuitively correct response to the cases mentioned in 8.3.3. In the case of the cheating husband, he has disrespected his wife in virtue of her capacity for friendliness. Such disrespect warrants the unfriendliness of failing to provide him with scarce medication when one has to choose between him and his wife. In some sense, the goal of morality on Metz's theory may well be to exercise friendliness (i.e., harmony), but never at the cost of disrespectful treatment of individuals. It is respectful treatment of individuals that constitutes, at least to some degree, harmony itself. Finally, in general, Metz's theory permits self- and other defence because those actions are intended to protect the dignity of innocents. Unprovoked aggressors act in unfriendly ways,

LIVELINESS AND HARMONIOUS RELATIONSHIPS   147

and therefore forfeit some of their rights to be treated with friendliness by others. Metz's moral relational theory avoids these objections to teleological harmony.

Notice that deontological liveliness also avoids the objections to teleological harmony in structurally similar ways to Metz's relational theory. According to deontological liveliness, a person has dignity in virtue of possessing liveliness or the capacity for liveliness. Defence of self and other is permitted on this view. The actions of unprovoked aggressors are disrespectful, and they forfeit some of their rights. Innocents cannot be sacrificed in order to save people because, again, the goal of morality on this view is not to simply maximize as much liveliness as possible. A person's dignity, which exists in virtue of their capacity for liveliness, cannot be compromised just to promote liveliness. The end of liveliness should be pursued, but not at the cost of disrespecting the dignity of persons. It should now be clear that, all else being equal, Metz's relational theory along with deontological liveliness ought to be preferred to teleological harmony in virtue of being able to accommodate the intuitions in the cases in 8.3.3.

Within this dialectical context, it would be fair to conclude that Metz's relational theory and deontological liveliness are equally plausible in that they are both able to avoid the problems associated with teleological harmony. However, in the next section, I outline three cases that serve as counterexamples to Metz's relational theory. Specifically, I believe his theory issues the intuitively wrong moral judgments when assessing them. While something close to these cases may obtain in the actual world, this need not be so in order to generate the relevant problem. It is enough that they are logically possible because they show that there are possibilities where Metz's theory issues the incorrect verdict. I suggest that though teleological liveliness faces similar problems dealing with these cases, deontological liveliness is able to accommodate them.

8.6 Clitoridectomy

The first case Metz's moral relational theory has some difficulty dealing with is that of the clitoridectomy of girls, which is still practiced in certain traditional African societies. I take it as granted that this practice is morally abhorrent and that it ought to be abolished in every place in which it is still

148 A MORAL THEORY OF LIVELINESS

practiced. Here's what Metz says his relational moral theory tells us about the practice:

> Note that since my conception of communal relationship includes cooperation, it is only practices that have been voluntarily adopted that merit moral consideration. So, for example, clitoridectomy imposed on girls is a tradition that does not merit respect insofar as minors are not competent to make free and informed decisions to undergo the procedure. Furthermore, the relational moral theory does not entail that voluntarily adopted customs should never change—for the solidarity element can sometimes provide all things considered reason not to do what identity would prescribe. Since, for all we can tell, killing innocent people did not in fact serve the function of appeasing the gods, considerations of communality on balance entail that the practice was right to challenge and overturn, even if everyone had been accepting of it for a long while. (2022, 135)

8.6.1 Metz's Relational Moral Theory on Clitoridectomy

However, I think that Metz's theory may have more trouble telling us why the practice is wrong than he surmises in this quote. While it is true that Metz's moral theory does not logically entail that voluntarily adopted customs can never change, imagine a possible world where there is a closed society (or almost closed) that practices clitoridectomy on girls. The society uniformly embraces this practice, creating immense unchallenged social pressure to participate in it. Suppose that the older female members of their community also participated in the practice and want the same for the younger members. Further suppose that clitoridectomy often marks the exit of the individual from the community as a girl and her entrance into it as a woman. It marks her full acceptance into the community as an adult. The practice is celebrated and embraced in this closed society.

In such a society, it is unclear how the solidarity element of Metz's theory could really provide an all things considered reason to abandon the custom. Recall that for Metz, the solidarity element fundamentally involves acts of service and empathizing with others. The challenge posed by this case is that *all* of the girls in this scenario genuinely *want* to participate in the practice. In this way, while Metz would probably want his solidarity component to forbid the practice, it appears to dictate the exact opposite in this case. Within this

LIVELINESS AND HARMONIOUS RELATIONSHIPS   149

particular community in question, participating in clitoridectomy is actually an act of solidarity.[5] While Metz is right to want his theory to support a ban of such practices, it fails to do so, at least in this society.[6] It is also difficult to see how pointing out that this case is about minors who by definition cannot consent really changes anything. Just imagine that all of the girls in question are nineteen years old. My intuitions about the immorality of the practice do not change when this modification is made to the case. I have the very strong moral intuition, and suspect that many others will, too, that the clitoridectomy of girls or young women in this closed society is still morally wrong. However, Metz's moral theory permits the practice in such a society, if not outright recommends it. Therefore, Metz's moral theory issues the intuitively wrong verdict in this case.

8.6.2 Teleological Liveliness on Clitoridectomy

At first glance, it might be tempting to respond that a person's *health* is an important constituent of liveliness. This includes sexual health, something that is damaged by clitoridectomy. There is thus a feature of teleological liveliness that can help to cast doubt on the practice where no similar feature exists in friendliness. On teleological liveliness the goal of morality is to promote liveliness. Since clitoridectomy degrades liveliness, it is wrong. However, I believe it is less than clear that teleological liveliness actually issues the correct verdict in this case. Recall that one potential challenge with teleological liveliness is that it is sometimes subject to similar problems facing utilitarianism (see 7.4.1). The difficulty has to do with unpalatable trade-offs and lack of human rights or related concepts. Clitoridectomy may well reduce the sexual health of girls who receive it, but it does not follow that the practice reduces the liveliness of the rest of the community, nor for that matter does it follow that it reduces the overall liveliness of the girls in question. If the community is supportive of the practice and sees it as a way of welcoming the girls into womanhood, the practice may well increase

---

[5] One challenge to African relational ethics is that while it works in small, closed communities, it is no longer applicable in contemporary society. See Matolino and Kwindingwi 2013 and Metz 2014 for a reply.

[6] Likewise, I do not think that making sacrifices to the gods can be handled very well on his account, either, for the same sort of reasons as the ones offered here. Though perhaps one relevant difference in these cases is that killing someone seems to be a paradigmatic case of unfriendliness, at least to the person in question.

150   A MORAL THEORY OF LIVELINESS

their liveliness. The same is true of girls who may desire to participate in the practice; it contributes to their sense of belonging. Admittedly, there might be ways of explicating teleological liveliness to forbid clitoridectomy. One way to accomplish this would be to appeal to considerations similar to rule utilitarianism such that it is more conducive to liveliness overall to forbid practices like clitoridectomy even if there are particular cases that do not conform to the rule. Of course, the worry here is that teleological liveliness becomes a subspecies of ruleutilitarianism and is therefore subject to all of the same worries.

8.6.3 Deontological Liveliness on Clitoridectomy

Deontological liveliness does not struggle with this case in the same way. This is because though liveliness is communitarian inasmuch as community fosters liveliness, it is not *essentially* communitarian as is Metz's moral relational theory. Friendliness is itself an inherently relational concept. While liveliness has important relational components, it is not fundamentally relational in the same way. On friendliness, the solidarity element is what creates the problem for dealing with this case. While exhibiting solidarity and identification with others does contribute to liveliness, it is not wholly constituted by such elements. Metz might respond that sexual health constitutes part of the capacity for friendliness and so needs to be respected. This is fair, but it is difficult to see how it could outweigh the kind of group solidarity and identification that is gained by the practice in the closed society described above. On deontological liveliness, a girl's right to sexual health cannot be sacrificed for the sake of the community, even if doing so would promote liveliness.

8.7 Religious Offence

The second unfriendly case for Metz's theory is about causing religious offence. What does his theory tell us about such cases? In a different work focussed on human rights, Metz explains that:

> [T]he Universal Islamic Declaration of Human Rights includes this article: 'No one shall hold in contempt or ridicule the religious beliefs of others or

LIVELINESS AND HARMONIOUS RELATIONSHIPS   151

incite public hostility against them".[7] Which approach is correct, if we must respect human dignity *qua* capacity to be party to friendly relationships? Is it "unfriendly" in the relevant sense to be blasphemous where one knows others would be offended? Is there a relevant difference between displeasing others by participating in a gay romantic relationship, which I argued is not unfriendly, and offending others by suggesting in a cartoon that a most beloved prophet is a terrorist? (Metz, Unpublished Manuscript)

8.7.1 Metz's Relational Moral Theory on Religious Offence

While Metz himself does not offer a definitive verdict on this case, I believe that it is fairly obvious what his theory says about it, at least if more details about the case are offered. Imagine a society where every single community member but one individual is a conservative Muslim. In such a society, causing religious offence, for example by depicting a beloved religious figure as a terrorist, is paradigmatically unfriendly. Imagine this one community member insists on spreading this depiction of the religious figure, causing widespread offence. On Metz's theory, this type of offence creates division (i.e., the opposite of identifying with others), and it also causes ill will (i.e., the opposite of solidarity). In other words, in such a society it is extremely unfriendly for the individual to cause religious offence. For now, suppose that Metz's theory has indeed issued the incorrect verdict.

I recognize that intuitions are likely to vary more about this case compared to the previous one. However, if at least *some* religious offence ought to be permitted in *any* society, then his theory issues the wrong judgment in this case, because it looks as if *all* religious offence is wrong in such a society. Furthermore, that Metz's own theory is by his own admission ambiguous on cases of religious offence is a strike against it. A superior moral theory would presumably be able to accommodate competing intuitions regarding the permissibility of religious offence. Finally, for those with strong moral intuitions that at least some religious offence (even if only incidental to some other purpose) is permissible, then for such a person Metz's theory again offers the intuitively wrong answer here.

---

[7] Islamic Council, *Universal Islamic Declaration of Human Rights* (1981) http://www.alhewar.com/ISLAMDECL.html.

152 A MORAL THEORY OF LIVELINESS

In fairness to Metz, it is important to recognize that his account preserves rights and so necessarily allows people to act in 'unfriendly' ways. For example, if I am walking down the sidewalk on the way to my favourite local coffee shop, I have the right not to be physically assaulted by you. Disliking my preference for naturally processed beans grown in Africa instead of washed beans from Central and South America is not a good reason to prevent my walk. More seriously, you are not permitted to prevent me from going to the coffee shop because of my ethnicity. In these and more severe cases, I am permitted to act in self- or other defence, and therefore in ways that would otherwise be deemed impermissible because they are unfriendly. An important question is whether there are similar types of overriding reasons that could possibly justify some unfriendliness in the case of religious offence. One immediate difference is that there is no physical harm in the case of religious offence. If physical harm or the threat of it is what justifies unfriendliness, then the kind of religious offence in question is still not permitted by Metz's theory.

Finally, think about what else might follow from the impermissibility of causing religious offence. Though in an almost universally conservative Muslim society, causing religious offence is unfriendly, consider that there would necessarily be no free speech, including freedom of the press (and other relevant forms of expression) in such a society. If these are rights that one is not inclined to give up, but I am correct that Metz's theory does not permit religious offence, then this is indeed a problem for his theory.

8.7.2 Teleological Liveliness on Religious Offence

Just as Metz is unsure what his theory dictates about the case of religious offence, what teleological liveliness says about it is also ambiguous. At first glance it appears that causing someone religious offence unnecessarily diminishes their liveliness and should therefore be avoided. All else being equal, if an individual has their deeply cherished beliefs mocked, their liveliness will be diminished. At least on the surface, then, it appears that teleological liveliness issues a verdict I believe is worth avoiding, because some religious offence ought to be permitted. Again, it is possible that if one is inclined to create a rule-based version of teleological liveliness that there would be rules designed to ensure a degree of freedom of expression, even when it causes offence. Still, it is difficult to see how this could outweigh the decrease in liveliness experienced in a society where all but one person is a religious conservative. At worst, teleological liveliness forbids causing religious offence and, at best, it is unclear what it says about religious offence and further clarification is needed.

8.7.3 Deontological Liveliness on Religious Offence

Deontological liveliness appears to issue a clearer verdict on the question of religious offence. I do not believe that deontological liveliness prohibits all religious offence. According to this version of liveliness as moral theory, every individual has dignity in virtue of possessing liveliness or the capacity for it. While a person may not be permitted to mock a religion just for the fun of it, they can participate in activities that may cause religious offence if they are exercising their liveliness. In other words, religious offence is at least permissible if it is an incidental result of some other activity aimed at respecting and promoting liveliness. For example, a scholar might be exercising their liveliness by conducting original research into the origins of a specific religion. This is a way of exercising their liveliness as it stimulates intellectual curiosity and has the potential to contribute important knowledge to society. If this scholars' research into the origins of a religion happens to offend adherents, then such offence appears to be permissible. It does not matter if a large number of people would be offended by such work, since the goal was not to cause offence. Unlike Metz's theory, then, deontological liveliness appears to clearly allow for some religious offence.

However, what I do think is unclear is the verdict deontological liveliness issues on Metz's specific case of religious offence. Depicting a beloved prophet as a terrorist is likely to decrease the liveliness of religious adherents. It is disrespectful to some degree. Furthermore, the goal of such a cartoon is to laugh at an important component of certain people's worldview. On the other hand, free speech, including the use of humour, is a plausibly important part of fostering liveliness in any society. With Metz, I am ultimately unsure whether deontological liveliness permits religious offence in this case, though I believe it clearly allows for it in cases of scholarly discoveries and disagreements where causing offence is merely incidental to the main goal of the activity in question.

154   A MORAL THEORY OF LIVELINESS

8.8 Homosexual Romantic Relationships

The third unfriendly case for Metz's moral relational theory is about the permissibility of homosexual romantic relationships. To begin, consider that Metz writes that:

> Regarding homophobia, those who have gay romantic relationships are not thereby being unfriendly or otherwise failing to relate communally. Those party to such relationships are not necessarily viewing anyone in 'us versus them' terms, subordinating others, harming them, or acting out of cruelty. They are not even necessarily being alienated from and indifferent to others. There is simply nothing immoral with homosexuality, if rightness is friendliness. If anything, insofar as a loving relationship is an intense realization of communality, there is good moral reason to support gay relationships as they suit people's needs. (2022, 142)

8.8.1 Metz's Moral Relational Theory on Homosexual Romantic Relationships

Contra Metz, it is actually easy to imagine cases in which it is false that there is nothing wrong with gay relationships according to his relational moral theory. Imagine a culture that almost universally eschews such relationships as unnatural, disgusting, and beyond the pale. Suppose that all of the millions of people in this society universally condemn homosexuality with the exception of two men who have fallen in love and are trying to decide whether to act on their feelings. If rightness is friendliness, in such a society, then, to engage in a gay romantic relationship (especially in public) is indeed unfriendly. In such a society, doing so would create widespread ill will (the opposite of solidarity) and widespread division (the opposite of identity). But if gay romantic relationships are intuitively permissible (as I imagine most professional philosophers these days will want to say), then Metz's moral relational theory fails to issue the correct verdict.

Part of what makes this case particularly challenging for Metz is that it does not need to rely on modal imagination in quite the same way as the previous cases. Though there might not be universal agreement about it, many traditional African societies do indeed forbid homosexuality. The practice is still shunned throughout many parts of Africa today, with even some African scholars declaring it 'un-African'. Consider that Molefi Kete Asante writes that '[h]omosexuality and lesbianism are deviations from Afrocentric thought because they often make the person evaluate his or her own physical needs above the teachings of national consciousness. . . . An Afrocentric perspective recognizes its existence but homosexuality cannot be condoned or accepted as good for the national development of a strong people' (Asante 2003, 72–73). Some of the motivation behind this comes from the fact that traditional societies tend to highly value life and hence procreation (through 'natural' means). For example, Bénézet Bujo observes that:

> It has been rightly noted that homosexuality is rare in traditional Black Africa, and the reason for this is precisely the communal dimension: south of the Sahara, the fundamental anthropological conception in Africa is both bipolar and tripolar. One is a human being only in the duality of man and woman, and this bipolarity generates the triad man-woman-child, which leads to full community. Against this background, a man-man or woman-woman relationship would not only be looked on as an egotistic isolationism which dares not take the step to full human existence; it also leads to a sexist discrimination against part of the human race and shows an unwillingness to accept the enrichment that comes from heterogeneity. (2001, 6)[8]

That the modal scenario in which homosexuality is universally condemned is much closer to the actual state of affairs in certain places on the African continent helps makes this a very forceful worry for Metz's moral relational theory.[9]

8.8.2 Teleological Liveliness on Homosexual Romantic Relationships

Teleological liveliness also struggles to issue the correct verdict on this case. For reasons that should be familiar by now, it is possible on teleological liveliness to generate cases in which the liveliness of the majority outweighs

---

[8] Interestingly, Bujo notes that a different ethical understanding of homosexuality is possible, but only if it was one arrived at by the community (Bujo 2001, 7).

[9] More 'unfriendly' cases abound. Consider that in many African societies it is considered very unfriendly not to procreate. Bujo writes that 'Africans argue against lifelong celibacy along precisely these lines: one who remains unmarried for life withdraws from solidarity with other human persons, offending against the law of life. He is like a magician who ruthlessly destroys life, since a celibate is unwilling to take a share in the growth of life on the biological level and refuses to take his place in the duality of man and woman, which alone constitutes full humanity' (Bujo 2001, 7).

the liveliness of a minority of people. In a case in which the actions of two individuals would cause the widespread degradation of the liveliness of millions of people, those actions are probably impermissible. It is difficult to show how the dignity or rights of two homosexual men could be preserved at the cost of the liveliness of literally millions of other humans. As with the other cases, I leave it as an open question whether there is a rule-based version of teleological liveliness that could be used to protect against such cases by arguing that protecting rights is the best overall strategy to promote liveliness in a society.

8.8.3 Deontological Liveliness on Homosexual Romantic Relationships

Unlike Metz's moral relational theory and teleological liveliness, deontological liveliness does a better job of issuing the intuitively correct verdict in this case. A person who is forbidden from pursuing a mutually loving homosexual romantic relationship has their liveliness degraded. Their liveliness does not matter any less than other members of the community. They have an inherent dignity that is disrespected by the prohibition of such relationships. As with Metz's relational moral theory, a key question is whether their inherent dignity justifies the relational disharmony that would result from their behaviour. But remember that according to liveliness, the community is valuable inasmuch as it produces liveliness; the community itself is neither the moral end nor the grounds of value. Provided that the goal of a homosexual relationship was simply to exercise the liveliness involved in a mutually loving relationship, the incidental offence that doing so may cause is likely permissible. The rights of a homosexual that are grounded in liveliness or the capacity for it cannot be trampled for the sake of the many.

8.9 Flourishing, Well-Being, and Self-Regarding Duties

I do not pretend that the above discussion of the three cases is exhaustive. However, it does provide some reason to prefer deontological liveliness to Metz's relational moral theory. But there is a general reply that could be made on behalf of Metz that deserves further consideration and comes by way of

LIVELINESS AND HARMONIOUS RELATIONSHIPS   157

reflecting on African conceptions of flourishing and well-being.[10] Though
in the relevant discussions, Metz does not belabour these ideas, it is clear
enough that on his theory a person can only be properly flourishing if they
are acting with friendliness towards others and also receiving friendliness
from others. A key theme across various African accounts of well-being is
that a person's well-being should be evaluated in light of the extent that their
needs are met (e.g., Metz 2019). Minimally, these needs are biological and
social.[11] This means that a person's sexual needs are severely harmed by a
clitoridectomy. Societies where the practice is widespread, or even in the
possible worlds where it is unanimously supported, ought to recognize that
this is the case. Once it is recognized that a woman's sexual needs are harmed
by this practice, it should be condemned, including in those societies where
it is (wrongly) embraced.

What about the case of religious offence? It could be that freedom of expression is a social need that would go unmet if all instances of religious offence were forbidden. Does this need take precedence over a person's need
to practice their religion free from offence? How should these seemingly
competing interests be balanced against each other?[12] If there are duties to
the self, they reasonably include duties to meet one's own needs. Now, it is
tempting to conclude that this shows that pursuing a gay romantic relationship would not in fact be wrong even in a society where it is universally or
almost universally condemned. If romantic needs are important, then one
has a duty to fulfil those needs when possible. In other words, in such a case
failing to pursue a gay romantic relationship would be an act of unfriendliness towards oneself. But why not think this is an instance in which a duty
to oneself conflicts with a duty to one's community?[13] An individual in this
case may have a duty to be friendly towards themselves. And yet it remains
difficult to see why pursuing a gay romantic relationship is not still a clear
instance of unfriendliness. Suppose the community I have been describing
consists of ten million people. All but the two men who are in love would be
distraught by the appearance of such a relationship in their society. Is it really

---

[10] The initial idea for this reply comes from discussions with Thaddeus Metz.

[11] Metz has argued that they should also include existential needs (2019).

[12] I say seemingly, because a popular view in African thought is that, though people may appear
to have competing needs, they *never* do. Metz himself also recognizes that how this case is parsed
fundamentally depends on the balance of harms and benefits in light of various social, psychological,
biological, and moral needs.

[13] Of course, many deontologists will claim that such conflicts are apparent, not actual. But even if
this is true, it does not clearly tell in favour of Metz.

158   A MORAL THEORY OF LIVELINESS

reasonable to conclude that the romantic needs of the two outweigh the millions of others in their community? Indeed, the health of the community is of paramount importance. Though there could be a way to motivate this or a related reply, more is required to do so than what I have offered here.[14]

8.10 Metz's Moral Relational Theory, Liveliness, and the Relevant Moral Community

To conclude, it is important to get clearer on the scope of the moral community for Metz's moral theory. Doing so will help to illuminate the relevant community for liveliness. According to Metz, all beings who can be both the subject and object of friendliness have a moral status and inherent dignity. On the other hand, those beings who can only be the object of friendliness have a moral status, but lack a dignity (Metz 2022, 110). Metz explains that:

> In particular, if an entity by its nature has the ability to identify with others and to exhibit solidarity with them, as well as the ability for us to do so with it, then it has a dignity, a superlative non-instrumental value that must be treated morally by us and specifically with respect. In contrast, if an entity cannot itself befriend others but we can befriend it, it matters morally but lacks a dignity. (Metz 2022, 153)

What this implies is that almost all humans have a dignity, while many animals enjoy at least some moral status (Metz 2022, 153). Metz also specifies that it is large, not small or incremental, differences in capacity to be the subject and/or object of friendliness that are morally relevant. This implies that 'if, by virtue of the nature of human beings, elephants, and molluscs, a moral agent were in principle much more able to identify with and exhibit solidarity towards elephants than molluscs, then elephants would have a greater moral status than molluscs' (Metz 2022, 153).

---

[14] Metz explains that 'Gyekye believes that there are human rights to life as well as to civil liberties regarding free expression of opinion (1992: 251), bodily integrity (2004: 36), and even lifestyles that the majority might frown upon (1997: 65)' (2022, 31). If human rights grounded in people's capacity for friendliness are a way out of these cases for Metz, he needs to explain what happens when such rights seem to run up against communal norms. Indeed, these difficult cases and this discussion in general could be formulated as a challenge to a conception of rights or dignity grounded in Metz's ethic. For more on the interaction between individual and communal rights, see Bujo 2001, 163.

The moral status of the disabled and otherwise impaired humans consistently poses a challenge to many moral theories. Kantians struggle to account for the moral status of humans who do not meet the requisite level of autonomy or rationality. Indeed, the implication is that such humans lack moral status altogether. Alternatively, utilitarianism seems to indicate that humans have full moral status on the assumption that they can experience happiness or pleasure (Metz 2022, 165).[15] Consider what Metz says about the case of extreme psychopaths:

> It might be that an extreme psychopath can in fact be a subject of a friendly relationship to some degree, viz., by virtue of being able to coordinate with and to aid others, even if we imagine that he cannot do so consequent to other-regarding propositional attitudes such as 'we-ness' or sympathy. Suppose, however, that this is not enough to count as being a subject of communality to the requisite extent for a dignity, or consider an extraordinarily autistic individual who by his nature cannot even engage in these kinds of behaviours. The relational view entails that, although these individuals would lack a dignity equal to ours, their moral status would be higher than that of animals. These persons would have the capacity for being an object of a friendly relationship with us to a much greater degree than that had by other beings such as mice and elephants. (Metz 2022, 164)

Metz believes that his relational theory establishes a middle ground where an extreme autist or psychopath has moral standing, though probably not a dignity. Such individuals have a higher status than animals, since we are better able to commune with them than with animals. Finally, Metz believes that 'such an approach well explains the intuition that in cases where one cannot save the lives of both a human being and an animal, one ought to favour the former, even supposing they have similar internal traits' (Metz 2022, 165).

In light of this discussion, it is interesting to explore the relevant moral community according to deontological liveliness. On the main approach I have taken, any individual who has the capacity for liveliness has full moral status, including a dignity. This status applies to the vast majority of humans. But what about extreme autists and psychopaths? Initially, it might appear that deontological liveliness says that they have full moral status and a dignity

---

[15] Alternatively, for the utilitarian, if a human had a severely diminished ability to experience happiness or pleasure, then their moral status could probably be called into question.

160 A MORAL THEORY OF LIVELINESS

simply in virtue of being alive. However, matters are likely more complicated. Liveliness is a multifaceted concept, and the capacity for it can clearly come in degrees. Though liveliness is not fundamentally a relational concept as is friendliness and (maybe) personhood, it still contains significant relational components. Indeed, it is reasonable to think that exhibiting friendliness contributes to liveliness. Thus, on the one hand, while the extreme psychopath is lively in the sense of being alive, they may well have a diminished capacity for important components of liveliness that most other humans do not lack. I leave it as an open question whether this implies that they might have a moral status but lack a dignity. Regarding the extreme psychopath's moral status in relationship to animals, liveliness probably issues a similar result to Metz's theory. Animals that have a capacity for some liveliness have moral status. However, humans are still going to be able to engage with the relational components of liveliness most meaningfully with other humans. I do not take any of this discussion to be definitive, but simply note the relevant moral community implied by liveliness is a topic that deserves more attention.

8.11 Conclusion

In the first half of this chapter, I explained that teleological harmony represents one of the most common approaches to African normative ethics, at least among its academic exponents. These views emphasize harmonious relationships as the end that must be sought above all else. A significant problem with these views is that they fail to account for human rights. They cannot justify acting in self- or other defence, when doing so would create disharmony. They also cannot always justify creating disharmony based on a person's past wrong actions. Metz's moral relational theory nicely avoids these objections by instead placing value on a person's capacity for harmonious relationships or friendliness. Deontological liveliness also avoids these worries by implying that people have a dignity in virtue of either possessing liveliness or the capacity for it.

In the second half of this chapter, I suggested that Metz's theory faces some difficult counterexamples where it appears to issue the intuitively wrong moral verdict. The upshot of this discussion was that deontological liveliness is more likely to issue the intuitively correct verdict in these cases. It clearly entails that female clitoridectomy is wrong, that some religious offence is permissible at least where the offence is incidental to some other end, and that romantic homosexual relationships are permissible even in those societies where there is widespread condemnation of the practice. This means that all else being equal, this chapter provides reasons for holding that deontological liveliness is superior to Metz's moral relational theory. This discussion is hardly conclusive, because there are numerous other axes along which these theories can be evaluated.

This concludes Part III of the book. I hope I have shown that the moral theory of liveliness deserves to be considered as a serious contender among the other major African moral theories. In Part IV: Liveliness, Metaethics, and Meaning, the books shifts gears to explore the metaethical grounds of life force and liveliness before turning to examine the question of meaning in life. For many other projects of a similar kind, it would have made better sense to include discussion of metaethics prior to normative ethics. However, in order to make this book accessible to audiences unfamiliar with the African tradition, it was important to first introduce life force, discussions of which tend to be dominated by normative ethics.

PART IV
LIVELINESS, METAETHICS, AND MEANING

9

The Metaethical Grounds of Life Force

9.1 Introduction

Though the main aim of this book is to develop a secular *normative* ethical theory based on life force, Part IV marks a foray into metaethics. It is fair for the reader at this stage of the book to have questions about the metaethical grounding of the normative theory of liveliness, and the purpose of Part IV is to answer some of these questions. In order to keep the scope of this and the next chapter manageable, I am going to assume that moral realism is true, and therefore will not discuss anti-realist theories. Anti-realists should see this as an invitation to explore what African ethics has to contribute to anti-realist understanding of ethics.

I begin this chapter by explaining the need for metaethics, along with the lack of metaethical discussion in contemporary African ethics (9.2). I then examine potential metaethical grounds of life force, exploring whether Divine Command Theory as found in the Anglo-American tradition could be leveraged to support it (9.3). After this, I outline a different position which takes life force itself as metaethical grounds. However, I argue that this is not fundamentally different from Divine Command Theory by showing it is also susceptible to the Euthyphro Dilemma (9.4). I close by considering whether solutions to the dilemma offered by proponents of Divine Command Theory might also apply to life force. Though in Part III I focussed almost exclusively on liveliness, this chapter focusses solely on life force and not liveliness, because, though as normative theories they might be quite similar, it turns out that the same cannot be assumed about their potential metaethical grounding given their vastly different metaphysical starting points.

A Moral Theory of Liveliness. Kirk Lougheed, Oxford University Press. © Kirk Lougheed 2025.
DOI: 10.1093/9780197782019.003.0009

9.2 The Is/Ought Gap and the Dearth of Metaethics in African Philosophy

The is/ought gap is plausibly the fundamental problem of metaethics. It is unjustified to move from descriptive observations to normative facts. The fact that the world *is* a certain way (observation) is not evidence that it *ought* to be that way (normative). More bluntly, the fact that society recognizes that murder is wrong is not in itself evidence that murder is in fact wrong. Or if it is, arguments are needed to explain why this is so. Metaethics seeks to provide the foundation for normative thinking in order to avoid committing the is/ought mistake. Moral realists say that truth values of ethical claims are independent of persons, while anti-realists say they are dependent on persons. Put differently, the realists say there are objective moral facts while anti-realists deny the existence of such facts.

While briefly exploring what might ground moral claims in African thought, Metz observes that '[w]hile contemporary African moral philosophy offers quite a lot to any open minded normative ethical theorist and applied ethicist, it currently has comparatively little to contribute to a metaethicist' (Metz 2017, 71). With respect to what one does find regarding metaethics, it is worth noting that in both secular and religious discussions, '[t]he default position amongst African philosophers is that ethics is to be grounded on metaphysics' (Metz 2022, 25).[1] This is not the minimal commonsense claim that an ethic ought to avoid making false metaphysical claims inasmuch as possible. Rather, it is the much stronger claim that normativity logically follows from (or at least is strongly implied) by ontology (i.e., by what exists) (Metz 2022, 25). In 'Chapter Two: Reconsidering Ontology's Relevance' of *A Relational Moral Theory* (2022), Metz focusses on two humanistic attempts in African philosophy to ground normativity.

The first of these is from Kwame Nkrumah's book *Consciencism* (1970). Nkrumah's main claim is that egalitarianism follows from a materialist metaphysics (Metz 2022, 26). The second is found in the highly influential work of Kwame Gyekye. Metz explains that 'Gyekye says, "Moral questions . . . may, in some sense, be said to be linked to, or engendered by, metaphysical conceptions of the person" (1997: 36), and "The natural relationality of the person thus immediately plunges her into a moral universe" (1997: 67)' (2022, 30). For Gyekye, his moral theory is communitarian, because it involves

---

[1] See also Imafidon and Bewaji et al. 2013; Mulago 1991.

participating in a culture and sharing in a way of life with one's community. The community is owed one's service because it is responsible for one's life. However, it is not extreme communitarianism, because it also protects individual rights, allowing people to pursue idiosyncratic lifestyles provided that they aren't harming anyone (Metz 2022, 30–31). Metz explains that 'Gyekye's main rationale for moderate communitarianism is that the self has a dual nature as partially independent of the community and partially dependent on it' (Metz 2022, 32). Individuals have obligations to support their society and culture, but they are also free to choose their own way of life and must not be used as a mere means to improving the community (Metz 2022, 32). According to Metz:

> Gyekye favours this combination of duties and rights because they are supposed to follow from the fact that there are two metaphysical aspects to ourselves—an individual nature and a social one. Our duties are a product of our nature as communal beings, whereas our rights follow from our nature as beings who are not utterly determined by the community. (2022, 32)

Metz's main criticism of both of these attempts to ground normativity is that nothing normatively automatically follows from ontology. Metz attempts to help the authors in question locate plausible intermediary premises which would allow one to move from the metaphysical fact of materialism to egalitarianism or from the dual nature of humans as social and individual to moderate communitarianism. However, I agree with Metz's conclusion that no such premises can be found (see Metz 2022, 28–30, 33–38). Indeed, '[t]he attempt to move from pure ontology to morality is not unique to these two Ghanian philosophers [i.e., Nkrumah and Gyekye], but is characteristic of the field of African philosophy more generally' (Metz 2022, 38). Such strategies ultimately appear to fall victim to the is/ought fallacy. Just because the world is a certain way, metaphysically speaking, nothing about normativity automatically follows.

9.3 Divine Command Theory in Context of African Metaethics

It is natural to understand life force as the main religious metaethical alternative to the humanistic theories described above, at least on the African

168 A MORAL THEORY OF LIVELINESS

continent. After all, life force is an imperceptible energy that flows from God and cannot be studied by the scientific method. However, it is noteworthy that according to Metz, accounts that attempt to ground normativity based on life force typically focus on the fact that it implies everything that exists is interconnected in virtue of sharing force (see 3.2.2). Everything is connected in virtue of being alive (i.e., in virtue of sharing life). Perhaps somewhat surprisingly to a reader steeped in the Anglo-American tradition, God is not appealed to as the grounds of morality on this view even though God is the ontological foundation (i.e., he is responsible for all that exists). Consider:

> Onyibor and Imafidon say that duties to help other persons are 'generated' from or 'implied' by this purely metaphysical view of the fundamental nature of reality, a view that several other philosophers appear to share. Here are additional examples of this approach: 'African morals lay a great emphasis on social conduct, since a basic African view is that the individual exists only because others exist' (Mbiti 1975: 175), and 'Existence in Africa cannot be any other thing outside 'in-relation', that is communal. The individual's life is inseparable from that of the other or his community. This breeds the idea of collective responsibility' (Ogugua 2007: 33; see also Nze 2007; cf. Oladipo 2004: 356; Ogbujah 2007) (Metz, 2022, 39).

As with the above humanistic theories, Metz finds such reasoning lacking because it attempts to move from metaphysical facts to normative facts. He asks: 'does necessary interdependence between an individual and his society really "breed" the idea of collective responsibility? How could it, logically speaking?' (Metz 2022, 39). In sum, for Metz, the 'problem with these rationales should be clear: from the bare fact that everything in the natural world is interrelated, nothing immediately follows about how to respond to nature' (2022, 40).

I agree with Metz's characterization of African metaethics. I believe that his description of the field is accurate and that it is illegitimate in the cases he describes to move from facts about what exists to normativity. However, when Metz writes that 'nothing moral *straightaway* follows from any *purely* ontological view, that is, a view about the nature of reality that includes no evaluative elements (about what is good/bad) or normative elements (about what an agent should/not do)', it sounds almost as if he intends this to be a universal law (Metz 2022, 26). But I think this is mistaken, because there is at least one important exception. Namely, if God exists, then it is reasonable to think a whole host of universal moral truths *could* follow from this fact. It is even possible that some moral facts may well be able to be inferred just from analyzing the concept of a perfect being. The reason that this is important in this context is that even though exponents of life force do not typically ground normativity in God, it is not unreasonable to suggest they *could* appeal more directly to God in order to ground normativity. Remember that all force is derived from God and that God is at the top of the chain of being. Thus, even if it is true that proponents of life force do not typically try to ground normativity in God's existence, I submit that it is possible to make the case for such grounds by focussing on God.

There is nothing *ad hoc* about this strategy, either—even in the context of life force and African Traditional Religion—because of God's importance in the hierarchy of being. In other words, Metz's criticisms do not necessarily apply to an account of normativity grounded in life force that focusses on God instead of on interdependence. Or, more modestly, an approach to metaethics grounded in God is the best approach to defeat Metz's claim that normativity can never follow automatically from ontology. This strategy is also not *ad hoc* because there is already a prominent account of metaethics grounded in God located in the Anglo-American tradition in the form of Divine Command Theory (from here on 'DCT'). Metz is well aware of DCT, since he mentions it as sharing the same motivation with a potential bridging premise for Gyekye's theory (2022, 37; see 9.2). However, he never explores how it could be used to help life force, presumably because this is not how African theorists themselves attempt to ground normativity (nor was such a project the focus of his book). Still, this suggests an area ripe for fruitful cross-cultural dialogue. In what follows I will outline a version of DCT as found in the work of Robert Adams, exploring along the way to what extent it can be applied to life force. This means exploring it in the context of the ontology of African Traditional Religion.

9.4 Divine Command Theory as the Metaethical Grounds of Life Force

Philosophers of religion in the Anglo-American tradition have spilt much ink in trying to explain how God can be said to ground normativity. One important answer has arisen in the form of DCT. It is tempting to think that inasmuch as this theory that has been developed in the context of the

170   A MORAL THEORY OF LIVELINESS

Abrahamic monotheistic traditions is successful, that it can be applied seamlessly to ground a normative theory based on life force. This is because life force implies the ontology of African Traditional Religion (ATR), with God serving as the common denominator among all of these views. But such a straightforward application cannot be assumed without sustained argument. Consider, for example, that recent work in African philosophy of religion has suggested that not all problems and solutions found in the Anglo-American philosophy of religion apply seamlessly to African Traditional Religion (e.g., Agada 2023; Lougheed, Molefe, and Metz 2024). It is therefore an open question whether work in DCT could be successfully leveraged to explain how God could ground a normative theory of life force. In this section I take up this question and related ones. I argue that DCT can indeed to a significant extent be appealed to as the metaethical grounds for life force.

DCT is the view, roughly, that if God commands action x, then agent s is obligated to perform x. God provides the objective grounds of morality which is entirely independent of humans. On the one hand, the view has experienced something of a renaissance in the last forty years or so, and so it may be unhelpful to leave the description of it in such generic terms (though I indeed choose this approach to utilitarianism in Chapter 6). But on the other hand, it is not possible to survey and evaluate every single possible variation of the theory found in the contemporary literature, as such a project would take me much too far afield. I therefore choose the middle ground and outline a version of DCT as found in Robert Adams' seminal *Finite and Infinite Goods* (1999), with a particular focus on 'Chapter 11: Divine Commands' and 'Chapter Twelve: Abraham's Dilemma'.[2] Adams' discussion helped to set the stage for much of the recent literature on DCT.

Adams suggests that DCT is a kind of idealized social requirement theory.[3] It is interesting that his view is not that of an isolated individual blindly following divine commands but rather one in which obligations arise in the context of one's social relationship with God (Adams 1999, 249). Part of what makes the social analogy apt here is that the concept of divine commands is analogous to human institutions (Adams 1999, 249). For Adams, DCT is not a general theory of moral properties, but is instead about the nature of moral obligations. He offers an account of the good earlier in his book that is grounded in *excellence* (Adams 1999, 250). However, Adams believes that

---

[2] Other prominent defenders of DCT that I could have chosen include William Wainwright (2005) or Phillip Quinn (1978, 1979, 1992).

[3] For Adams on the benefits of DCT, see 1999, 256–257.

though this makes the scope of his theory perhaps different, it is consistent with many early modern approaches to DCT, including Locke's, in which 'the nature of nonmoral good and evil (as pleasure and pain) is understood independently of God's commands, and is used to explain the nature of obligation imposed by divine commands' (1999, 251).

Adams emphasizes the 'reasons for compliance that arise from a social bond or relationship with God' (1999, 252). The nature of the social bond in question will dictate the level of force the reasons for obeying them possess. In the context of a relationship with God, the strength of such reasons will be very strong. Adams explains that '[i]f God is our creator, if God loves us, if God gives us all the good that we enjoy, those are clearly reasons to prize God's friendship' (1999, 252). These might be considered reasons of *gratitude*. The reasons for compliance will also track the excellence of the commander, which in the case of God is supreme excellence. For Adams, God is wholly just in the sense of being supremely excellent, instead of just regarding, say, in virtue of the fulfilling of obligations (1999, 254). This means that 'God's justice, so understood, grounds obligation, rather than being grounded in it' (Adams 1999, 255).

God's commands arise from his social interactions 'and it is partly because the latter [i.e., God] is taken to be an ideal candidate for the role of definitive exemplar of the relevant sort of excellence, that God's commands can plausibly be taken as constituting moral obligation' (Adams 1999, 255). This means that 'God's commands spring from a design and purpose that is good, and that the behavior that God commands is not bad, but good, either intrinsically, or by serving a pattern of life that is very good' (Adams 1999, 255). The commands in question need to be actual, not counterfactual; they need to be based on the actual excellence of God (Adams 1999, 256).[4]

Two potential worries immediately arise when asking of the degree to which this description can apply to life force, which rests on the metaphysics of ATR. First, consider there is controversy in ATR about how best to define the attributes of God. Early expositors of ATR tended to attribute the omni-properties to God such as omnipotence, omnibenevolence, and omniscience to the God of ATR (e.g., Mbiti 1975, Evans-Pritchard 1965). However, later work suggested that such descriptions were largely impacted by the fact that the early expositors were Christians and perhaps trying to show

---

[4] Adams is careful to explain why divine commands are to be preferred to the divine will. For discussion, see Adams 1999, 258–262.

172   A MORAL THEORY OF LIVELINESS

that the Africans already held the 'correct' understanding of God prior to colonialization (e.g., p'Bitek 1971; Sogolo 1993). As such, the second wave of scholars in ATR often considered themselves to be decolonizing the previous interpretations. For example, some suggest that though God is the greatest being who exists in terms of knowledge, love, and power, this does not mean such properties are infinite or maximal (e.g., Wiredu 1998). This has come to be known as the 'limited-God' thesis. Ada Agada has argued that despite the rather fierce disagreement over which conception of God is more accurate to the African tradition(s), both conceptions can indeed be found in different oral traditions (2023). More radically, some have gone so far as to suggest that God is indeed omnipotent and therefore can do evil to accomplish his plans, since to suggest otherwise puts a limitation on God's power (1998).

The reason that this has the potential to create a worry is that, according to Adams, the force of commands tracks the excellence of the person issuing the commands. A maximal God with all of the relevant omni-properties is presumably more excellent than the limited God, and far more excellent than a God capable of evil.[5] However, this does not mean that the proponent of life force must abandon any appeals to Adams' account. On the limited-God view, God is still the most excellent being that exists. His commands therefore come with considerable force, even if it is indeed weaker than that of the maximal God. However, as I will explain below, a God capable of evil is not worth following for Adams. Since this view is a minority position (perhaps the extreme minority position), I will not consider whether it is compatible with DCT any further.

Second, however, a different problem remains even on the assumption that Adams' version of DCT is compatible with the limited-God view. This is because on both the maximal-God and limited-God views, it is close to universally agreed upon in ATR that God is distant from humans. God is wholly other from humans and has little direct interaction with them. God never dictated commandments onto stone tablets, nor did he inspire anyone to write any holy books. It is therefore difficult to know just *how* God could issue commands if ATR is true. DCT works only if there are divine commands. This worry is, however, less strong than it appears to be given Adams' permissive view of what constitutes a divine command.

Adams casts an extremely wide net in identifying divine commandments, including that they can come not only from scripture, but also from natural

---

[5] There are probably ways to challenge this assumption, but I will not explore them here.

THE METAETHICAL GROUNDS OF LIFE FORCE   173

law, ecclesiastical bodies, direct extrabiblical commands, and even from conscience or natural inclination (Adams 1999, 263).[6] All of this implies that 'the
ethical obligations whose nature I [i.e., Adams] propose to analyze in terms
of divine commands are not just those of some particular sort of Christian,
or even adherents of all the theistic religions, but those of human beings
in general' (Adams 1999, 263–264). This explains why the theory does not
confine morality to a segment of humans, and instead understands 'divine
commands as cognitively accessible to human beings quite generally, and
hence in a wide variety of ways' (Adams 1999, 264). For example, a divine
command such as 'thou shall not murder' is revealed through 'human social
requirements'. However, Adams also believes that it is always an open question the extent to which human social requirements perfectly track divine
commands (1999, 264–265).

Notice what this implies about divine commands and ATR. Human social
requirements exist in every society and as such divine commands exist in
ATR, even if God is quite distant. Furthermore, in ATR, God has a significant amount of *indirect* communication with humans. God communicates
with humans through the living dead and departed ancestors. They are the
conduits by which humans are able to access God's will and hence divine
commands. All of this is perfectly consistent with Adams' broad description
of divine commands.[7]

Part of what may separate Adams' version of DCT from others is that he
stresses the need to evaluate God's character and the content of any specific
divine commands. This is different than a DCT being grounded solely in alle-
giance to something like the Good, which is further grounded in God. There
seems to be much room in Adams' account to question whether a command
is indeed from God. For Adams, 'a conception of devotion to God in terms of
a teleological subordination of other values does not allow the devout really
to love anything other than God; for instance, it does not allow them really

---

[6] Adams borrows these from Mouw 1990, 8. Also note that Adams does not allow for counterfactuals
about commandments, since this would amount to needing to guess at what God commands, and
possibly being condemned for getting it wrong.

[7] For Adams, the issuing of a divine command needs to include the following three
requirements: '(1) A divine command will always involve a *sign*, as we may call it, that is intentionally caused by God. (2) In causing the sign God must intend to issue a command, and *what* is
commanded is what God intends to command thereby. (3) The sign must be such that the intended
audience could understand it as conveying the intended command' (1999, 265). Notice that all of this
implies that 'it is enough for God's commanding if God intends the addressee to recognize a requirement as extremely authoritative and as having imperative force. And that recognition can be present
in nontheists as well as theists' (Adams 1999, 268).

174 A MORAL THEORY OF LIVELINESS

to love their neighbor, as commanded in Judaism and Christianity' (1999, 275). Instead, the devotion to God that is advocated for by Adams is one 'in which love for God is an organizing principle into which one integrates genuine love for other goods that one is to prize for their own sake, as God does' (1999, 275).

This is perhaps the part of Adams' theory that is the least obviously compatible with ATR and life force. In the African tradition it is typically frowned upon to question authority. Elders possess greater forced than other members of the community, and so their wisdom should not be questioned. Typically, a person tries to maintain a good relationship with departed ancestors and the living dead, as they are ultimately reflective of God's attitude. If some ill befalls a person, it is perhaps because they have displeased an ancestor (and so ultimately God). Now, Adams wants to leave much room to question whether a command is indeed genuinely good and hence from God. However, questioning a departed ancestor is beyond the pale for much of the African tradition. Questioning communal norms is viewed as disruptive to communal harmony. This is not an insurmountable challenge with respect to squaring ATR and life force with Adams' theory, but it is a noteworthy difference. Indeed, as noted above, it is what separates his version of DCT from many others.

This discussion hardly exhausts the topics relevant to assessing whether DCT can be appealed to as the metaethical grounds for a normative theory based on life force which necessarily has the ontology of ATR. However, in outlining one of the best contemporary versions of the theory on offer as located in the work of Adams, I hope it is clear to the reader that a strong case is emerging that DCT could indeed ground life force. In the next section, I explore a potential objection which says I have mischaracterized the best way to understand how to ground life force.

9.5 Life Force Itself as the Metaethical Grounds

At this juncture, it might be objected that I have been unfair to try to ground life force in DCT. Indeed, an objector might say there is something rather 'un-African' about attempting to ground life force in a theory from the Western or Anglo-American tradition. They could further insist that I have presented a misreading of life force because the view actually implies that *life itself* is the metaethical grounds of normativity, nothing else. One reason to prefer this type of account is that some have suggested it avoids the longstanding Euthyphro Dilemma. In the rest of this section, I will attempt to motivate this view in more detail (9.5.1), before demonstrating that it turns out to be fundamentally no different from DCT and hence does no better at avoiding the Euthyphro Dilemma (9.5.2).

9.5.1 Molefe on Life Force and the Euthyphro Dilemma

In this section I use the work of Motsamai Molefe as a foil in order to show why attempting to say that life force itself is the metaethical grounds of the normative theory of life force fails. Specifically, I appeal to Molefe's work to show that while it might be tempting to think life force can avoid the Euthyphro Dilemma better than DCT can, the reasons for this claim ultimately fail. Molefe explains that '[i]f DCT is correct in asserting that *rightness* is entirely a function of what God commands then morality is strictly about *obeying* God. In the African tradition, however, morality is about a positive or negative relation to a divine energy [i.e., life force]' (2017b, 31). Though Molefe claims that divine commands are not incompatible with an ethic grounded in life force, he suggests that they are not necessary for it. Rather, morality is located in a '*property* of God, life force' (Molefe 2017b, 31; emphasis mine). According to Molefe, or the proponent of this sort of objection, life force is not ultimately a theory about what God commands, no matter how permissive an account of what constitutes divine commands one adopts.

It might seem opaque what precisely it means to say that life force itself acts as the grounds for normativity. Understanding why Molefe believes that such an account avoids the Euthyphro Dilemma will, I think, shed light on the nature of the theory itself. Briefly, the Euthyphro Dilemma asks whether an action is right (or good or permissible) because God recognizes it as good or because God decides that it is right. The former answer implies that morality is independent from God, which poses a challenge to divine sovereignty and aseity. The latter answer implies that morality is arbitrary. Therefore, the dilemma suggests that either morality is independent of God or is arbitrary. Neither horn of the dilemma is supposed to be very palatable to the monotheist attempting to explain how God grounds morality.

In thinking about the dilemma, Molefe says that DCT implies that if God commands infanticide, then it is right. However, on a life force ethic,

176 A MORAL THEORY OF LIVELINESS

infanticide remains wrong because it promotes death, something which ought to be avoided at all costs (Molefe 2017b, 31). Notice, however, that this claim has more to do with how to address commands from God that one finds problematic than with addressing the Euthyphro Dilemma itself.[8] Consider that just because a person finds a divine command counterintuitive, it does not necessarily follow that morality must be either independent of God or arbitrary.

Later on, Molefe says:

> [A]n African religious ethic locates morality on something intrinsic to an individual, [life force]. One does not have to go to any institution, prophet or God to understand that they have life; one is required to deal with an assumption that one has life and one is expected to relate positively with this life. (2017b, 33)

This is interesting but again does not actually explain how an ethic grounded in life force avoids the Euthyphro Dilemma. I believe that Molefe's main claim is just that if morality is based on divine commands, then morality is not an intrinsic part or property of God. If morality is not an intrinsic part or property of God, then it is subject to the Euthyphro Dilemma. Molefe's description of African religious ethics avoids all of this by being grounded in life force, which just flows from God without any commands. This, then, is how an objector might insist the metaethical picture of life force ought to look.[9]

9.5.2 Why Life Force Does Not Avoid the Euthyphro Dilemma

There are at least two problems with the suggestion that an ethic grounded in life force is not susceptible to the Euthyphro Dilemma. The first is that such a claim, as represented in Molefe's comments above, has to assume a

---

[8] Or perhaps this applies to someone who is just exclusively worried about the arbitrary horn of the dilemma.

[9] Molefe also complains that DCT makes morality mysterious, since we do not need to appeal to divine commands to know why something like child abuse is wrong (2017, 32). He also says that even if one accepts DCT, we still have to identify the correct commands (Molefe 2017b, 33). The former becomes less of a worry when the understanding of divine commands is widened to include social norms, strong moral intuitions, etc., apart from what we might call explicit commands. The latter is an epistemological worry that is not particularly unique to DCT. Or, it could perhaps be generated as a problem based on the existence of religious diversity; this would not be a unique challenge to DCT. In any case, I will not address them further, as they are distinct from the Euthyphro Dilemma.

THE METAETHICAL GROUNDS OF LIFE FORCE 177

rather unnuanced approach to DCT. For example, consider that the version of DCT defended by Adams includes a very expansive view of what counts as divine commands. Adams includes the idea that divine commands can come not only from scripture, but also from natural law, ecclesiastical bodies, direct extrabiblical commands, and even from *conscience* or *natural inclination* (1999, 263). God's commands arise from his social interactions with humans in addition to human interests, 'and it is partly because the latter is taken to be an ideal candidate for the role of definitive exemplar of the relevant sort of excellence, that God's commands can plausibly be taken as constituting moral obligation' (Adams 1999, 255). This means that 'God's commands spring from a design and purpose that is good, and that the behavior that God commands is not bad, but good, either *intrinsically*, or by serving a pattern of life that is very good' (Adams 1999, 255; emphasis mine). The devotion to God that is advocated for by Adams is one 'in which love for God is an organizing principle into which one integrates genuine love for other goods that one is to prize for their own sake, as God does' (1999, 275). This theory comes in the broader context of Adams' account of the Good as *excellent*, and his identification of God as the Good. This description gets much closer to saying that commands are grounded in something like a property or character of God (i.e., they somehow inhere in God), which makes them closer to a concept like life force than Molefe and others may suspect.

If Adams is right that God is the Good, then there is a version of DCT that clearly grounds divine commands in a property of God (if not identifies them with God himself). This is hardly different from saying that life force is grounded in and derived from God. More charitably, perhaps Molefe would insist that a difference remains by claiming that on DCT it is logically possible that infanticide *could* be commanded and hence *could* be right. On life force, however, it is logically impossible that something leading to death could ever be good. Fancy interpretive footwork is not necessary here; it is just obvious what acts will protect life and what acts will diminish or end it. Maybe this is all that Molefe means when he suggests that life force fares better than DCT with respect to the Euthyphro Dilemma. After all, there might be a difference between recognizing God as the Good and recognizing life force as the Good. The actions permitted by the latter are just obvious or self-evident, and so in some sense are entirely disconnected from the evaluative judgments of humans in a way that is impossible for Adams' DCT.

178 A MORAL THEORY OF LIVELINESS

Such reflections, however, lead to the second and more pressing problem with respect to claiming that life force avoids the Euthyphro Dilemma. The problem quickly arises from reflecting on the possibility of an inverted moral spectrum. What if what we know to be life-giving were to suddenly cause death? What if what we know to cause death were suddenly to be life-giving? Even though all life force flows from God, it is still possible to ask why one set of actions strengthens life as opposed to some other set. Defenders of life force could respond by doubling down, so to speak, on the above considerations that life force is just life itself; life is life. But what does this precisely mean? Surely the view is not that what is life-giving is just an eternal law or brute fact or necessary truth of the universe. This would be to make morality independent of God.

Yet to say that life force is a property or component or just exudes from God hardly seems different from just identifying God as the Good. Goodness just exudes from God. Importantly, it is also still possible to ask why God used life force instead of something else. Why does one set of actions have a certain effect on life force instead of a different set? Consider the terrible case of rape. On an ethic grounded in life force, rape is wrong because it diminishes the life of the victim (and plausibly the perpetrator's life, too). But what if God had set up the world such that rape increased life force? What if unconsenting sexual intercourse which makes the perpetrator feel a sense of power or sexual gratification increased life force? Would this make rape right? What if the actions that would normally kill a person turned out to strengthen life force? Or, staying within the African tradition, what if murdering someone actually helped to ensure that they would become a departed ancestor with very strong life force?[10]

Once it is recognized that these and similar questions can be asked of a metaethical theory grounded in life force itself, the Euthyphro Dilemma and related worries re-emerge. Either God recognizes that it was good to create and structure the world using life force in addition to recognizing the actions associated with promoting life force as good, or God decided that creating the world in such a way was good. The former entails that an ethic grounded in vitality is independent of God, while the latter implies that such an ethic is arbitrary. In sum, there is little reason to think that an African religious ethic grounded in life force instead of divine commands avoids the Euthyphro Dilemma any better than does the Adams' version of DCT.

---

[10] For more on ancestors, see Bujo 2005; Hamminga 2005; Mbiti 1975.

9.6 Divine Command Theory, Life Force, and Abraham's Dilemma

I now briefly take stock. I have outlined Adams' version of DCT, suggesting that much of it is compatible with life force and the ontology of ATR (9.4). I then addressed an objection which said that this is a misreading of life force and it is life force or life itself that is the metaethical grounds of normativity (9.5.1). While it might be thought that one reason to prefer this view is that it avoids the Euthyphro Dilemma, I argued that this is mistaken. Life force as the grounds of morality is also subject to the dilemma (9.5.2). So where does this leave us regarding the metaethical grounds of life force? Notice that in the above I did not issue a verdict on whether I thought the dilemma was successful. My point was just that life force does no better at avoiding it than does DCT. At this stage I think it is helpful to explore Adams' response to a slightly different problem he labels 'Abraham's Dilemma'.

Though Adams doesn't explicitly address the Euthyphro Dilemma, he addresses an adjacent worry in Abraham's Dilemma, the failure or success of which at least partially maps onto the Euthyphro problem. The basic problem for Adams arises when one asks: what if God commands something evil? The binding of Isaac in the book of Genesis is a paradigmatic case of such a command that theologians and philosophers have puzzled over for centuries. Did Abraham do the right thing when he obeyed God's instructions to bind and prepare Isaac for sacrifice (Adams 1999, 278)? Does not DCT imply that it would have been right for Abraham to sacrifice Isaac, had God not rescinded the original command? Adams acknowledges that if in fact God really did command Abraham to sacrifice his son, then it would have been right for Abraham to do it. In a fascinating move, Adams ultimately says that he agrees 'with Jeremiah that the true God never commanded any such thing—never even thought of doing so, as Jeremiah put it' (1999, 279). Now, as fascinating as this claim is, entering into debates about biblical interpretation is not only far beyond my expertise, but it would take this discussion too far afield. Remember that I am wanting to know about the philosophical plausibility of DCT, and so it is ultimately irrelevant whether God in fact commanded Abraham to sacrifice Isaac. I want to know the implications *if* God issues such a command.

Adams claims that '[t]here is nothing in my metaethics to keep me from saying that child sacrifice was and is a hideous evil in the life of any individual or culture that has practiced it, despite any religious virtues that they

180 A MORAL THEORY OF LIVELINESS

may have exemplified in the practice' (1999, 280). He insists that his account does not have to be relativistic. To understand how he arrives at this conclusion, it is helpful to be more precise about the specific dilemma in question. Adams formulates Abraham's Dilemma as comprising the following inconsistent set:

(1) If God commands me to do something it is not morally wrong for me to do it.
(2) God commands me to kill my son.
(3) It is morally wrong for me to kill my son. (1999, 280)

Adams begins by rejecting the idea that (1) can be given up. What is wrong cannot be necessarily and eternally wrong apart from God (Adams 1999, 280). Notice that this clearly takes a stance on the Euthyphro Dilemma in rejecting the horn which says morality can stand apart from God. Adams explains that he believes 'there are points on which it is contingent what a perfectly good God would or would not determine to be wrong. That is not to say that I think such a deity could ordain sacrifice. The divine nature may be such that it is impossible for God to want such a thing' (1999, 280). For Adams, wrongness is not simply disobeying divine commands. Instead, it is obeying the commands of a perfectly loving God (Adams 1999, 281). Accordingly, '[i]f there were no loving God, then (on an adequately qualified version of my view) no acts (either of obedience or of disobedience) would have the property that I identify with moral wrongness' (Adams 1999, 281–282). (1) is true because on Adams' DCT, wrongness does not exist apart from what is contrary to divine commands.[11]

Adams notes that Kant believes that (2) must be rejected, in part because it is impossible to be certain that it is really God issuing the command (Adams 1999, 284).[12] This points to an epistemological issue, and Adams is

[11] It might be asked at this point if there can be conflicting divine commands such that it would be wrong to follow one command if doing so were to break another (Adams 1999, 282). Adams explains that moral philosophers tend to agree that there can in fact be at least *prima facie* conflicting obligations, where '[s]ome philosophers think it is best to deal with such cases by saying sometimes no available action which it is not *wrong, all things considered* to perform, and that full, genuine guilt is then inevitable' (Adams 1999, 283). However, he rejects this opinion, claiming that there may be cases in which every option is bad 'but there must always be at last one that is not *wrong*. This view is strongly supported by a conception of moral obligation, and of the corresponding possibility of moral wrongness, as constituted by demands of a deity or other persons or a society' (Adams 1999, 283). Moral obligations need to be reasonable in order to generate requirements, and conflicting obligations are not reasonable (Adams 1999, 283).
[12] See Kant, 1798, 283n (Ak VIi, 63) and Kant 1793, 100f., 179f (Ak, VI, 87, 186f).

THE METAETHICAL GROUNDS OF LIFE FORCE   181

in agreement with Kant here (Adams 1999, 284). Earlier in the book, Adams describes God as the Good, which he articulates in more detail through an account of excellence. He explains that '[t]his theological conception is not offered as a way of discovering goodness for the first time, but as an account of the nature of a goodness with which we are assumed to have some acquaintance' (Adams 1999, 284). This implies that '[h]olding such a conception [of goodness], we must test purported messages from God for their coherence with ethical judgments formed in the best ways available to us' (Adams 1999, 284). Adams claims that moral theorizing should reason from ought to is, not is to ought (Adams 1999, 285).

However, this does not mean that (2) should be rejected quickly. If it were, then 'Religion's connection with the transcendent would be threatened if it could not demand costly sacrifices for distinctly religious reasons, or if one's acts of faith and devotion could not be allowed to be costly in any way to anyone besides oneself. If we believe in divine commands at all, we should not want to hold that they can never be surprising' (Adams 1999, 285). Notice that sacrifice for religious reasons is not always wrong. For instance, people have sacrificed themselves at extremely high costs to themselves and to their families for political ideals. Such cases tend to be thought of as at least *prima facie* permissible. This means that sacrifice needs to be permissible in at least some religious cases (Adams 1999, 285). Suppose that Isaac was old enough and consented to being sacrificed. The Jewish tradition often describes him as a consenting adult who welcomed being chosen as a sacrifice (Adams 1999, 288). While this might alleviate some concerns, Adams suggest that it is still the case that '[w]e want to know whether one should believe that God really commanded the sacrifice; and thinking of the sacrifice as suicidal rather than homicidal is hardly enough to remove the objection to regarding the command as genuinely issued by God' (Adams 1999, 288).

Adams' main problem with the binding of Isaac is that it does not arise as a response to a crisis that already exists (1999, 289). For example, the situation is not forced on Abraham or Isaac in having to choose death instead of renouncing their religious loyalty (Adams 1999, 289). What good is the act supposed to have? Commentators often stress the importance of obedience, which may well be very highly valued by God. However, Adams asks, "[b]ut why would God want to be obeyed in such a horrible way?" (1999, 289). Adams claims that dishonours to God to think that he would desire the killing of an innocent person (Adams 1999, 290).

182   A MORAL THEORY OF LIVELINESS

Adams concludes 'that in any cultural context in which it is possible to worry about Abraham's Dilemma it will hardly be credible that a good God has commanded the sort of sacrifice that is envisaged there' (1999, 290). He further recognizes that '[t]o this conclusion it may be objected that an omnipotent deity would have the power to cause a sign that we could not credibly fail to interpret as a genuine command from God to offer otherwise unnecessary human sacrifices. I am not sure this is true' (Adams 1999, 290). But what if it were a certainty that the command came from God? Adams claims that it would then depend on whether the deity in question could reasonably be identified as the supreme God. Adams believes that it is a 'waste of spiritual energy' to consider cases in which God has given an abhorrent command (1999, 290). Though perhaps arriving at this verdict more carefully than Kant, Adams' solution to the dilemma is ultimately to reject (2).

Now Adams is clear enough that *if* God in fact commanded human sacrifice, then God could not be identified as the Good, and therefore would not really be God as such but an entirely different being altogether. It is interesting to consider whether Adams would even consider (2) a logical possibility, given his identification of God as the Good. I myself believe this response is insufficient. Where does the concept of the Good come from? Well, Adams believes we must check the character of God (i.e., the Good) against commonsense moral intuitions. How do these intuitions arise? Different answers have been given, but regardless of what account of them one chooses, it feels like God is being tested against a standard independent of God. Yet at the same time God just *is* that standard. This *might* constitute a middle path of the dilemma, but not one I find very convincing.

How, if at all, does this map onto life force itself as a metaethical theory? Abraham's dilemma as stated by Adams could be reformulated to apply to life force in the following way:

(1)* If something promotes life, it is not morally wrong for me to do it.
(2)* Killing my son promotes life.
(3) It is morally wrong for me to kill my son.

Though I believe that life force itself as the metaethical grounds suffers from the Euthyphro Dilemma because it is possible to ask similar questions of it that one can ask of divine commands, it might fare better than DCT with respect to Abraham's Dilemma. Consider (1)*. If life force exudes from God, it is possible that in the same way God might not ever issue a command

THE METAETHICAL GROUNDS OF LIFE FORCE   183

ordaining child sacrifice, that it might be impossible for child sacrifice to ever be life-giving. Regarding (2)*, it is tempting to say that it is a contradiction in terms. What snuffs out a life cannot simultaneously be life-promoting. It is possible to ask why one set of actions is life-giving as opposed to some other (a problem for the Euthyphro Dilemma), but *if* some action kills, then it can never be permissible on life force. It can never be recommended by life force. Rejecting (2)* may well be easier for the defender of life force than it is for the DCT theorist to reject (2). Much more remains to be said on the relationship between the Euthyphro Dilemma and Abraham's Dilemma, Adams' proposed solution, and the degree to which these dilemmas and solutions apply to life force.

9.7 Conclusion

In this chapter I explained that there is a dearth of literature on metaethics in contemporary African philosophy. What little one can find are attempts to move from claims about metaphysics to normativity. Though I agree with Metz as a general rule that nothing normative follows from metaphysics, this is not true of God's existence. If God exists, this would have a significant impact on normativity. This led me to explore the extent to which, if at all, life force (and ATR) is compatible with DCT. I argued that if Adams' wide conception of what counts as commands is right, then life force could indeed be grounded by a theory like DCT. However, the Euthyphro Dilemma is a serious challenge to it, and claiming that life force itself is the ethical grounds does not successfully avoid this challenge. I concluded by exploring Abraham's Dilemma, and suggested it may be easier for life force to navigate than DCT. My work in this chapter is exploratory and should be taken as an invitation for philosophers who might defend life force to think more about the metaethical architecture it requires to succeed.

I conclude by observing that Adams' theory is strongly grounded in commonsense moral intuitions. In his discussion of the binding of Isaac, Adams is clear that commands that are wrong ought to be rejected. Either they did not really come from God, or God is actually not the Good and hence not worthy of our worship. Intuitions play a very important role in Adams' account, because we're supposed to evaluate God based on them. This naturally raises questions about the reliability of intuitions. Adams might circle back to the claim that moral intuitions typically track the Good,

184 A MORAL THEORY OF LIVELINESS

and God should be identified with the Good. Setting aside worries about whether this is circular, this move is clearly not available for grounding a secular theory of liveliness, because it appeals to God. However, the value that Adams places on intuitions might prove to be a boon for grounding a secular theory of liveliness. At the very least, there is a well-developed metaethical theory known as *intuitionism* that could potentially be employed to ground liveliness. This is the idea that I will explore in the next chapter (10.4).[13]

[13] It's a further interesting question whether Adams' theory itself just reduces to a theory of a kind of intuitionism.

10

The Metaethical Grounds of Liveliness

10.1 Introduction

In this chapter I turn to exploring the potential metaethical grounds of liveliness. Since liveliness is consistent with metaphysical naturalism, the options discussed in the previous chapters of Divine Command Theory or life force itself as potential metaethical grounds are not available here. Remember that I continue to assume that moral realism is true. As such, I believe there are three main possible metaethical theories that could be used to ground liveliness as located in Ideal Observer Theory, Ethical Intuitionism, and Naturalism (i.e., reductionism). I will begin by briefly examining the Ideal Observer Theory, explaining that I am doubtful of its prospects because objections to Divine Command Theory apply to it with more force (10.2). I then observe that the groundwork for an appeal to Ethical Intuitionism already exists in at least one African normative theory found in the work of Thaddeus Metz (10.3), before outlining the basics of the view as located in the work of Michael Huemer (10.4). After this, I tentatively argue that Ethical Intuitionism can be used as the metaethical grounds of liveliness (10.5), and I observe that it should be particularly appealing to moral realists (10.6). I will not, however, discuss the naturalistic view which says that all moral properties can be reduced to non-moral properties (i.e., reductionism). I believe there are good reasons for thinking this is false, though I will not defend this claim here. For those who disagree, this can be taken as an invitation for future research.

10.2 The Ideal Observer Theory

The Ideal Observer Theory became known in the contemporary literature primarily through the work of Roderick Firth (1952, 1955, 1978) and Richard B. Brandt (1955a, b). In this section I explain the theory (10.2.1)

A Moral Theory of Liveliness. Kirk Lougheed, Oxford University Press. © Kirk Lougheed 2025.
DOI: 10.1093/9780197782019.003.0010

186   A MORAL THEORY OF LIVELINESS

before clarifying why I think it would be a mistake to attempt to appeal to it as the metaethical grounds of liveliness (10.2.2).

10.2.1 Firth's Ideal Observer

Firth's description of the ideal observer is that it is objective and dispositional. This means that the truth of ethical claims is independent of humans and that they imply a disposition to act in a certain way (Firth 1952, 317–321). Firth's analysis focuses on 'assertions about the dispositions of all *possible* beings of a certain kind (of which there might in fact exist only one or none at all)' (1952, 320). An ideal observer is a logically possible being who, by definition, knows the truth value of all ethical statements (Firth 1952, 322–323). This is an objective theory because 'it construes ethical statements to be assertions about the reactions of an ideal observer—an observer who is conceivable but whose existence or non-existence is logically irrelevant to the truth or falsity of ethical statements' (Firth 1952, 323). Such a being is relational in that it reacts to ethical statements and is empirical inasmuch as these are psychological reactions. Firth also suggests that ethical properties are natural (1952, 324–329).[1]

Firth believes an Ideal Observer Theory primarily needs to explain the characteristics of such an observer in addition to the conditions under which they will determine the truth value of ethical claims. With respect to the former, he writes that an ideal observer must be *omniscient*, because it is impossible otherwise to know which facts are moral or relevant for moral knowledge (Firth 1952, 333–335). They must also be *omnipercipient*, which means they are able to imagine or visualize all relevant facts and details. The observer needs to be *disinterested* and *dispassionate*, which means they are completely impartial and free from any biases. They are not able to experience emotions that according to Firth would bias their decision-making (1952, 335). The observer needs to be *consistent*, which means having consistent reactions to like ethical claims. Finally, the ideal observer is *normal* in all other respects, which just means that they do not suffer from physical or mental fatigue when evaluating ethical claims. Charles Taliaferro nicely summarizes Firth's ideal observer by explaining that it implies that 'an act

---

[1] Firth's theory may ultimately be a version of the type of reductionism I dismissed in 10.1, but I set this aside.

is morally right if and only if it would be approved of by a being in virtue of his omniscience of the nonethical, omnipercipience, and his approval is not prompted by particular interests and passions' (1988, 129).

Richard Brandt observes that Firth's theory has merit for a variety of reasons, including that it allows us to take a wide selection of facts as relevant to ethical situations. Also, 'it enables us to explain the heterogeneousness of the actions which we regard as right or wrong' (1955a, 407). It can explain why ethical disagreement occurs even when there is agreement about the nature of the act in question. Firth's theory allows our ethical claims to be subject to objective criticism and also takes seriously our 'feelings and attitudes', nicely explaining why 'exceptions' often feel intuitively justified (Brant 1955a, 407). Yet that humans tend to value impartial and unbiased ethical judgments is also well explained. Finally, Brandt suggests that 'it enjoys advantages over the emotive theory such as the capacity to give a satisfactory analysis of "ethically relevant", and the ability to explain why ethical judgments do not always correspond with favorable or unfavorable attitudes on the part of the judge' (1995a, 407).

10.2.2 Problems for the Ideal Observer

I now briefly consider some problems for the Ideal Observer Theory in order to explain why I will not appeal to it as the metaethical grounds of liveliness. One potential worry is that the theory implies relativism. For example, Brant argues that psychological and ethnological evidence suggests that two ideal observers could have completely different responses to the same act (1955a, 408–410). Firth responds that 'it would never be possible to untangle and compare all their [i.e., the ideal observers'] beliefs about psychological, biological, sociological, and theological facts; yet any of these beliefs might make a difference to their interpretation of the situation as a whole' (1955, 415). According to Firth, by hypothesis, if two purported ideal observers issued conflicting ethical verdicts, then at least one of them is necessarily non-ideal. One of them must not have complete knowledge or be completely disinterested and dispassionate (Firth 1955, 416). Though more remains to be said here, I do not believe this is the most troublesome objection to the theory and so I will not spend more time on it.[2]

---

[2] For more, see Brant 1955b; Postow 1978; Firth 1978; Carson 1989.

188   A MORAL THEORY OF LIVELINESS

I believe that a more serious objection to the Ideal Observer Theory is epistemic. Although he ultimately defends the theory, Jason Kawall helpfully explains this worry by asking: '[h]ow are we, as mere humans, ever to know what is morally right on an ideal observer theory? We are not omniscient; nor do we possess unlimited reasoning abilities. The perspective of an ideal observer seems distant and removed at best' (2006, 361). Kawall offers a threefold response. First, he suggests that other theories also suffer from similar problems. Second, he believes that morality is so complex that it is not realistic to expect to know the details of it at all times (2006, 362–363). Third, he claims that the theory is really about showing that objective morality exists, and not about demonstrating how humans are supposed to arrive at moral knowledge. Indeed, he believes that '[t]here is not a devastating epistemic gap here. In most situations we will be adequately informed and of sufficiently good character (or have exemplars to whom we can turn) to reliably anticipate the reactions of ideal observers' (Kawall 2006, 363).

But this epistemic problem is more serious than Kawall suspects. This is especially so given that other metaethical theories are not also subject to it. Consider that Divine Command Theory (DCT), at least as described by Robert Adams, allows for numerous ways of God communicating moral truths, including through things like social norms and institutions (9.4). Likewise, the next theory I will discuss in Ethical Intuitionism does not suffer from this worry, since it suggests that ethical truths are, roughly, directly apprehended (10.4). I also believe that Kawall does not take seriously enough the possibility of genuine moral dilemmas. There could be cases in which there are no people with sufficiently good characters to help us determine the ethical judgements of an ideal observer. Other times, we lack key pieces of information necessary to determine the judgements. Consider an example employed by Jean-Paul Sartre.[3] Pierre lives on a farm outside of Paris during World War II. He can either stay and look after his ailing mother, or he can leave the farm and join the French resistance to help undermine the Nazis. It seems like both options are morally good, and maybe even morally obligatory. And yet it also seems that in the future Pierre will look back on what he decides and know that it was either right or wrong. By hypothesis, Firth's ideal bbserver knows which choice Pierre should make. But there is a significant epistemic gap here, since it is unclear how Pierre should discover which course of action to pursue. Now, it is also possible in this case that a

---

[3] I take Satre's example from Putnam 1992: 191–192.

THE METAETHICAL GROUNDS OF LIVELINESS   189

person may not be able to discern any divine commands that will be of help, nor may they be able to simply intuit the relevant ethical truths. However, it seems to me that this sort of epistemological gap is more fundamentally a part of the Ideal Observer Theory than these alternatives.[4]

Finally, it is unclear how this theory could be used to support liveliness as a normative theory. Perhaps one way is to say that pursuing and prioritizing liveliness is the best way to determine the judgements of an ideal observer. This means that pursuing liveliness helps to solve the epistemic challenge. But I do not see a principled way of defending this claim without already assuming the truth of liveliness. Alternatively, and more to the point, to ground liveliness in an Ideal Observer Theory, it needs to be the case that the judgements of the ideal observer affirm and prioritize liveliness. But I do not know how to show that an ideal observer would make such judgements, at least not in a non-circular way. Indeed, I am tempted to appeal to intuition to ground the judgements of an ideal observer, which only strengthens my motivation to appeal to Ethical Intuitionism.

10.3 Intuition as the Metaethical Grounds of Metz's Friendliness

Before continuing in my exploration of the metaethical grounds of liveliness, it is worth briefly noting how Thaddeus Metz grounds his secular theory of liveliness as rightness for two reasons. First, as shown in the previous chapter (9.2), Metz rejects the tendency in African philosophy to ground normativity in metaphysics. Second, I believe that Metz himself may well be implicitly committed to Ethical Intuitionism. This is noteworthy because he defends a deontological theory of friendliness as rightness (see 7.4). Though I have tried to spell out different ways of thinking about liveliness as a normative theory, it should be clear to the reader that I am partial to deontological approaches to liveliness. It is therefore interesting to see whether the purported grounds of Metz's friendliness could be leveraged as the grounds of liveliness.

What leads me to suspect Metz of being committed to intuitionism? Metz explains that he follows the influential Paulin Hountondji in sidestepping

---

[4] There is also debate about whether omniscience is necessary for the theory, including the worry that if it is necessary, humans cannot possess it (see Bandt 1955a, 409; Firth 1955; Taliaferro 1998).

190 A MORAL THEORY OF LIVELINESS

metaphysical controversies to 'normative approaches to moral disputes in African philosophy' (Metz 2022, 42).[5] He therefore wants to evaluate the general moral principles of his theory against specific moral claims (Metz 2022, 42). For Metz, a general moral principle is plausible to the extent that it 'can make sense of particular cases of right and wrong that are less controversial than it' (Metz 2022, 42). But what precisely are these less controversial and more specific moral claims? It appears that for Metz, these just are intuitions:

> [A]n intuition counts as a judgement that a particular act has some moral feature such as permissibility or a certain degree of wrongness, where that judgement is meant to be less controversial than the principles it is being invoked to evaluate. I do not consider intuitions to be beyond doubt, *self-justifying, or anything so strong as a foundationalist epistemology would suggest.* Instead, they are beliefs that are firmly and commonly held by most informed interlocutors, and for this reason are sensibly taken as provisional starting points for debate; they are judgements that could be overridden in principle, but only with substantial evidence. (2022, 50-51; emphasis mine)[6]

He then adds:

> Although there is fair debate about which intuitions are reliable (with those about remote possible worlds being prima facie more dubious), it looks difficult, if not impossible, to make philosophical headway without them. How else can one provide substantial evidence either in favour of or against a general principle without appealing to its implications for a wide array of particular cases deemed to be less contested than it? (Metz 2022, 51)

Metz believes that what justifies his own theory is that it best explains both African and global intuitions (1.5). So intuitions are doing the work of underpinning his theory at multiple levels. I therefore need to know more about what an intuition is, and how it can plausibly ground a normative theory, in

---

[5] See Hountondji 1996.

[6] The italicized comments suggest that Metz would not accept the version of Ethical Intuitionism I discuss below. However, it is an open question whether he can reasonably appeal to intuitions without making stronger claims about their epistemic status than he is comfortable doing. Indeed, I suspect Metz is committed to Huemer's principle of phenomenal conservatism that underpins the latter's entire theory of Ethical Intuitionism.

THE METAETHICAL GROUNDS OF LIVELINESS   191

order to better assess Metz's claim. More important for my purposes, I need this information in order to discover whether a similar appeal to intuitions can be successfully employed by liveliness.[7]

10.4 Ethical Intuitionism

Ethical Intuitionism can be found in British moral philosophy from the eighteenth century to the 1930s (see Stratton-Lake 2020). From these centuries, I could have chosen to elaborate on the work of Richard Price (1758), Henry Sigwick (1874), or W. D. Ross (1927, 1930, 1939), among others. Instead, however, I choose to explain a contemporary defense of intuitionism as found in Michael Huemer's book *Ethical Intuitionism* (2008). Rather than attempting to summarize the contemporary literature on Ethical Intuitionism, I choose to focus mostly on one work, since my main purpose in this chapter is not to conduct a systematic evaluation of Ethical Intuitionism.[8] Rather, I am attempting to discover whether Ethical Intuitionism can be successfully employed as the metaethical grounds of liveliness, and so exploring one comprehensive statement of it is sufficient for this purpose.[9]

10.4.1 The Basics of Huemer's Ethical Intuitionism

Huemer explains that the view he defends:

> [H]olds that there are objective evaluative facts—facts such as that it is wrong to cause gratuitous suffering to others—over and above the natural, non-evaluative facts; that we have a kind of intellectual insight into some of these evaluative facts; and that they provide us with reasons for behaving in certain ways, irrespective of what we desire. (2008, XXIV)[10]

---

[7] I raise similar points in Lougheed forthcoming.

[8] For a comprehensive survey of intuitionism, see Stratton-Lake 2020.

[9] Of course, it is possible that Huemer's version of ethical intuitionism is not well suited to ground liveliness while a different version of it fits better. I am hopeful that the variances between different versions of ethical intuitionism are not so fundamentally different as to allow for different answers regarding its fit with liveliness.

[10] The typical way of sorting theories in metaethics is between anti-realism and realism. However, Huemer believes a better distinction is between dualism and monism. He explains that 'dualism is the idea that there are two fundamentally different kinds of facts (or properties) in the world: evaluative facts (properties) and non-evaluative facts (properties). Only the intuitionists embrace this'

192   A MORAL THEORY OF LIVELINESS

According to Huemer, Ethical Intuitionism endorses three theses. First, it implies a *semantic* thesis that says '[e]valuative predicates like "good" function to attribute objective features to things' (Huemer 2008, 9). This is just a semantic thesis about what we think we are doing with language; we think language references objective value properties regardless of whether in fact it does reference them. Second, it embraces a *metaphysical* thesis that there are objective values. Certain things really are good and bad (Huemer 2008, 10). Third, it endorses an *epistemological* thesis that helps to justify the metaphysical one. It says that '[w]e are justified in believing some evaluative statements on the basis of rational intuitions. Our knowledge of moral truths is not wholly derived from sensory perception, nor are moral truths all derived from non-moral truths. At least some moral truths are self-evident' (Huemer 2008, 10).

Huemer explains that:

> Intuitions, in my sense, are a sort of mental state or experience, distinct from and normally prior to belief, that we often have when thinking about certain sorts of propositions, including some moral propositions. They are the experiences we report when we say a thing is 'obvious' or 'seems true'. Why are we justified in believing propositions on the basis of such experiences? I argue that, in general, it makes sense to assume things are the way they appear, until proven otherwise. All reasoning and judgment proceed upon this principle, and even the arguments of the moral anti-realists rest upon intuitions. I also argue that many of the objections to the use of ethical intuitions would, if consistently applied, require abandoning sensory perception as well and renouncing all knowledge of the world. (2008, 10)

Huemer also claims that intuitionism implies that sometimes evaluative beliefs are good reasons for actions and can be independent of desires. These moral beliefs sometimes just are the actual motives for action (Huemer 2008, 10).[11]

(Huemer 2008, 8). Huemer believes that all other theories on offer are monist, because they either suggest that there are no value facts (eliminativism) or that value facts necessarily reduce to other facts (reductionism). In the former group there are non-cognitivists or value nihilists, while in the latter there are subjectivists, relativists, and naturalists.

[11] Of course, this means that Huemer rejects Hume's influential account of action which says that actions are always motivated by desires.

THE METAETHICAL GROUNDS OF LIVELINESS   193

Huemer denies the reductionist thesis, which says that any moral property can ultimately be described in natural non-evaluative terms (2008, 66). He rejects reductionism, because he believes that (all) moral claims cannot be known either through deduction from non-moral properties or by the scientific method (via inferences from observation) (Huemer 2008, 96–97). If it turns out that moral 'properties are irreducible, non-natural properties, then it seems that the only way we might be aware of them is by "intuition"— a faculty that contemporary philosophers have been reluctant to embrace' (Huemer 2008, 67).

Though Huemer spends a significant portion of the book purporting to show the defects with other metaethical theories, I am going to mostly focus on his positive case for Ethical Intuitionism. Part of his motivation for rejecting those theories is to show that 'moral claims are assertions about a class of irreducible, objective properties, which cannot be known on the basis of observation' (Huemer 2008, 99).

10.4.2 Huemer's Principle of Phenomenal Conservatism

Huemer's main defense of Ethical Intuitionism rests on what he calls the Principle of Phenomenal Conservatism. This principle says that 'Other things being equal, it is reasonable to assume that things are the way they appear' (Huemer 2008, 99).[12] This is a mental state that Huemer calls an 'appearance'. Appearances have propositional content but are not beliefs and are reflected by statements such as 'it seems that', 'it is obvious that', and 'it appears that' (Huemer 2008, 99). Appearances typically cause beliefs and include things like sense perception, memory, introspection, and intellection. Only appearances can vary in strength and only appearances can overrule initial appearances (Huemer 2008, 100). Huemer acknowledges that '[t]hings can become complicated when many different beliefs and/or appearances are involved, but the basic principle is that we are more inclined to accept what more strongly seems to us to be true' (2008, 100).

There are also what Huemer calls 'intellectual appearances'. For example, '[i]t seems to us that the shortest path between any two points must be a straight line; that time is one dimensional and totally ordered' (Huemer 2008, 100). Logical judgements (e.g., modus ponens) are based on intellectual

---

[12] For more on this principle, see Bonjour 2004 and Huemer 2007.

194 A MORAL THEORY OF LIVELINESS

appearances. A rational person believes what *seems* to be the case to them. This implies that 'The function of arguments is to change the way things seem to one's audience, by presenting other propositions (premises) that seem true and seem to support something (the conclusion) that may not initially have seemed true to the audience' (Huemer 2008, 101). Furthermore:

> Intellectual inquiry presupposes Phenomenal Conservatism, in the sense that such inquiry proceeds by assuming things are the way they appear, until evidence (itself drawn from appearances) arises to cast doubt on this. Even the arguments of a philosophical skeptic who says we aren't justified in believing anything rest upon the skeptic's own beliefs, which are based upon what seems to the skeptic to be true. (Huemer 2008, 101)

This is why Huemer argues that trying to deny Phenomenal Conservatism is self-defeating. It therefore turns out that one has to be an extreme sceptic in order to reject it (Huemer 2008, 101).[13]

To be more precise, 'an intuition that p *is* a state of its seeming to one that p that is not dependent on inference from other beliefs and that results from thinking about p, as opposed to perceiving, remembering, or introspecting' (Huemer 2008, 102). This means that 'An ethical intuition is an intuition whose content is an evaluative proposition' (Huemer 2008, 102). Huemer believes that this description answers those critics who claim that we don't know what an intuition is or that it is an empty concept. For others who wonder whether ethical intuitions exist, Huemer offers the following examples:

- Enjoyment is better than suffering.
- If A is better than B and B is better than C, then A is better than C.
- It is unjust to punish a person for a crime he did not commit.
- Courage, benevolence, and honesty are virtues.
- If a person has a right to do something, then no person has a right to forcibly prevent him from doing that thing. (2008, 102)

Before conducting any arguments, these propositions just *seem* to be true. These are intellectual appearances because they are observed by the senses. Here are some examples of what Huemer says are *not* intuitions:

---

[13] Huemer is clear throughout the book that he is assuming scepticism is false.

THE METAETHICAL GROUNDS OF LIVELINESS 195

- The United States should not have gone to war in Iraq in 2003.
- We should privatize Social Security.
- Abortion is wrong. (2008, 102)

The reason that these are not intuitions is that their truth value depends upon other beliefs. Consider that:

> the sense that the United States should not have invaded Iraq depends on such beliefs as that the war predictably caused thousands of deaths, that this is bad, that Iraq did not have weapons of mass destruction, and so on. This is not to deny that intuition has a role in one's coming to the conclusion that the U.S. should not have gone to war. It is intuition that tells us that killing people is *prima facie* wrong. (Huemer 2008, 102)

Intuitions are not the product of prior held beliefs. If this were the case, they would fail to explain the origin of moral beliefs in the first place. Notice that moral intuitions cannot be caused by prior moral beliefs, since they 'often either conflict with our antecedently held moral theories, or are simply unexplained by them' (Huemer 2008, 103). The case of conflicting intuitions simply shows that additional beliefs are in play. Finally, 'intuitions should not be embraced uncritically, and that conflicting intuitions should be weighed against each other taking into account our best judgments as to their relative levels of reliability' (Huemer 2008, 105).

A number of clarifications are in order. Ethical intuitionists do not need to be dogmatic; intuitions are subject to revision (Huemer 2008, 105–106). Huemer does not rule out the possibility that some intuitions might be infallible but claims that nothing in his theory necessitates them being infallible. Intuitionism does not imply that all moral truths are self-evident. Moral principles can rest on others. It is also not the case that arguments have no role in moral reasoning. This is because '[o]nce we have a fund of *prima facie* justified moral beliefs to start from, there is great scope for moral reasoning to expand, refine, and even revise our moral beliefs, in exactly the manner that the contemporary literature in philosophical ethics displays' (Huemer 2008, 106). Finally, some claim that intuitionism requires an infallible foundation, but Huemer has not discovered any good reason why this should be the case.

There are a handful of epistemological objections to Ethical Intuitionism. One such objection says that we need a reason for trusting ethical intuitions.

196 A MORAL THEORY OF LIVELINESS

However, there is no principled reason why this worry should not also be applied to memory, sense perception, and reason itself, with the result being global scepticism (Huemer 2008, 107). If the objection is really that ethical intuitions require some special justification that these other types of intuition do not, Huemer claims to be unable to identify a principled reason why this is the case (2008, 108). Another epistemic objection worries that intuitions cannot be checked without reliance on intuitions, while empirical beliefs can be checked. However, it is doubtful that all non-moral knowledge can be 'checked'. For example, Huemer asks how introspection could be checked through non-introspective means (2008, 108–109). Finally, another objection is that Ethical Intuitionism can justify any moral belief. However, all intuitionism does is claim that some things are *prima facie* justified, not every belief. That some people may refuse to give reasons or to report their intuitions sincerely says nothing about the possibility of moral knowledge (Huemer 2008, 110).

It is important to recognize that:

> Intuitionism does not hold that from 'I have an intuition that *p*' one may infer '*p*'; nor does the principle of Phenomenal Conservatism hold that 'It seems to me that *p*' is a reason for '*p*'. Those would be claims about *inferential* justification. Phenomenal Conservatism and my version of intuitionism are forms of *foundationalism*: they hold that we are justified in some beliefs without the need for supporting evidence. (Huemer 2008, 120)

This is a type of *non-inferential* justification. Huemer believes that intuitionists should appeal to direct realism in the philosophy of perception, with intuitions not being taken as evidence for moral claims (2008, 121–122). Instead, we are just directly aware of certain moral claims; no evidence is needed in order for them to be justified. Likewise, '[i]ntuitions are not the objects of our awareness when we do moral philosophy; they are just the vehicles of our awareness, which we 'see through' to the moral reality' (Huemer 2008, 122). Finally, this account does not imply that ethical intuitions are infallible. When they are mistaken, then they do 'not constitute direct awareness of moral facts. But this does not prevent the remaining intuitions, those that are true, from constituting direct awareness of moral facts' (Huemer 2008, 122).

10.4.3 Huemer on Disagreement and Error

The strongest objection to Ethical Intuitionism is the existence of moral disagreement. Huemer explains that '[t]here are three versions of the argument. One is that the occurrence of disagreement entails that morality is not objective. Another is that intuitionists cannot plausibly *explain* disagreement or error. The last is that intuitionists have no method of *resolving* disagreements' (2008, 128). But he believes there are answers to these worries.

Regarding the prevalence of moral disagreement, Huemer believes that examples of moral disagreements tend to be cherry-picked and overemphasized. Likewise, many apparent moral disagreements are fundamentally matters of disagreement about some non-moral issue and so are not genuine moral disagreements. There are many more paradigmatic cases of moral agreement (Huemer 2008, 129–131).

With respect to the ability to explain the existence of moral disagreement, anti-realists say they can explain it more readily than can intuitionists. Since there are no objective moral facts, it is unsurprising there is moral disagreement. But intuitionists never say that intuitions are infallible such that everyone will always agree on moral matters (Huemer 2008, 133–134). More charitably, maybe the worry is that 'intuitionism *renders improbable* disagreements *of the kind and number* that we find in moral philosophy' (Huemer 2008, 134). Huemer suggests that intuitionism is not incompatible with long-standing and persistent moral disagreements. Consider that such disagreements exist in other fields where we still insist there is truth (e.g., history, anthropology, economics).

Finally, maybe the problem is that widespread disagreement suggests widespread error. Huemer considers a number of possible sources of error: bias, miscalculation, confusion, misunderstanding and lack of understanding, oversight, hasty judgments, false or incomplete information, stubbornness, fallacies, forgetfulness, intrinsic difficulty of issues, inarticulate evidence, mental defects, etc. (2008, 137–139). There are so many ways for humans to go wrong in their moral thinking that offer an explanation of disagreement that does not involve denying the existence of objective moral facts.

Intuitionism does not predict there will not be lots of moral disagreement. In fact, Huemer actually argues that intuitionism predicts disagreement. This is because disagreements are likely to exist where there are biases in play, and biases are likely to exist about controversial moral subjects

198   A MORAL THEORY OF LIVELINESS

(Huemer 2008, 140). Those pushing objections from disagreement also tacitly assume that metaethical theories must be able to explain and solve the existence of moral disagreement (Huemer 2008, 142). But such an assumption needs to be defended. There needs to be some reason given for holding that a metaethical theory needs to resolve moral disagreements, especially given that intuitionism does not appear to be any worse off than its competitors in this regard.

10.5   Ethical Intuitionism as the Grounds of Liveliness

I submit that Ethical Intuitionism provides a plausible metaethical grounds for the normative theory of liveliness. In the rest of this section, I do more work to explain this claim by addressing a series of questions, some of which may also be taken as initial objections.

10.5.1   Lively Intuitions?

I submit that intuitionism supports liveliness because it establishes the judgement that not only is there something to be strongly preferred to liveliness over unliveliness, but that it is an objectively better state. It is objectively better for a person to exhibit strength, health, energy, and creativity, than depression, anxiety, sickness, weakness, and decay. It is better to be alive than dead. I further submit that these judgements are ethical intuitions in the sense Huemer uses the term. They are seemings, or self-evident. They are directly apprehended but not through observation.

Notice that if I am wrong, and some of these judgments (e.g., strength is better than weakness) are not ethical intuitions, it does not follow that Ethical Intuitionism cannot support liveliness. This is because the various judgements needed to support liveliness could rest on judgements that ultimately rest on intuitions that support liveliness. It could be that the best way to think about normativity is with the liveliness normative moral theory, even if liveliness itself is not directly supported with ethical intuitions. Liveliness may simply be the best outworking of ethical intuitions.

Still, I think there is a case that there are ethical intuitions that demonstrate the truth of liveliness as a normative theory. Consider: life is better than

THE METAETHICAL GROUNDS OF LIVELINESS   199

death. I suppose one could attempt to support this judgement by appealing to all of the goods associated with living. However, these goods would have to be weighed against the harms that come with living.[14] As someone who is rather pessimistic about the human condition, I am perhaps not quite as sure as many others might be about the results of such a weighting. Yet I still have the intuition that living is better than dying, and I think this may well be an intuition in Huemer's technical sense of the term.

10.5.2 Is Ethical Intuitionism Inconsistent with Naturalism?

At first glance it might sound as if Ethical Intuitionism is incompatible with metaphysical naturalism. Ethical Intuitionism implies that ethical properties are not supposed to be able to reduce to natural properties, and so it cannot be appealed to as the explanation of the ethical grounds of liveliness because such an explanation must be naturalistic. However, this type of objection is too quick. It is not quite right to say that ethical properties are not supposed to be reducible to natural properties. Instead, the idea is that they are not supposed to reduce to *non-evaluative* natural properties. This is perfectly consistent with claiming that there are *natural evaluative* properties. It is just that natural moral facts cannot be reduced to natural non-moral facts. My basic point here is just that nothing spooky or supernatural needs to be appealed to in order to deny reductionism.[15]

Now, the objector might respond by reminding us that Huemer defends the thesis that 'moral claims are assertions about a class of irreducible, objective properties, which cannot be known on the basis of observation' (Huemer 2008, 99). If moral properties cannot be observed, then their existence is inconsistent with metaphysical naturalism. But this is false. Metaphysical naturalism does not imply that everything that exists is observable. Consider that the long course of evolution or black holes are not observable and are obviously consistent with Naturalism. The only way this type of objection gets off the ground is by making further assumptions; for example, such as the truth of verificationism.[16]

---

[14] For a discussion of the harms in question see, for example, Benatar 2006.
[15] Also notice that Metz is a naturalist and has no qualms about appealing to intuitions.
[16] See Popper 2002.

10.5.3 Ethical Intuitionism Explains the Possibility of Moral Knowledge, Not Morality Itself

There is an epistemic objection that I suspect some readers will have had earlier in this chapter. Ethical Intuitionism is a theory about how we come to *know* ethical truths. It is a theory about the possibility of moral knowledge. It does not actually tell us where ethical truths come from or how, if at all, they are grounded. Consider how this differs from Divine Command Theory. The latter explains where moral knowledge comes from by suggesting it comes from divine commands. This is so even if it suffers from epistemic problems such as not having enough divine commands, or not being able to accurately identify divine commands, or not being able to deal with (apparently) conflicting divine commands, etc.

The force of this objection depends on what one expects a successful metaethical theory to accomplish. That Ethical Intuitionism establishes the possibility of knowledge of objective moral claims seems to me like a rather significant accomplishment. In other words, I do not deny this objection in the sense that Ethical Intuitionism is indeed a theory about moral knowledge. However, what it purports to establish should not be downplayed. With respect to my purposes, it establishes the possibility of moral knowledge regarding liveliness. This means that it provides a framework for showing the objective truth of the moral claims made by the normative theory of liveliness.

Still, if an objector insists on having a specific metaethical theory that could serve as the grounding for normative claims about liveliness, I recommend to them the work of Erik J. Wielenberg. He defends a view which says that certain ethical truths are necessary truths (Wielenberg 2005, 51). For example, Wielenberg believes that the claim 'suffering is intrinsically evil' is true in every possible world. These exhibit much the same properties as other necessary truths, such as that there are no possible worlds where $2+2 = 5$. Wielenberg claims that the truth of these ethical claims are based on their *essential natures*. Consider that '[i]t is the essential character of the numbers 2 and 5, and of the relations addition and identity, that make it the case that necessarily, $2 + 2$ is not equal to 5. It is the essential nature of pain that makes it the case that it is intrinsically evil' (Wielenberg 2005, 51). He further explains that '[t]hese necessary ethical truths constitute the ethical background of every possible universe. It is within this framework

THE METAETHICAL GROUNDS OF LIVELINESS 201

that all beings and their actions, divine and human alike, are to be evaluated'
(Wielenberg 2005, 52).

Another way of thinking about this is in terms of brute facts. For
Wielenberg, certain ethical facts are brute facts. This is an ontological commitment, not an epistemological one. There is nothing in this view implying
that brute facts cannot be known or inferred from other items of knowledge
(Wielenberg 2014, 36). For Wielenberg:

> Such facts are the foundation of (the rest of) objective morality and rest
> on no foundation themselves. To ask of such facts, "where do they come
> from?" or "on what foundation do they rest?" is misguided in much the
> way that, according to many theists, it is misguided to ask of God, "where
> does He come from?" or "on what foundation does He rest?" The answer is
> the same in both cases: they come from nowhere, and nothing external to
> themselves grounds their existence; rather, they are fundamental features
> of the universe that ground other truths. (2014, 38)

Of course, it would take a significant amount of work to unpack this view
further. My point is just that there is a realist and objective metaethical view
on offer that is consistent with Naturalism.

10.6 Anti-Realism, African Communitarianism, and the Alternative of Liveliness

Some suggest that many theories one finds in African Communitarian
ethics entail cultural relativism. Metz confirms this when he writes that
'[s]ometimes the communitarianism of the African tradition has been
interpreted to mean that a given community's standards constitute what is
right or wrong for its members, where different communities have different
standards, some of which are intuitively wrong for most twenty-first-century
moral philosophers' (2022, 137).[17] Notice that this claim entails anti-realism,
because it implies that the truth value of ethical claims is dependent on persons. The African Communitarian theories in question say that morality is

---

[17] For some specific examples, Metz refers the reader to Mungwini 2019b, 145; Ogbujah 2007,
133–135; Menkiti 1984; Oyowe 2013; Oyowe and Yurkivska 2014.

202 A MORAL THEORY OF LIVELINESS

dependent on the community, which is made up of persons. For example, two of the normative theories I discussed earlier in personhood and teleological harmony suggest themselves as particularly susceptible to implying something like cultural relativism (see 6; 7.2). With respect to the former, morality is about exercising other-regarding virtues in the context of community. Just which traits are considered virtues or vices in the context of community seems to be a function of communal norms that are established over an extended period of time. Regarding the former, morality is about pursuing whatever fosters harmonious relationships within one's community. Presumably, the actions that tend to promote either harmony or disharmony are determined by how the other people in one's community react to those actions. In both cases, the truth of ethical claims is clearly dependent on other persons; their truth value does not depend on God, on the dictates of a logically possible ideal observer, and finally on directly apprehending moral truths (i.e., on intuitions).

That liveliness is amenable to moral realism as demonstrated throughout this chapter is a very attractive feature for anyone who is already inclined towards realism. A committed moral realist is not going to be able to (consistently) adopt a normative theory that entails anti-realism in metaethics. As I have already said elsewhere (1.6, 9.1), I am simply assuming the truth of moral realism in this book. Anti-realists are not going to be very impressed by my claim that a virtue of liveliness is that it is amenable to moral realism. Indeed, what I claim is that a favourable feature of the theory will be viewed by them as an undesirable bug. But since I am not evaluating the debate between moral anti-realists and moral realists, my point is just that if one already accepts moral realism, then liveliness will be even more appealing to them than some of the other African moral theories.

10.7 Conclusion

The purpose of this chapter was to explore possible realist metaethical grounds for liveliness. The Ideal Observer Theory could supply such grounds if the judgements of the observer turned out to support liveliness. However, I suggested that epistemic challenges levelled against Divine Command Theory apply with more force to the ideal observer, and so did not endorse it. Instead, I suggested that a more promising metaethical theory for liveliness is Ethical Intuitionism. I outlined the version of it as found in the work of Michael Huemer, who holds that ethical claims can be directly apprehended. This is a type of non-inferential knowledge that does not need evidence in order to be justified. I claimed that this theory can be used to ground liveliness because at least some of the truth claims of liveliness are known by intuition. Even if this is incorrect, it can still support liveliness, provided judgements supporting liveliness ultimately rests upon ethical intuitions. I further claimed that this account is consistent with metaphysical naturalism, and the fact that it is a theory about moral knowledge should not be trivialized as insignificant.

As I said in the previous chapter (9.3), there is a dearth of metaethical work in contemporary African philosophy, especially compared to the rich discussions one finds in normative and applied ethics. Perhaps more than any other part of the book, this and the previous chapter should be taken by the reader as exploratory. I am well aware that there is a significant amount of literature in metaethics that I did not interact with here. This is because my primary aim was to construct a plausible realist metaethics for life force (Ch. 9) and especially for liveliness (Ch. 10). I have merely scratched the surface of many important topics in metaethics, some of which could easily merit their own full-length books.

Finally, it is also worth noting that I focussed on exploring the extent to which metaethical theories from the Anglo-American philosophical tradition could be used to ground liveliness. Two topics readily present themselves for further development. First, it is an open question what existing theories, if any, could be used to support other African normative theories. Second, notice that I have focused on using already available theories in the Anglo-American tradition. But it is highly likely that there are resources in the African philosophical tradition that can be appealed to in order to establish unique African metaethical theories. This is all the more reason to believe that this discussion is just the beginning for African metaethical ethics.

11

Liveliness and Meaning in Life

11.1 Introduction

The last aspect of a moral theory of liveliness I aim to develop has to do with the meaning of life. Though considerations about the meaning in life are sometimes referenced in the African tradition, an explicit body of literature devoted to this topic has emerged only quite recently. Given the explosion of work on the meaning of life in Anglo-American philosophy over the past twenty years, the time is undoubtedly ripe for cross-cultural dialogue on this important topic. In this chapter, I aim to improve upon the current literature on African theories of meaning in life by more fully developing a theory of meaning based on liveliness, noting relevant differences between it and a theory that appeals to life force instead.

I begin by explicating the basic ideas involved in the life force theory of meaning (11.2). This includes explaining the meaning implied by both liveliness and life force. I then turn to outlining two objections developed by Thaddeus Metz to the liveliness theory of meaning (11.3). The first is based on the claim that liveliness cannot account for intuitions about the value of certain types of knowledge, because in the African philosophical tradition knowledge or understanding is not usually thought of as valuable in itself. The second is that liveliness cannot account for the value arising from certain types of progress. I counter that there are resources in the African philosophical tradition to respond to these objections, thereby filling out the liveliness theory of meaning in important ways. Specifically, I respond by noting that in other work Metz has developed a defense of the intrinsic value of knowledge that is consistent with certain African traditions by appealing to the idea that meeting a person's existential needs can be important for self-realization and hence for their meaning (11.4). I conclude by suggesting that the relationship between knowledge and liveliness is not causal (11.5). However, I tentatively argue that the relationship between them could plausibly be construed as constitutive. It is an appealing feature of liveliness in that not only does it offer a comprehensive normative

A Moral Theory of Liveliness. Kirk Lougheed, Oxford University Press. © Kirk Lougheed 2025.
DOI: 10.1093/9780197782019.003.0011

LIVELINESS AND MEANING IN LIFE   205

theory for moral decision-making, but it also provides a plausible account of meaning in life.

11.2 Life Force, Liveliness, and Meaning in Life

The purpose of this section is to focus on what constitutes a theory of meaning in life based on life force. Before doing so, however, a clarifying caveat about methodology is in order. I am intentionally writing of African theories of meaning *in* life as opposed to meaning *of* life. The latter tends to denote questions about the meaningfulness of the entire human species. Is there a purpose for which humanity was created? Is there something beyond us that we ought to seek connection with? The former, however, is typically about the meaningfulness of an individual's life. This chapter focusses on meaning *in* life, as this tends to be the focus of discussions of meaning in African philosophy (Metz 2020b: 114). Though it should be clear from Chapter 3 that the protecting and strengthening of life force or liveliness is the most important way in which a person's life can be meaningful, I briefly pause to make this connection explicit.

K. C. Anyanwu says that 'ultimate reality' would be without value if it did not contain life force, because life itself is the highest value. The way in which a person lives their life is supposed to recognize this fact (Anyanwu 1987b, 37, cited in Metz 2020b, 119). Noah Dzobo claims there is a 'creative energy in life' that helps people achieve wholeness and health. He writes that 'the essence of the ideal life is regarded as power and creativity, growth, creative work and increase have become essential values. Powerlessness or loss of vitality, unproductive living, and growthlessness become ultimate evils in our indigenous culture' (Dzobo 1992, 227, 230, quoted in Metz 2020b, 119). This implies that procreation is one of the highest values because it is a way to create and increase life force. Likewise, productive work is a way to exercise one's creative potential. A meaningful life is therefore about participating in life-giving activities.

Turning to additional thinkers beyond those cited by Metz, there are numerous other statements that affirm the connection between life force and meaning. For example, according to E. Elochukwu Uzukwu, a person's destiny or purpose is about trying to protect and increase life itself, which is synonymous with life force (1982, 196). Pantaleon Iroegbu holds that the highest purpose of life is to *live* for others and God (2005b, 448). Bert

Hamminga claims that the highest aim in life is to have children with strong life force (2005, 58). For Peter Kasenene, 'supreme happiness' amounts to having the strongest life force, while the worst thing that can befall a person is the weakening of their life force through illness or injustice and the like (1998, 140). Bénézet Bujo declares that the meaning of life is about the flourishing of life itself (2001, 62). Finally, Laurenti Magesa suggests that meaning is fundamentally about creation, which necessarily involves life (1997, 285). According to these thinkers, the purpose of life is to develop the life force in oneself and in others.

Regarding secular liveliness, the more that one protects or promotes liveliness, the more their life is meaningful (Metz 2020b, 119). On this view, the purpose of life is to develop liveliness in oneself and in others, implying that 'one's purpose is to produce in them properties such as health, growth, reproduction, creativity, vibrancy, activity, self-motion, courage, and confidence' (Metz 2020b, 119). On the other hand, one ought to avoid and seek to reduce 'disease, decay, barrenness, destruction, lethargy, passivity, submission, insecurity, and depression' (Metz 2020b, 119). These ideas combine to form the following theory that I will call the *liveliness theory of meaning in life*: 'A human person's life is more meaningful, the more that she promotes liveliness in herself and others' (Metz 2020b, 119–120).

11.3 Two Objections to the Secular Liveliness Theory of Meaning in Life

Though Metz advocates that an African theory of meaning in life based on liveliness ought to be considered as a legitimate contender on a global stage, he claims that it struggles to accommodate certain global intuitions about what confers meaning. The first set of intuitions rests on the idea that some knowledge is intrinsically valuable, while the second set affirms the value of progress.

11.3.1 Knowledge as Intrinsically Valuable

The first set of global intuitions that liveliness struggles to explain has to do with the idea that certain instances of knowledge are intrinsically valuable (Metz 2020b, 121). Considering that false beliefs can sometimes detract from meaning, there is something intuitively sad about cult members (Metz 2020b, 120–121). Consider the members of the Heaven's Gate cult who committed suicide based on the belief that they would be taken to a spacecraft ultimately going to paradise. We also rightly pity the schizophrenic who thinks the devil or evil spirits are controlling them. His key claim is that the appropriateness of our reactions is well explained by the fact that having false beliefs about the fundamental nature of reality partly contributes to a reduction of meaning in life (Metz 2020b, 120–121).

The problem is that according to Metz, false beliefs do not necessarily reduce a person's liveliness (2020b, 21). It is tempting to reply that in the cases of the false beliefs mentioned above, the harmful results would clearly decrease a person's liveliness. But the reply would be that if a false belief does not lead to harmful consequences, then it does not reduce the meaning of a person's life (Metz 2020b, 121). However, Metz insists that it is the false beliefs themselves, not just their consequences, that at least partly contribute to a loss of meaning. Suppose a person believes a Flying Spaghetti Monster created the human species ten thousand years ago. Metz claims that a person who believes this has a less meaningful life in light of such a belief, even if it does not harm them and in fact makes them feel good (2020b, 121).

Alternatively, another problem for liveliness is that it cannot capture global intuitions about how true beliefs can confer meaning on a person's life. Consider Charles Darwin and the theory of natural selection. Presumably, 'the theory of natural selection conferred great meaning on Darwin's life, most plausibly in virtue of what the theory is about and not so much in virtue of whether it has made (or had been likely to make) people more healthy, creative, or the like' (Metz 2020b, 121). Furthermore, the ideas were deemed 'dangerous' by some, uprooting their important beliefs about how human life arose. Even if the theory caused people to feel worse, it was still very important knowledge (Metz 2020b, 121). The same would be true of a cosmologist who discovered the fate of the universe, even if that fate was that it would end and this knowledge caused people's lives to lose meaning and they became depressed (Metz 2020b, 121). In short, it is intuitively obvious that the discovery of true beliefs can confer meaning on a person's life but that liveliness has a difficult time explaining why this is the case (Metz 2020b, 121).

These two cases have to do with knowledge, and the heart of the problem here is that the majority of African philosophers tend to deny that knowledge is valuable for its own sake. Knowledge, understanding, true belief, and so on ought to be pursued only if they can be reasonably expected to yield

208 A MORAL THEORY OF LIVELINESS

practical benefits (Metz 2020b, 122–123). Metz concludes this objection by asking, '[i]s there really no loss of meaning insofar as one, say, believes that a Flying Spaghetti Monster created us not long ago? Was there really nothing to admire about Darwin's life simply in virtue of his deep insight into how humanity arose?' (Metz 2020b, 123).

Elsewhere, Metz addresses five justifications given for using public funds to support a university in an African context. These are that universities foster development (socioeconomic), support culture (preserve and transmit it), rectify injustices, foster (normative) personhood, and realize the majority's aspirations (Metz 2009, 185–187). Metz suggests that the latter two justifications should be replaced with the justifications that universities help to realize equal opportunity and facilitate cooperation (2009, 191–192). His discussion is illuminating, because none of his justifications appeal to the fact that knowledge is intrinsically valuable. Indeed, Metz writes that 'in a critical survey of dozens of works by African thinkers on the point of higher education, I [i.e., Metz] could not find one that extolled knowledge for its own sake.... It might be, however that Léopold Senghor would, upon reflection, do so' (Metz 2019, 2 fn1; e.g., Balogun 2008a, 2008b, 2013; Dowling and Seepe 2003; Nabudere 2006; Nwakaeze-Ogugua 2006; Oladipo 1992; Seepe 1998; Wiredu 2004).

11.3.2 The Value of Progress

Arguably, liveliness also has difficulty explaining the value of progress (Metz 2020b, 121–123). Consider that many will share the intuition that there is something uniquely valuable about being the first to make a discovery about an item of knowledge. For example:

> Consider Albert Einstein's revelation that space and time are affected by the mass of objects in them. He was the first person, if not to have conceptualised general relativity, then at least to have provided a solid justification of it. Making that breakthrough was meaningful, not merely because of what it was about [. . .], but also because of its novelty. Einstein *advanced* our understanding of the nature of reality, as have those who have recently discovered species of hominids.... It is hard to see how . . . liveliness . . . can explain the importance of novelty relative to what other enquirers have done in the past. (Metz 2020b, 121)

It is tempting to reply that such discoveries would indeed increase the liveliness of the discoverer. For instance, on those admittedly rather rare occasions when I feel I have discovered an important philosophical insight or made an interesting conceptual connection, it is reasonable to describe what I experience as an increase in liveliness. But the point here is that it is not just the lively *effect* of making a discovery but the accomplishment of making the discovery itself that confers meaning. Imagine a person who fifty years after Einstein, having somehow never heard of his discoveries, replicates them by coincidence. Though the same intellectual labour could have been involved, there is something less impressive in virtue of it occurring after Einstein had already made the discoveries. This is so even if making the discoveries after Einstein would have the same impact on one's liveliness (Metz 2020b, 122).

There is, therefore, a difference between the feelings that might result in liveliness and the fact of making an actual novel discovery. Again, I recall those rather rare occasions when I believe I have made a genuinely novel and interesting philosophical insight, only to have a referee inform me that the claim was already made elsewhere in work I overlooked while conducting research. Metz says that the false belief of having made an original discovery is enough to produce relevant feelings of liveliness (Metz 2020b, 122). Conversely, someone could make a discovery without knowing it and so feel no increase in liveliness. Yet such a discovery remains meaningful (2020b: 122). This is not to deny that the realization that one has made a discovery will increase liveliness. Instead, the point is just that it is the discovery itself that is valuable and so confers meaning, irrespective of whether it also happens to bring an increase in the person's liveliness.

The final problem for the liveliness theory of meaning is its purported inability to account for the ways in which the overall pattern of a life can make it more or less meaningful. Consider that there is *pro tanto* reason to think a life with less repetition is better than one with a lot of repetition, but that liveliness cannot explain why this is the case (Metz 2020b, 122). Additionally, consider that if the total sum of a life is held fixed, a life is more meaningful if it gets better over time instead of worse. Liveliness cannot explain this intuition (Metz 2020b, 122). Now, Metz acknowledges that awareness of the fact that one's life is repeating or that it is gradually improving can affect liveliness. However, the worry is that liveliness cannot explain the intuition behind the idea that all else being equal, a repetitive life is less meaningful than one that is not, even if one is unaware of the repetition. Nor can it explain why a life that gets better over time is more meaningful than a life that

210 A MORAL THEORY OF LIVELINESS

gets worse or stays the same over time even if one is aware of this fact (Metz 2020b, 122). The strength of these examples about repetition and structure:

> Turns on an appeal to the importance of progress. Being the first to have made a certain accomplishment and living in a way that consistently improves until the end are both well understood as kinds of advancement. African philosophers do of course distinguish between better and worse ways of living for human beings, and so are committed to maintaining that a human life can usually admit of improvement. However, that point is different from prizing original contributions or linear development in a person's life as meaning-conferring. (2020b, 123)

Though Metz says that his appeals to knowledge and progress in these ways are more typical of the Modern Western tradition than of the African intellectual tradition, he believes that many of his readers, including Africans, will feel the strength of the examples he has offered. In what follows, I am simply going to assume that Metz is correct about this point. If there are African or other readers who do not see the intuitive plausibility of the examples offered by Metz and are simply happy to 'bite the bullet' and deny their implications for meaning, I presume that at least some who are sympathetic to liveliness feel the weight of the examples. The rest of this chapter addresses these objections, thereby expanding the liveliness theory of meaning in life in important ways.

11.4 Knowledge and Progress as a Form of Self-Realization

My primary response to these worries is based on the claim that knowledge and progress can constitute an important form of self-realization. This is a particularly powerful response, because Metz himself defends this claim in other work.[1] There he explores different approaches to defend the claim that knowledge is intrinsically valuable in ways that are consistent with African thought (Metz 2019: 11–13). Metz accomplishes this by observing that though the needs that tend to be emphasized in the African tradition are biological or social, there is a third set of 'existential' needs that is also important

---

[1] I cannot locate any place where he himself considers it as a potential response to his objections to liveliness as a theory of meaning.

(Metz 2019, 14). Accomplishments that are deserving of lasting admiration and esteem are an important form of self-realization and thereby meet what might be called an existential need. According to Metz:

> If people's dignity gives us moral reason to go out of our way to help them, then the help should include assistance in achieving what is particularly worth having in life, which includes meaning. And if part of caring about people's good is indeed a matter of enabling them to live meaningfully, and if that includes understanding certain objective truths about humanity and the world in which we live, then it follows that we have some reason to promote some knowledge for its own sake. (Metz 2019, 14)

I believe Metz is correct that caring about existential needs is important, and I agree that pursuing knowledge (or the type of progress he describes) can contribute to a person's self-realization, and merit admiration and esteem, and therefore contribute positively to the meaning in their life.[2]

If existential needs are indeed legitimate, then meeting them is important on a liveliness theory of meaning. Notice that Metz has (perhaps inadvertently) provided a solution to his own objections to the liveliness theory of meaning in life. This is because if a person achieves self-realization, accomplishing something that merits admiration and esteem, their liveliness will be increased. Consider that Noah Dzobo writes, 'to our people, value is primarily the power to satisfy human needs' (1992, 224). Knowledge and progress are important forms of self-realization. The sort of pride and self-worth one might feel is an indication of liveliness although such feelings are not strictly necessary in order for self-realization itself to occur. It is having one's existential needs met that plausibly contributes to liveliness.

Now, recall the case of the cosmological discovery about the end of the universe. According to Metz, if people found the discovery to be depressing, then it would detract from the meaning in their life (2020b, 121). But there is no tension between this fact and the claim that the discovery increases the cosmologist's liveliness. The consequences of her research may well depress others, but this does not change the fact that discovering knowledge or making progress is reasonably connected to her self-realization and hence to

---

[2] Notice that even if this is false, I can still appeal to this as a solution for Metz because it is located within his own work. Assuming what I say next is right, then someone else could raise this objection, but not Metz himself (on pains of inconsistency).

the meaning in her life. Indeed, that liveliness can explain both the increase and the decrease of the different parties in this case seems to be a theoretical virtue.

For certain individuals, it is reasonable that knowledge and progress are part of their self-realization. This is an existential need that ought to be recognized by their community in addition to the social or biological needs more typically recognized in the African tradition. If such needs are indeed genuine, then they plausibly contribute positively toward a person's liveliness. Thus, Metz's own work on why knowledge is intrinsically valuable in an African context provides the solution to his own problem cases for liveliness.

11.5 Liveliness and Knowledge: Constitutive or Causal?

The idea that knowledge increases liveliness has recently been explicitly defended by Ada Agada:

> Since vital force is the energy of life, determining the mode and extent of survival, it stands to reason that a meaningful life will be one that maximises vital force in all aspects of a person's life. Positive states of mind and affects like optimism, hopefulness and joy are to be maximised, while negative states of mind and affects like pessimism, nihilism, fearfulness and sadness are to be minimised. Knowledge must be pursued and ignorance rejected. (Agada 2020b, 103, quoted in Metz 2023, 349)

Metz claims that Agada is unclear on whether the relationship between liveliness and knowledge is causal or constitutive and that there are problems for either position. On the former view, obtaining knowledge causes an increase in a person's liveliness. Since I agree that this position will have difficulty explaining why knowledge is intrinsically valuable instead of only valuable as a means, I am going to focus on developing the latter position that says acquiring knowledge constitutes a form of liveliness (see Metz 2023, 349). I therefore build on Agada's account by expanding it and defending it from objections offered by Metz.

Metz writes that if knowledge is constitutive of liveliness, then 'certain kinds of awareness, say, accurately apprehending the fundamental nature of reality and of humanity are themselves instances of robust vitality, where vitality is what accounts for the intuitive meaning involved' (Metz 2023, 349).

More precisely, the view can be defined as follows: It is an instance of liveliness when S becomes aware at T_1 that proposition P, where the content of P is important. Metz also adds that establishing greater coherence across one's set of beliefs would come with an increase in life force (Metz 20223, 349).

According to Metz, the problem with this approach is that it cannot tell us the difference between truths that are important for meaning and those that are trivial (2023, 349). If a person changes their mind about whether God exists, it is reasonable to think this might come with an increase in liveliness. However, there is no principled way on this view to explain why awareness of how many redheads live in Beiseker, Alberta, would not be an instance of liveliness.[3] But of course, it is absurd to think that such knowledge is important. Metz claims that the topic in question is what matters regarding meaning. It is the propositional content that explains why holding a particular belief happens to be meaningful. But the propositional content is logically distinct from liveliness (Metz 2023, 349). This is interesting, because the worry in this most recent work from Metz is that positing a constitutive relationship between knowledge (or progress) and liveliness is not that liveliness cannot accommodate the claim that certain types of knowledge are intrinsically valuable. Instead, Metz worries that liveliness cannot accommodate the strong intuition that some types of knowledge are more valuable than others.

Recall that the values indicative of liveliness are 'health, growth, reproduction, creativity, vibrancy, activity, self-motion, courage, and confidence' (Metz 2020b, 119). While a person could insist that counting blades of grass or discovering how many redheads there are in Beiseker contributes to their creativity, vibrancy, courage, confidence, and so on, and therefore to their self-realization, there is nothing in the liveliness theory that rules out a person being mistaken about what is lively. It is doubtful that awareness of the number of blades of grass or the number of redheads is really an instance of liveliness. But that a person can be mistaken about what is meaningful merely implies that human beings are fallible judges with respect to meaning. This fallibility seems to accord well with the common human experience about sometimes being mistaken about what sorts of activities would confer meaning on our lives (e.g., Penner 2015, 335). Though acknowledging the fallibility of our judgments should help assuage this worry, it is instructive to consider briefly two alternative responses to account for the difference

---

[3] Metz borrows this case from Hurka 1993, 155.

214 A MORAL THEORY OF LIVELINESS

between trivial and important knowledge, responses that could be appealed to by the proponent of the liveliness theory of meaning. I suggest that the first alternative is not very promising but that the second is worth serious consideration.

The first alternative account can be found in recent discussions in epistemology to help explain the difference between trivial and important beliefs. For example, Jane Friedman explores the consequences of a principle first offered by Gilbert Harmen about what to believe: 'Clutter Avoidance. One should not clutter one's mind with trivialities' (Friedman 2018, 568; see also: Christensen 1994; Feldman 2000; Williamson 1998). According to Friedman, a belief is trivial for a person if they have no interest in it (Friedman 2018, 569). What makes her discussion normative is the suggestion that people should avoid forming beliefs on trivial matters. Yet, it is quickly apparent that a defense of this principle will be of no help here. Suppose that a person insists that identifying the number of redheads is important for self-realization, or, in Friedman's terminology, they insist that it is in their interests. This discussion in epistemology is not addressing the more fundamental question about what in fact is trivial and what is important.

The second alternative approach is to attempt to offer a more tangible set of criteria about how to differentiate between important and trivial knowledge. Interestingly, Metz's own theory of meaning in life could be appealed to for such criteria. According to his account of meaning, what confers meaning on our life transcends our animal nature, is worth pursuing for its own sake, and merits our esteem and admiration (see Metz 2013b). Not only can meriting esteem and admiration help explain why knowledge and progress are valuable in the first place (as shown above), but they are also intuitively helpful criteria for distinguishing between important and trivial types of knowledge. Knowledge about the number of redheads in a small town in northern Canada does not merit esteem and admiration. However, discovering who created and controls the universe, if anyone does (assuming such a discovery is even possible), does merit esteem and admiration. Again, this means that meriting esteem and admiration can be understood as indicators of whether awareness of a certain truth should be considered an instance of liveliness. This account need not deny that humans are fallible about what merits esteem and admiration. Of course, much more remains to be said, but this is the makings of a way to tell the difference between trivial and important types of knowledge that is consistent with the claim that knowledge is constitutive of liveliness. Once again a potential solution appears in Metz's own work.

Finally, if it turns out that liveliness really is worse off regarding distinguishing between trivial and important knowledge than are other theories of meaning, it does not follow the theory ought to be rejected. Remember that my purpose has been to explore the plausibility of a theory of meaning grounded in liveliness. If the theory turns out to be deficient in this matter, it does not mean the theory should be jettisoned altogether. After all, there were reasonable answers to all of Metz's other objections, and that may be reason enough to consider the liveliness theory of meaning.

11.6 Conclusion

The liveliness theory of meaning in life says that a life is more meaningful the more it promotes liveliness in others and in oneself. Metz believes that this theory has difficulty accommodating two sets of intuitions. He claims that a liveliness theory of meaning cannot explain why pursuing knowledge because of its intrinsic value can confer meaning on a life nor can it explain a similar claim regarding the value of progress. I argued that a solution to this problem can be found in other parts of Metz's work. Elsewhere he suggests that African theories of meaning should also consider existential needs beyond just the social and biological. Pursuing knowledge or progress for its own sake is an existential need that can contribute to a person's self-realization and thus confer meaning on their life. But an accomplishment that merits admiration and esteem plausibly increases a person's liveliness. Thus, liveliness can explain how pursuing knowledge and progress can confer meaning on a person's life once such pursuits are recognized as an existential need. I conclude that, contra Metz, it is reasonable to think that the knowledge that would increase one's liveliness is constitutive of it. The sort of knowledge that is valuable will be closely connected to a person's self-realization. This means that discovering this type of knowledge is likely to merit our esteem and admiration. Still, human beings are ultimately fallible judges about meaning and can therefore be mistaken about what instances of knowledge are constitutive of liveliness. In keeping with the spirit of much of the rest of the book, my conclusions in this chapter are tentative. As it stands, I have shown that there are reasonable responses to Metz's objections to the liveliness theory of meaning in life and, as such, that theory merits consideration among both African theories of meaning and globally better-known alternatives.

12
Conclusion

12.1 Introduction

The purpose of this book has been to construct a moral theory of liveliness that deserves to be considered as a serious competitor to the other African moral theories in those that focus on personhood or harmony. In the future, I hope it will be considered alongside moral theories on a global stage. While this book is not a work of ethnophilosophy, it is difficult to see how philosophy can proceed without any reference to cultural norms and beliefs. In explicating life force, I focused mostly on accounts from contemporary African scholars (Part I). This work tends to be merely descriptive and so does not usually offer explicit moral theories. Still, from them I was able to glean the following principles of right action:

- An action is right if and only if it strengthens, preserves, and protects the life force of oneself and one's community.
- An action is wrong if and only if it weakens and degrades the life force of oneself and one's community.
- An action is permissible inasmuch as it strengthens, preserves, and protects the life force of oneself and one's community.
- An action is impermissible inasmuch as it weakens and degrades the life force of oneself and one's community (see 3.3.3).

I then sought to naturalize this theory by appealing to what I call liveliness (Part II). A person is lively if they exhibit qualities such as confidence, creativity, reproduction, and health. This I construed in terms of force, not substance. I addressed whether naturalizing life force is legitimate, since doing so appears to deny ontological holism. Though I offered no conclusions, it is interesting that panpsychism may offer a potential solution to this problem.

The ethical principles that emerged from naturalizing life force are teleological and deontological. Regarding the former:

A Moral Theory of Liveliness. Kirk Lougheed, Oxford University Press. © Kirk Lougheed 2025.
DOI: 10.1093/9780197782019.003.0012

CONCLUSION 217

- An action is right inasmuch as it increases (or can reasonably be expected to increase) the life force in oneself and in others.
- An action is wrong inasmuch as it decreases (or can reasonably be expected to decrease) the life force in oneself and in others (see 5.2.1).

With respect to the latter:

- An action is right inasmuch as it respects individuals in virtue of their capacity to be lively.
- An action is wrong inasmuch as it degrades those with the capacity to be lively (see 5.2.2).

I suggested that a more complete deontological theory would explicitly incorporate a teleological component in order to better account for moral motivation and various intuitions regarding certain cases:

- An action is right inasmuch as (i) it increases (or can reasonably be expected to increase) the liveliness in oneself and in others and (ii) only inasmuch as it also respects individuals in virtue of their capacity to be lively.
- An action is wrong inasmuch as (iii) it decreases (or can reasonably be expected to decrease) the liveliness in oneself and in others and (iv) inasmuch as it degrades those with the capacity to be lively (see 6.8).

These imply an account of moral value, but I focussed mostly on what they have to say about right action. Though I explored both teleological liveliness and deontological liveliness, I tended to favour the answers to various cases and problems provided by the latter. I argued that liveliness is superior to the other major African moral theories on offer, at least in the context of certain problems (Part III). With respect to normative personhood, it does not face the same difficulties in explaining how to balance competing interests between the individual and the community. Regarding teleological harmony, it avoids cases that seem to trample on human rights or dignity. With respect to Metz's moral relational theory, it does not struggle as much in issuing the intuitively correct verdict regarding certain difficult cases.

To conclude, I shifted the discussion towards exploring the possible metaethical grounds of liveliness, moving well beyond what one normally finds in African philosophy (Part IV). I suggested that it is not entirely clear

218 A MORAL THEORY OF LIVELINESS

how to ground an ethic based on life force, particularly given that it does not avoid the Euthyphro Dilemma any better than Divine Command Theory. With respect to the metaethical grounding of liveliness, I appealed to ethical intuitionism. To conclude, I showed that liveliness lends itself nicely to a coherent account of meaning in life.

My hope is that I have offered the most systematic discussion of the moral implications of life force and liveliness found in the literature to date. Given that work on life force in the philosophical literature has tended to be descriptive, I hope to have moved the discussion forward in focussing on moral theory. I would like to re-emphasize to the reader that my goal has not been to defend any moral theory of liveliness as true, but instead to show that a serious moral theory can be derived from the life force tradition. In what follows, I conclude the book by discussing the future of liveliness as a moral theory (12.2), and why global moral philosophy is important (12.3)

12.2 The Future of Liveliness as a Moral Theory

Despite my hope that this is the most systematic work on the ethics of life force and liveliness to date, numerous topics for further research remain. In this section, I briefly touch on the ones that appear as the most obvious candidates for future development.

12.2.1 Anti-Realism

As I mention in 9.6, anti-realists could seek ways of reinterpreting the results of this book into anti-realist terms. It is not lost on me that some readers will consider my assumption of moral realism to be a very large and untenable one. I do not know whether a moral theory based on liveliness could be consistent with moral anti-realism, but I would be very curious to see such anti-realist models of it.

12.2.2 Other Moral Theories

Though I have discussed liveliness in comparison to other African moral theories (Part III), there are numerous other theories worthy of serious consideration. For example, though Chapter 6 contains some treatment of utilitarianism, I noted that there are far more nuanced versions of it in the literature. Likewise, I said very little, if anything, about the various versions of deontology and virtue ethics that one finds in the Anglo-American literature. All of this is to say that there are numerous other theories that the moral theory of liveliness ought to be evaluated against. Furthermore, this says nothing of the other moral theories outside of the African and Anglo-American traditions. Mastering all of the relevant literature would be a very tall order for any individual, and so it is best to understand this book as a modest contribution to the collaborative project of globalizing ethics.

12.2.3 Life Force across Different Indigenous Societies

As suggested in 3.4, life force or similar concepts arise in many other indigenous cultures around the globe. Various indigenous cultures appear to affirm some type of animism. This is not just an interesting sociological fact. That life force has not been taken up as a plausible way of understanding morality by Anglo-American philosophers runs the risk of missing out on important ethical truths. Many interesting projects arise here. Is the normativity implied by these different indigenous cultures similar, or are there morally relevant differences? If yes, do such differences make it easier or more difficult to naturalize? Indeed, it is difficult to even know the appropriate questions to ask without doing the comparative work itself.

12.2.4 Applied Topics

When I first began drafting this book, I planned for the final part to be focussed on applying the theory of liveliness to various applied topics. However, the project began to grow in unexpected places, and the book would have become far too large and unwieldly to include extensive coverage of applied issues.[1] Some of the success of a moral theory is based on the degree to which it issues the intuitively correct results in applied cases. It also ought to issue consistent verdicts and so treat like cases in like ways. Thus,

---

[1] Indeed, I plan to write a follow-up book devoted to applying liveliness to a wide range of applied ethical topics.

220 A MORAL THEORY OF LIVELINESS

not only would it be inherently interesting to see a liveliness moral theory tackle various applied cases, but it would also be yet another way to evaluate it against competing normative ethical theories.

12.3 Global Approaches to Moral Philosophy

Though the focus of this book is clearly African moral philosophy, given my formal training in analytic or Anglo-American philosophy, it is no surprise that there are frequent citations of and connections to that tradition. Though I am proud of the cross-cultural dialogue that takes place in this monograph, I have pointed out numerous places for further discussion. At this point, one may wonder why I am so keen for these different traditions to speak to each other. Does it really matter if they do not?

It is a matter of epistemic justice that philosophical traditions that have been ignored, particularly in the global south, are taken into consideration (see Fricker 2007; Ndlovu-Gatsheni 2018). Consider that the reasons why these traditions have been neglected thus far are *not* because they have been carefully considered and then discarded by philosophers working in the Anglo-American tradition. Instead, I suspect that colonization, among other problematic reasons, plays a significant role in the causal story of their neglect. Additionally, elsewhere I have argued that there are epistemic benefits to be gained from disagreements in certain contexts (Lougheed 2020, 2022c). A diversity of views in ethics may well foster the kind of disagreement that will help us arrive at the truth. Finally, at the risk of recommending an approach that would paralyze the philosopher who is open to global approaches but does not know where to begin, let me reiterate what I say above: Globalizing the field needs to be understood as a collaborative project. We are (epistemically) better together.

12.4 Conclusion

The moral theory of liveliness I have developed in this book is a serious competitor to the main African alternatives in normative personhood and harmonious relationships. Defenders of those theories need to contend with the African alternative I have put forth in this book. I believe this approach also deserves to be considered alongside the better globally known moral theories from the Anglo-American tradition such as consequentialism, deontology, and virtue theory. I look forward to seeing such interactions.

Bibliography

Adams, Robert. 1999. *Finite and Infinite Goods: A Framework for Ethics*. New York: Oxford University Press.

Agada, Ada. 2015. *Existence and Consolation: Reinventing Ontology, Gnosis, and Values in African Philosophy*. St. Paul, MN: Paragon House.

Agada, Ada. 2019. The Sense in Which Ethno-Philosophy Can Remain Relevant in 21st Century African Philosophy. *Phronimon* 20: 1–20. http://dx.doi.org/10.25159/2413-3086/4158.

Agada, Ada. 2020a. Grounding the Consolationist Concept of Mood in the African Vital Force Theory. *Philosophia Africana* 19 (2): 101–121. http://doi.org/10.5325/philafri.19.2.0101.

Agada, Ada. 2020b. The African Vital Force Theory of Meaning in Life. *South African Journal of Philosophy* 39: 100–112. http://doi.org/10.1080/02580136.2020.1770416

Agada, Ada. 2022a. *Consolationism and Comparative African Philosophy: Beyond Universalism and Particularism*. New York: Routledge.

Agada, Ada. 2022b. Kwame Gyekye as a Pan-Psychist. *Philosophia Africana* 21 (1): 28–44. http://doi.org/10.5325/philafri.21.1.0028.

Agada, Ada. 2023. Rethinking the Concept of God and the Problem of Evil from the Perspective of African Thought. *Religious Studies* 59: 294–310. http://doi.org/10.4314/ft.v11i4.1s.

Allias, Lucy. forthcoming. *Relations, Communing, and Intuitions – a response to Metz's Relational Moral Theory*.

Anyanwu, K. C. 1984. The Meaning of Ultimate Reality in Igbo Cultural Experience. *Ultimate Reality and Meaning* 7: 84–101. https://doi.org/10.3138/uram.7.2.84.

Anyanwu, K. C. 1987a. The Idea of Art in African Thought. *Contemporary Philosophy: A New Survey* 5: 235–260.

Anyanwu, K. C. 1987b. Sound as Ultimate Reality and Meaning: The Mode of Knowing Reality in African Thought. *Ultimate Reality and Meaning* 10: 29–38. http://doi.org/10.4324/9781003451495.

Asante, Molefi Kete. 2003. *Afrocentricity*, rev. ed. Chicago: African American Images.

Attoe, Aribiah D. 2020. A Systematic Account of African Conceptions of the Meaning of/in Life. *South African Journal of Philosophy* 39: 127–139. https://doi.org/10.1080/02580136.2020.1771822.

Attoe, Aribiah D. 2021. Accounts of Life's Meaningfulness from a Contemporary African Perspective. *Philosophia Africana* 20: 168–185. http://doi.org/10.5325/philafri.20.2.0168.

Attoe, Aribiah D. 2019. *An Inquiry into African Conceptions of the Meaning of Life*, PhD diss. University of Johannesburg.

Bacin, Stefano. 2022. Lying, Deception, and Dishonesty: Kant and the Contemporary Debate on the Definition of Lying. In *Kant and the Problem of Morality: Rethinking the Contemporary World*, eds. Luigi Caranti and Alessandro Pinzani, 73–91. New York: Routledge Chapman & Hall. https://philpapers.org/rec/CARKAT-9.

Balogun, Oladele Abiodun. 2008a. Philosophy: What Social Relevance? *Philosophia Africana* 11: 103–116. http://doi.org/10.5840/philafricana20081122.

Balogun, Oladele Abiodun. 2008b. The Idea of an 'Educated Person' in Contemporary African Thought. *Journal of Pan-African Studies* 2: 117–128. https://www.academia.edu/71771001/The_Idea_of_an_Educated_Person_in_Contemporary_African_Thought?uc-sb-sw=12357598.

222 BIBLIOGRAPHY

Balogun, Oladele Abiodun. 2013. Philosophy in an African Culture: A Light in the Darkness. *68th Inaugural Lecture at Olabisi Onabanjo University*. Ago-Iwoye, Nigeria: Olabisi Onabanjo University Department of Mass Communication.

Barnett, Cassandra. 2017. Te Tuna-Whiri: The Knot of Eels. In *Animism in Art and Performance*, ed. Christopher Braddock, 23–44. Switzerland: Springer.

Behrens, Kevin Gary. 2014. Toward an African Relational Environmentalism. In *Ontologized Ethics: New Essays in African Meta-Ethics*, eds. Elvis Imafidon and John Ayotunde Isola Bewaji, 55–72. Lanham, MD: Lexington Books.

Bell, Richard H. 1989. Narrative in African Philosophy. *Philosophy* 64: 363–379. http://doi.org/10.1017/s0031819100044715.

Benatar, David. 2006. *Better Never to Have Been: The Harm of Coming to Existence*. New York: Oxford University Press.

Bennett, Jane. 2010. *Vibrant Matter: A Political Ecology of Things*. Durham, NC: Duke University Press.

Bergson, Henri. 1907. *Creative Evolution*. Trans. Donald Landes. New York: Routledge, 2022.

Bewaji, J. A. I. 1998. Olodumare: God in Yoruba Belief and the Theistic Problem of Evil. *African Studies Quarterly* 2: 1–17.

Biko, Steve. 2004. *I Write What I Like*. Johannesburg: Picador Africa.

Bikopo, Deogratias, and Louis-Jacques van Bogaert. 2010. Reflection on Euthanasia: Western and African Perspectives on the Death of a Chief. *Developing World Bioethics* 10: 42–48. http://doi.org/10.1111/j.1471-8847.2009.00255.x.

Bird-David, Nurit. 1993. Tribal Metaphorization of Human–Nature Relatedness: A Comparative Analysis. In *Environmentalism: The View from Anthropology*, ed. D. K. Milton, 112–125. New York: Routledge.

Bird-David, Nurit. 1999. "Animism" Revisited: Personhood, Environment, and Relational Epistemology. *Current Anthropology* 40 (S1): S67–S79. http://www.jstor.org/stable/10.1086/200061.

Bird-David, Nurit. 2017. *Us, Relatives: Scaling and Plural Life in a Forager World*. Berkeley, CA: University of California Press.

Bird-David, Nurit. 2018. Size Matters! The Scalability of Modern Hunter-Gatherer Animism. *Quaternary International* 464 (A): 305–314. https://doi.org/10.1016/j.quaint.2017.06.035.

Bishop, Paul. 2018. *Ludwig Klages and the Philosophy of Life: A Vitalist Toolkit*. New York: Routledge.

Bodunrin, P. O. 1981. The Question of African Philosophy. *Philosophy* 56: 161–179. http://doi.org/10.1017/s0031819100050014

Bonjour, Laurence. 2004. In Search of Direct Realism. *Philosophy and Phenomenological Research* 69: 349–367. http://doi.org/10.1111/j.1933-1592.2004.tb00398.x.

Bouissac, Paul. 1989. What Is a Human? Ecological Semiotics and the New Animism. *Semiotica* 77 (4): 497–516. https://doi.org/10.1086/200061.

Brandt, Richard. 1955a. The Definition of an Ideal Observer Theory in Ethics. *Philosophy and Phenomenological Research* 15 (3): 407–413. http://doi.org/10.2307/2103510.

Brandt, Richard. 1955b. Some Comments on Professor Firth's Reply to My The Definition of an 'Ideal Observer' Theory in Ethics. *Philosophy and Phenomenological Research* 15 (3): 422–423. http://doi.org/10.2307/2104223.

Bujo, Bénézet. 2005. Differentiations in African Ethics. In *The Blackwell Companion to Religious Ethics*, ed. William Schweiker, 423–437. Malden, MA: Blackwell.

Bujo, Bénézet. 1997. *The Ethical Dimension of Community*. Trans. Cecilia Namulondo Nganda. Nairobi: Paulines Publications.

Bujo, Bénézet. 2001. *Foundations of an African Ethic: Beyond the Universal Claims of Western Morality*. Trans. Brian McNeil. New York: Crossroad Publishers.

Burley, Mikel. 2023. New Animism as Cultural Critique? In *Animism and Philosophy of Religion*, ed. Tiddy Smith, 123–151. Cham, Switzerland: Palgrave Macmillan.

BIBLIOGRAPHY 223

Calvo, Paco. 2016. The Philosophy of Plant Neurobiology: A Manifesto. *Synthese* 193 (5): 1323–1343. http://doi.org/10.1007/s11229-016-1040-1.

Capper, Daniel S. 2016. Animism among Western Buddhists. *Contemporary Buddhism* 17 (1): 30–48. http://doi.org/10.1080/14639947.2016.1189130.

Carson, Thomas L. 1989. Could Ideal Observers Disagree: A Reply to Taliaferro. *Philosophy and Phenomenological Research* 50 (1):115–124. https://doi.org/10.2307/2108112

Carson, Thomas L. 2010. *Lying and Deception: Theory and Practise.* Oxford: Oxford University Press.

Chachage, C. S. L. 1994. Discourse on Development among African Philosophers. In *African Perspectives on Development*, eds. Ulf Himmelstrand, Kabiru Kinyanjui, and Edward Mburugu, 51–60. Tanzania: Mkuki na Nyota.

Chalmers, David. 1995. Facing Up to the Problem of Consciousness. *Journal of Consciousness Studies* 2 (3): 200–219. https://doi.org/10.1093/acprof:oso/9780195311105.003.0001.

Chalmers, David. 2015. Panpsychism and Panprotopsychism. In *Consciousness in the Physical World: Perspectives on Russellian Monism*, eds. Torin Alter and Yujin Nagasawa, 246–276. New York: Oxford University Press.

Chemhuru, Munamato. 2014. The Ethical Import in African Metaphysics: A Critical Discourse in Shona Environmental Ethics. In *Ontologized Ethics: New Essays in African Meta-Ethics*, eds. Elvis Imafidon and John Ayotunde Isola Bewaji, 73–88. Lanham, MD: Lexington Books.

Christensen, David. 1994. Conservatism in Epistemology. *Noûs* 28: 69–89. https://doi.org/10.2307/2215920.

Clifton, Chas, and Graham Harvey, eds. 2004. *The Paganism Reader.* New York: Routledge.

Cornelli, Evaristi Magoti. 2022. The Origin of Tempel's *Bantu Philosophy*. In *Beyond Bantu Philosophy: Contextualizing Placide Tempels's Initiative in African Thought*, eds. Frans Dokman and Evaristi Magoti Cornelli, 7–25. New York: Routledge.

Davies, Owen. 2011. *Paganism: A Very Short Introduction.* Oxford: Oxford University Press.

Delgado Rosa, Frederico. 2023. Edward Tylor's Animism and Its Intellectual Aftermath. In *Animism and Philosophy of Religion*, ed. Tiddy Smith, 63–93. Cham, Switzerland: Palgrave Macmillan.

Diagne, Souleymane Bachir. 2011. *African Art as Philosophy: Senghor, Bergson, and the Idea of Negritude.* Trans. Chike Jeffers. New York: Seagull Books.

Dokman, Frans, and Evaristi Magoti Cornelli, eds. 2022. *Beyond Bantu Philosophy: Contextualizing Placide Tempels's Initiative in African Thought.* New York: Routledge.

Dowling, Dolina, and Sipho Seepe. 2003. Towards a Responsive Curriculum. In *A Tale of Three Countries: Social Sciences Curriculum Transformations in Southern Africa*, eds. Piet Naude and Nico Colete, 41–53. Lansdowne: Juta and Co.

Dzobo, Noah. 1992. Values in a Changing Society: Man, Ancestors, and God. In *Person and Community; Ghanaian Philosophical Studies, I*, eds. Kwasi Wiredu and Kwame Gyekye, 223–240. Washington, DC: Council for Research in Values and Philosophy.

Ebo, Socrates, and Yimini Shadrack George. 2022. A Critical Take on the Debate on African Philosophy. *Social Science and Humanities Journal* 6 (03): 2594–2604. https://sshjournal.com/index.php/sshj/article/view/788/299.

Ehiakhamen, Justina O. 2014. Beyond Culpability: Approaching Male Impotency through Legitimated Adultery in Esan Metaphysics. In *Ontologized Ethics: New Essays in African Meta-Ethics*, eds. Elvis Imafidon and John Ayotunde Isola Bewaji, 97–106. Lanham, MD: Lexington Books.

Etieyibo, Edwin. 2017a. Anthropocentrism, African Metaphysical Worldview, and Animal Practices: A Reply to Kai Horsthemke. *Journal of Animal Ethics* 7 (2): 145–162. http://doi.org/10.5406/janimalethics.7.2.0145.

Etieyibo, Edwin. 2017b. Ubuntu, Cosmopolitanism, and Distribution of Natural Resources. *Philosophical Papers* 46 (1): 139–162. http://doi.org/10.1080/05568641.2017.1295616.

224 BIBLIOGRAPHY

Etieyibo, Edwin. 2022. Beyond Placide Tempels' *Bantu Philosophy* and in Defence of the Philosophical Viability of Ethnophilosophy. In *Ethnophilosophy and the Search for the Wellspring of African Philosophy*, ed. Ada Agada, 87–103. Switzerland: Springer.

Etieyibo, Edwin, and Polycarp Ikuenobe, eds. 2020. *Menkiti on Community and Becoming a Person*. Lanham, MD: Lexington Books.

Evans-Pritchard, E. E. 1965. *Theories of Primitive Religion*. London: Oxford University Press.

Eze, Michael, and Thaddeus Metz. 2016. Emergent Issues in African Philosophy: A Dialogue with Kwasi Wiredu. *Philosophia Africana* 17: 73–86. http://doi.org/10.5840/philafricana2 015/20161728.

Fabian, Johannes. 1969. Charisma and Cultural Change: The Case of the Jamaa Movement in Katanga (Congo Republic). *Comparative Studies in Society and History* 11 (2): 155–173. https://www.jstor.org/stable/i209265.

Feldman, Richard. 2000. The Ethics of Belief. *Philosophy and Phenomenological Research* 60: 667–695. http://doi.org/10.2307/2653823.

Firth, Roderick. 1952. Ethical Absolutism and the Ideal Observer. *Philosophy and Phenomenological Research* 12 (3):317–345. http://doi.org/10.2307/2103988.

Firth, Roderick. 1955. Reply to Professor Brandt's the Definition of an Ideal Observer Theory in Ethics. *Philosophy and Phenomenological Research* 15 (3): 414–421. http://doi.org/ 10.2307/2103511.

Firth, Roderick. 1978. Comment on Professor Postow's Paper: Ethical Relativism and the Ideal Observer. *Philosophy and Phenomenological Research* 39 (1):122–123. http://doi.org/ 10.2307/2107035.

Fliksuch, Katrin. 2016. The Arc of Personhood: Menkiti and Kant on Becoming and Being a Person. *Journal of the American Philosophical Association* 2 (3): 437–455. http://doi.org/ 10.1017/apa.2016.26.

Fricker, Miranda. 2007. *Epistemic Injustice: Power and the Ethics of Knowing*. Oxford: Oxford University Press.

Friedman, Jane. 2018. Junk Beliefs and Interest-Driven Epistemology. *Philosophy and Phenomenological Research* 97:568–583. http://doi.org/10.1111/phpr.12381.

Gbadegesin, Segun. 1991. *African Philosophy: Traditional Yoruba Philosophy and Contemporary African Realities*. American University Studies 5.5. New York: Peter Lang.

Gewirth, Alan. 1982. *Human Rights: Essays on Justification and Applications*. Chicago: The University of Chicago Press.

Giddy, Patrick. 2012. The Ideal of African Scholarship and Its Implications for Introductory Philosophy: The Example of Placide Tempels. *South African Journal of Philosophy* 31 (2): 504–516. http://doi.org/10.1080/02580136.2012.10751790.

Goff, Philip. 2015. Against Constitutive Panpsychism. In *Consciousness in the Physical World: Perspectives on Russellian Monism*, eds. Torin Alter and Yujin Nagasawa, 370–400. New York: Oxford University Press.

Goff, Philip. 2017. *Consciousness and Fundamental Reality*. New York: Oxford University Press.

Goff, Philip. 2019. Did the Universe Design Itself? *International Journal for the Philosophy of Religion* 85: 99–12. http://doi.org/10.1007/s11153-018-9692-z.

Goff, Philip. 2023. *Why? The Purpose of the Universe*. New York: Oxford University Press.

Goff, Philip, William Seager, and Sean Allen-Hermanson. 2022. Panpsychism. In *The Stanford Encyclopedia of Philosophy*, ed. Edward N. Zalta. Standford, CA: Stanford University.

Goodin, Robert E. 1995. *Utilitarianism as a Public Philosophy*. Cambridge: Cambridge University Press.

Green, Mark A. 2019. *Atheopaganism: An Earth-honoring Path Rooted in Science*. Green Dragon Press.

Gyekye, Kwame. 1992. Person and Community in African Thought. In *Person and Community: Ghanaian Philosophical Studies*, eds., Kwasi Wiredu and Kwame Gyekye, 1, 101–122. Washington, DC: Council for Research in Values and Philosophy.

BIBLIOGRAPHY 225

Gyekye, Kwame. 1995. *An Essay on African Philosophical Thought: The Akan Conceptual Scheme.* Philadelphia: Temple University Press.

Gyekye, Kwame. 1997. *Tradition and Modernity: Philosophical Reflections on the African Experience.* New York: Oxford University Press.

Gyekye, Kwame. 1999. The Concept of a Person. In *Philosophy and Choice,* ed. Kit R. Christensen, 215–225. Mountain View, CA: Mayfield Publishing Company.

Gyekye, Kwame. 2004. *Beyond Cultures: Ghanaian Philosophical Studies, III.* Washington, DC: The Council for Research in Values and Philosophy.

Hallen, Barry. 2006. *African Philosophy: The Analytic Approach.* Trenton, NJ: Africa World Press.

Hamminga, Bert. 2005. Epistemology from the African Point of View. In *Knowledge Cultures: Comparative Western and African Epistemology,* ed. Bert Hamminga, 57–84. Amsterdam: Rodopi.

Harding, Sandra. 1998. The Curious Coincidence of Feminine and African Moralities. In *African Philosophy: An Anthology,* ed. E. C. Eze, 360–372. Malden, MA: Wiley-Blackwell.

Harvey, Graham. 2005. *Animism: Respecting the Living World.* London: Hurst.

Harvey, Graham. 2006. Animals, Animists, and Academics. *Zygon* 41 (1): 9–19. http://doi.org/10.1111/j.1467-9744.2006.00723.x.

Harvey, Graham. 2010. Animism Rather than Shamanism: New Approaches to What Shamans Do (for Other Animists). In *Spirit Possession and Trance: New Interdisciplinary Perspectives,* eds. Bettins E. Schmidt and Lucy Huskinson, 16–30. London and New York: Continuum.

Harvey, Graham, ed. 2013. *The Handbook of Contemporary Animism.* New York: Acumen.

Harvey, Graham. 2017. *Animism: Respecting the Living World,* 2nd ed. London: Hurst.

Horsthemke, Kai. 2015. *Animals and African Ethics.* Cham, Switzerland: Palgrave Macmillan.

Hountondji, Paulin J. 1996. *African Philosophy: Myth and Reality.* Trans. Henri Evans. Bloomington and Indianapolis: Indiana University Press.

Hountondji, Paulin J. 2018. How African Is Philosophy in Africa? *Filosofia Theoretica* 7 (3): 9–18. http://doi.org/10.1007/978-3-030-70436-0_2.

Huemer, Michael. 2007. Compassionate Phenomenal Conservatism. *Philosophy and Phenomenological Research* 74 (1): 30–55. http://doi.org/10.1111/j.1933-1592.2007.00002.x.

Huemer, Michael. 2008. *Ethical Intuitionism.* Cham, Switzerland: Palgrave Macmillan.

Hurka, Thomas. 1993. *Perfectionism.* New York: Oxford University Press.

Hursthouse, Rosalind. 1991. Virtue Theory and Abortion. *Philosophy & Public Affairs* 20 (3): 223–246. https://www.jstor.org/stable/2265432

Ikuenobe, Polycarp. 2006. *Philosophical Perspectives on Communalism and Morality in African Traditions.* Lanham, MD: Lexington Books.

Ikuenobe, Polycarp. 2015. Relational Autonomy, Personhood, and African Traditions. *Philosophy East and West* 65 (4): 1005–1029. http://doi.org/10.1353/pew.2015.0101.

Imafidon, Elvis. 2014a. On the Ontological Foundation of a Social Ethics in African Traditions. In *Ontologized Ethics: New Essays in African Meta-Ethics,* eds. Elvis Imafidon and John Ayotunde Isola Bewaji, 36–54. Lanham, MD: Lexington Books.

Imafidon, Elvis. 2014b. Life's Origin in Bioethics: Implications of Three Ontological Perspectives: Judeo-Christianity, Western Secularism, and the African Worldview. In *Ontologized Ethics: New Essays in African Meta-Ethics,* eds. Elvis Imafidon and John Ayotunde Isola Bewaji, 133–149. Lanham, MD: Lexington Books.

Imafidon, Elvis, Benard Matolino, Lucky Uchenna Ogbonnaya, Ada Agada, Aribirah David Attoe, Fainos Mangena, and Edwin Etieyibo. 2019. Are We Finished with the Ethnophilosophy Debate? A Multi-Perspective Conversation. *Filosofia Theoretica* 8 (2): 111–138. http://doi.org/10.4314/ft.v8i2.9.

Imafidon, Elvis, and John Aytunde Isola Bewaji, eds. 2013. *Ontologized Ethics: New Essays in African Meta-Ethics.* Lanham, MD: Lexington Books.

Ingold, Tim. 2000. *The Perception of the Environment.* New York: Routledge.

226 BIBLIOGRAPHY

Iroegbu, Pantaleon. 2005a. Beginning, Purpose and End of Life. In *Kpim of Morality Ethics*, eds. Pantaleon Iroegbu and Anthony Echekwube, 440–445. Ibadan: Heinemann Educational Books.

Iroegbu, Pantaleon. 2005b. Right to Life and the Means to Life: Human Dignity. In *Kpim of Morality Ethics*, eds. Pantaleon Iroegbu and Anthony Echekwube, 446–449. Ibadan: Heinemann Educational Books.

Iroegbu, Pantaleon. 2005c. Do All Persons Have a Right to Life? In *Kpim of Morality Ethics*, eds. Pantaleon Iroegbu and Anthony Echekwube, 78–83. Ibadan: Heinemann Educational Books.

Jahn, Janheinz. 1961. *Muntu: An Outline of Neo-African Culture*. Trans. Marjorie Greene. London: Faber and Faber.

Janz, Bruce B. 2022. *African Philosophy and Enactivist Cognition*. London: Bloomsbury.

Kagan, Shelly. 1998. *Normative Ethics*. Boulder, CO: Westview.

Kant, Immanuel. 1798. *The Conflict of the Faculties*. Trans. Mary J. Gregor and Robert Anchor. In *Religion and Rational Theology, Immanuel Kant*, eds. Allen W. Wood and George Di Giovanni, 233–327. Cambridge: Cambridge University Press.

Kant, Immanuel. 1793. *Religion within the Boundaries of Mere Reason: and Other Writings*. Trans. and ed. Allen W. Wood and George di Giovanni, with introduction by Robert Merrihew Adams. Cambridge: Cambridge University Press, 1998.

Kanu, Ikechukwu Anthony. 2013. Trends in African Philosophy: A Case for Eclectism. *Filosofia Theoretica* 2 (1): 275–288.

Kanu, Ikechukwu Anthony. 2018. A Review of 'Philosophie Bantou' by Placide Templs. *NASARA Journal of Philosophy* 3 (1): 194–201.

Kamm, Frances Myrna, ed. 2015. *The Trolley Problem Mysteries*. New York: Oxford University Press.

Kasenene, Peter. 1994. Ethics in African Theology. In *Doing Ethics in Context: South African Perspectives*, eds. Charles Villa-Vicencio and John de Gruchy, 138–147. Cape Town, South Africa: David Philip.

Kasenene, Peter. 1998. *Religious Ethics in Africa*. Kampala, Uganda: Fountain Publishers Ltd.

Kawall, Jason. 2006. On the Moral Epistemology of Ideal Observer Theories. *Ethical Theory and Moral Practice* 9 (3): 359–374. http://doi.org/10.1007/s10677-006-9016-8.

Kehinde, Elizabeth Oluwafunmilayo. 2014. A Critical Analysis of Eldership-Based Ethics in African (Yoruba) Thought. In *Ontologized Ethics: New Essays in African Meta-Ethics*, eds. Elvis Imafidon and John Ayotunde Isola Bewaji, 151–162. Lanham, MD: Lexington Books.

Keller, Simon. 2009. Welfarism. *Philosophy Compass* 4 (1): 82–95. http://doi.org/10.1111/j.1747-9991.2008.00196.x.

Khoza, Reuel. 2006. *Let Africa Lead: African Transformational Leadership for 21st Century Business*. Johannesburg: Vezubuntu.

Kitcher, Philip. 1990. The Division of Cognitive Labor. *Journal of Philosophy* 87: 5–22. http://doi.org/10.2307/2026796.

Klages, Ludwig. 2013. *The Biocentric Worldview*. Budapest, Hungary: Arktos Media Ltd.

Korsgaard, Christine M. 1983. Two Distinctions in Goodness. *Philosophical Review* 92 (2):169–195.

Kraft, Siv Ellen. 2010. The Making of a Sacred Mountain: Meanings of 'Nature' and 'Sacredness' in Sápmi and Northern Norway. *Religion: An International Journal* 40 (1): 53–61. http://doi.org/10.1016/j.religion.2009.08.011.

Kraft, Siv Ellen. 2015. Sámi Neo-Shamanism in Norway: Colonial Grounds, Ethnic Revival and Pagan Pathways. In *Contemporary Pagan and Native Faith Movements in Europe: Colonialist and Nationalist Impulses*, ed. Kathryn Rountree, 25–42. Oxford, New York: Berghahn Books.

LenkaBula, Puleng. 2008. Beyond Anthropocentricity—Botho/Ubuntu and the Quest for Economic and Ecological Justice in Africa. *Religion and Theology* 15: 375–394. http://doi.org/10.1163/157430108X376591.

Lougheed, Kirk. 2020. *The Epistemic Benefits of Disagreement*. Switzerland: Springer.

BIBLIOGRAPHY 227

Lougheed, Kirk. 2022a. *Ubuntu and Western Monotheism: An Axiological Investigation.* New York: Routledge.

Lougheed, Kirk. 2022b. *African Communitarianism and the Misanthropic Argument for Anti-Natalism.* Cham, Switzerland: Palgrave Macmillan.

Lougheed, Kirk. 2022c. The Epistemic Benefits of Diversifying the Philosophy of Religion. *European Journal for Philosophy of Religion* 14 (1): 77–94. http://doi.org/10.24204/ejpr.2022.3396.

Lougheed, Kirk. 2024. *A Relational Theory of the Atonement: African Contributions to Western Philosophical Theology.* New York: Routledge.

Lougheed, Kirk. *Unfriendly Cases for Metz's Moral Relational Theory.* Social Theory and Practice. Forthcoming.

Lougheed, Kirk, Motsamai Molefe and Thaddeus Metz. 2024. *African Philosophy of Religion and Western Monotheism.* Cambridge: Cambridge University Press.

Lucas, Jonathan Olumide. 1970. *Religions in West Africa and Ancient Egypt.* Lagos: The Nigerian National Press.

Lupa. 2021. *Nature Spirituality from the Ground Up: Connect with Nature Spirits in Your Ecosystem.* Amazon Publishing. ISBN-13 9798502263894.

Magesa, Laurenti. 1997. *African Religion: The Moral Traditions of Abundant Life.* Maryknoll, NY: Orbis Books.

Maher, Chauncey. 2017. *Plant Minds: A Philosophical Defence.* New York: Routledge.

Mahon, James Edwin. 2009. The Truth about Kant on Lies. In *The Philosophy of Deception,* ed. Clancy W. Martin, 201–224. Oxford: Oxford University Press.

Mangena, Fainos. 2014. Ethno-philosophy Is Rational: A Reply to Two Famous Critics. *Thought and Practice: A Journal of the Philosophical Association of Kenya* 6 (2): 23–38. http://doi.org/http://dx.doi.org/10.4314/tp.v6i2.3.

Masolo, D. A. 1994. *African Philosophy in Search of Identity.* Bloomington: Indiana University Press.

Matolino, Bernard. 2009. Radicals Versus Moderates: A Critique of Gyekye's Moderate Communitarianism. *South African Journal of Philosophy* 28 (2): 160–170. http://doi.org/10.4314/sajpem.v28i2.46674.

Matolino, Bernard. 2011. Tempels' Philosophical Racialism. *South African Journal of Philosophy* 30 (3): 330–342. http://doi.org/10.4314/sajpem.v30i3.69579.

Matolino, Bernard. 2014. *Personhood in African Philosophy.* Pietermaritzburg, South Africa: Cluster Publications.

Matolino, Bernard. 2022. Placid Temepels's Legacy in the Bantustanisation of Philosophy in Africa. In *Beyond Bantu Philosophy: Contextualizing Placide Tempels's Initiative in African Thought,* eds. Frans Dokman and Evaristi Magoti Cornelli, 65–77. New York: Routledge.

Matolino, Bernard and Wenceslaus Kwindingwi. 2013. The End of Ubuntu. *South African Journal of Philosophy* 32 (2):197–205.

Mbiti, John. 1969. *African Religions and Philosophy.* New York: Praeger.

Mbiti, John. 1975. *Introduction to African Religion.* New York: Praeger.

Menkiti, Ifeanyi. 1984. Person and Community in African Traditional Thought. In *African Philosophy: An Introduction,* 3rd ed., ed. Richard Wright, 171–181. Lanham, MD: University Press of America.

Menkiti, Ifeanyi. 2004. On the Normative Conception of a Person. In *A Companion to African Philosophy,* ed. Kwasi Wiredu, 324–331. Oxford: Blackwell.

Menkiti, Ifeanyi. 2018. Person and Community—A Retrospective Statement. *Filosofia Theoretica* 7 (2): 162–167. http://doi.org/10.4314/ft.v7i2.10.

Metz, Thaddeus. 2007. Toward an African Moral Theory. *The Journal of Political Philosophy* 15 (3): 321–341. http://doi.org/10.1111/j.1467-9760.2007.00280.x.

Metz, Thaddeus. 2009. The Final Ends of Higher Education in Light of an African Moral Theory. *Journal of Philosophy of Education* 43: 179–201. http://doi.org/10.1111/j.1467-9752.2009.00689.x

228 BIBLIOGRAPHY

Metz, Thaddeus. 2011. Ubuntu as a Moral Theory and Human Rights in South Africa. *African Human Rights Law Journal* 11 (2): 532–559.

Metz, Thaddeus. 2012. African Conceptions of Human Dignity: Vitality and Community as the Grounds of Human Rights. *Human Rights Review* 13: 19–37. http://doi.org/10.1007/s12 142-011-0200-4.

Metz, Thaddeus. 2013a. The Western Ethic of Care or an Afro-Communitarian Ethic? Specifying the Right Relational Morality. *Journal of Global Ethics* 9 (1): 77–92. http://doi.org/10.1080/17449626.2012.756421.

Metz, Thaddeus. 2013b. *Meaning in Life: An Analytic Study*. New York: Oxford University Press.

Metz, Thaddeus. 2014. Just the Beginning for Ubuntu: Reply to Matolino and Kwindingwi. *South African Journal of Philosophy* 33 (1): 65–72.

Metz, Thaddeus. 2015. An African Egalitarianism: Bringing Community to Bear on Equality. In *The Equal Society: Essays on Equality in Theory and Practice*, ed. George Hull, 185–208. Lanham, MD: Rowman & Littlefield.

Metz, Thaddeus. 2017. An Overview of African Ethics. In *Themes, Issues and Problems in African Philosophy*, ed. Issac E. Ukpokolo, 61–75. Cham, Switzerland: Palgrave Macmillan.

Metz, Thaddeus. 2018. African Values and Capital Punishment. In *Moral Reasoning: A Text and Reader on Ethics and Contemporary Moral Issues*, ed. David R. Morrow, 372–377. Oxford University Press.

Metz, Thaddeus. 2019. Pursuing Knowledge for Its Own Sake Amidst a World of Poverty: Reconsidering Balogun on Philosophy's Relevance. *Filosofia Theoretica: Journal of African Philosophy, Culture and Religions* 8: 1–18.

Metz, Thaddeus. 2020a. African Communitarianism and Difference. In *Handbook of the African Philosophy of Difference*, ed. Elvis Imafidon, 31–51. Switzerland: Springer.

Metz, Thaddeus. 2020b. African Theories of Meaning in Life: A Critical Assessment. *South African Journal of Philosophy* 39: 113–126. http://doi.org/10.1080/02580136.2020.1770429.

Metz, Thaddeus. 2021. Recent Work in African Philosophy: Its Relevance Beyond the Continent. *Mind* 130 (518): 639–660. http://doi.org/10.1093/mind/fzaa072.

Metz, Thaddeus. 2022a. *A Relational Moral Theory: African Ethics in and beyond and the Continent*. Oxford: Oxford University Press.

Metz, Thaddeus. 2022b. Why Reconciliation Requires a Punishment but Not Forgiveness. In *Conflict and Resolution: The Ethics of Forgiveness*, eds. Paula Satne and Krisanna M. Scheiter, 265–281. Springer.

Metz, Thaddeus. 2022c. A Reconciliation Theory of State Punishment: An Alternative to Protection and Retribution. *Royal Institute of Philosophy Supplement* 91: 119–139.

Metz, Thaddeus. 2023. How African Conceptions of God Bear on Life's Meaning. *Religious Studies* 59: 340–354. http://doi.org/10.1017/s0034412522000488.

Metz, Thaddeus. A Relational Theory of Human Rights: Contributions from African Ethics. (Unpublished Manuscript).

Metz, Thaddeus & Molefe, Motsamai. 2021. Traditional African Religion as a Neglected Form of Monotheism. *The Monist* 104 (3): 393–409.

Miller, Sarah Clark. 2017. Reconsidering Dignity Relationally. *Ethics and Social Welfare* 11 (2): 108–121. http://doi.org/10.1080/17496535.2017.1318411.

Mkhize, Nhlanhla. 2008. Ubuntu and Harmony: An African Approach to Morality and Ethics. In *Persons in Community: African Ethics in a Global Culture*, ed. Ronald Nicolson, 35–44. Pietermaritzburg: University of KwaZulu-Natal Press.

Mlungwana, Yolanda. 2020. An African Approach to the Meaning of Life. *South African Journal of Philosophy* 39: 153–165. http://doi.org/10.1080/02580136.2020.1771824.

Mokgoro, Yvonne. 1998. *Ubuntu* and the Law in South Africa. *Potchefstroom Electronic Law Journal* 1: 15–26. http://doi.org/10.4314/pelj.v1i1.43567.

Molefe, Motsamai. 2015. A Rejection of Humanism in African Moral Tradition. *Theoria* 62: 59–77. http://doi.org/10.3167/th.2015.6214304.

Molefe, Motsamai. 2016a. African Ethics and Partiality. *Phronimon* 17 (1): 104–122. http://doi.org/10.25159/2413-3086/1988.

BIBLIOGRAPHY 229

Molefe, Motsamai. 2016b. Revisiting the Menkiti-Gyekye Debate: Who Is a Radical Communitarian? *Theoria: A Journal of Social and Political Theory* 63 (149): 37–54. http://doi.org/10.3167/th.2016.6314903.

Molefe, Motsamai. 2017a. Critical Comments on Afro-Communitarianism: Community versus the Individual. *Fliosofia Theoretica* 6 (1): 1–22. http://doi.org/10.4314/ft.v6i1.1.

Molefe, Motsamai. 2017b. An African Religious Ethics and the Euthyphro Problem. *Acta Academica* 49 (1): 22–38. http://doi.org/10.18820/24150479/aa49i1.2.

Molefe, Motsamai. 2018. African Metaphysics and Religious Ethics. *Filosofia Theoretica: Journal of African Philosophy, Culture, and Religions* 7 (3): 19–37. http://doi.org/10.4314/ft.v7i3.3.

Molefe, Motsamai. 2019. *An African Philosophy of Personhood, Morality, and Politics.* Cham, Switzerland: Palgrave Macmillan.

Molefe, Motsamai. 2020. *An African Ethics of Personhood and Bioethics: A Reflection on Abortion and Euthanasia.* Cham, Switzerland: Palgrave Macmillan.

Molefe, Motsamai, and Mutshidzi Maraganedzha. 2023. African Traditional Religion and Moral Philosophy. *Religious Studies* 59: 355–370. http://doi.org/10.1017/S0034412522000543.

Moore, Andrew, and Roger Crisp. 1996. Welfarism in Moral Theory. *Australasian Journal of Philosophy* 74: 598–613. http://doi.org/10.1080/00048409612347551.

Mosima, Pius. 2022. The African Debate on Tempels's *Bantu Philosophy.* In *Beyond Bantu Philosophy: Contextualizing Placide Tempels's Initiative in African Thought,* eds. Frans Dokman and Evaristi Magoti Cornelli, 81–104. New York: Routledge.

Mouw, Richard. 1990. *The God Who Commands.* Notre Dame, IN: University of Notre Dame Press.

Mulago, Vincent. 1991. Traditional African Religion and Christianity. In *African Traditional Religions in Contemporary Society,* ed. Jacob Olupona, 119–134. New York: Paragon House.

Mulgan, Tim. 2007. *Understanding Utilitarianism.* Stocksfield: Acumen.

Mungwini, Pascah. 2014. Postethnophilosophy: Discourses of Modernity and the Future of African Philosophy. *Phronimon* 15 (1): 16–31. http://doi.org/10.25159/2413-3086/2210.

Mungwini, Pascah. 2019a. The Critique of Ethnophilosophy in the Mapping and Trajectory of African Philosophy. *Filosofia Theoretica* 8 (3): 1–20. http://doi.org/10.4314/ft.v8i3.1.

Mungwini, Pascah. 2019b. *Indigenous Shona Philosophy: Reconstructive Insights.* Grahamstown, South Africa: NISC [Pty] Ltd.

Mungwini, Pascah. 2022. *Beyond Bantu Philosophy: Contextualizing Placide Tempels's Initiative in African Thought,* eds. Frans Dokman and Evaristi Magoti Cornelli, 51–64. New York: Routledge.

Murove, Munyaradzi Felix. 2007. The Shona Ethic of Ukama with Reference to the Immorality of Values. *Mankind Quarterly* 48 (2): 179–189. http://doi.org/10.46469/mq.2007.48.2.4.

Nabudere, Dani. 2006. Towards an Afrokology of Knowledge Production and African Regeneration. *International Journal of African Renaissance Studies* 1: 7–32. https://doi.org/10.1080/18186870608529704.

Nagasawa, Yujin, and Khai Wager. 2016. Panpsychism and Priority Cosmopsychism. In *Panpsychism,* eds. Godehard Brüntrup and Ludwig Jaskolla, 113–129. New York: Oxford University Press.

Ncgoya, Mvuselelo. 2015. *Ubuntu:* Toward an Emancipatory Cosmopolitanism? *International Political Sociology* 9: 248–262. http://doi.org/10.1111/ips.12095.

Ndlovu-Gatsheni, Sabelo J. 2018. *Epistemic Freedom in Africa: Deprovincialization and Decolonization.* New York: Routledge.

Nkemnkia, Martin Nkafu. 2022. *Bantu Philosophy* P. Tempels as the Expression of African Philosophy in Front of African Vitalogy. In *Beyond Bantu Philosophy: Contextualizing Placide Tempels's Initiative in African Thought,* eds. Frans Dokman and Evaristi Magoti Cornelli, 26–47. New York: Routledge.

Nkondo, Fessler Muxe. 2007. Ubuntu as Public Policy in South Africa: A Conceptual Framework. *International Journal of African Renaissance Studies* 2 (1): 88–100. http://doi.org/10.1080/18186870701384202.

230 BIBLIOGRAPHY

Nkrumah, Kwame. 1970. *Consciencism*, 2nd edn. New York: Monthly Review Press.

Nkulu-N'Sengha, Mutombo. 2022. Tempels and the 'Bumuntu Paradigm': Prolegomenon to an African Philosophy of Dialogue among Civilizations in the Twenty-first Century. In *Beyond Bantu Philosophy: Contextualizing Placide Tempels's Initiative in African Thought*, eds. Frans Dokman and Evaristi Magoti Cornelli, 105–130. New York: Routledge.

Nozick, Robert. 1974. *Anarchy, State, and Utopia*. New York: Basic Books.

Nussbaum, Martha. 2011. *Creating Capabilities*. Cambridge, MA: Harvard University Press.

Nwakaeze-Ogugua, Ikechukwu. 2006. The Tragedy of Pseudo-democracy and Social Disorder in Contemporary Africa: Any Philosophical Rescue? In *Philosophy and Africa*, ed. Ike Odimedgwu. Amawbia: Lumos.

Nwala, T. Uzodinma. 1985. *Igbo Philosophy*. Lagos, Nigeria: Lantern Books.

Nze, Chukwuemeka. 2007. Aspects of African Communalism. In *Perspectives on African Communalism*, ed. Ike Odimegwu, 588–604. Victoria: Trafford Publishing.

Ochieng-Odhiambo, Frederick. 2021. Cesaire's Contribution to African Philosophy. *Filosofia Theoretica* 10 (1): 35–54. http://doi.org/10.4314/ft.v10i1.3.

Ogbujah, Columbus. 2007. The Individual in African Communalism. In *Perspectives on African Communalism*, ed. Ike Odimegwu, 127–141. Victoria: Trafford Publishing.

Ogugua, Ikechukwu. 2007. The Metaphysical Basis of African Communalism. In *Perspectives on African Communalism*, ed. Ike Odimegwu, 24–33. Victoria: Trafford Publishing.

Okafor, Fidelis. 1997. African Philosophy in Comparison with Western Philosophy. *The Journal of Value Inquiry* 31: 251–267. http://doi.org/10.1023/a:1004259125528.

Okafor, Stephen O. 1982. Bantu Philosophy: Placide Tempels Revisited. *Journal of Religion in Africa* 13 (2): 83–100. https://doi.org/10.2307/1581204.

Okeja, Uchenna. 2019. On Kant's Duty of State Entrance. *Philosophy and Public Issues* 9 (3): 83–108.

Oladipo, Olusegun. 1992. *The Idea of African Philosophy: A Critical Study of the Major Orientations in Contemporary African Philosophy*. Ibadan, Nigeria: Molecular Publications.

Oladipo, Olusegun. 2004. Religion in African Culture: Some Conceptual Issues. In *A Companion to African Political Philosophy*, ed. Kwasi Wiredu, 356–363. Oxford: Blackwell Publishing Ltd.

Onah, Godfrey. 2012. The Meaning of Peace in African Traditional Religion and Culture. *The Monist* 104: 393–409. http://beeshadireed.blogspot.com/2012/08/the-meaning-of-peace-in-african.html.

Oppy, Graham. 2023. Animism: Its Scope and Limits. In *Animism and Philosophy of Religion*, ed. Tiddy Smith, 199–226. Cham, Switzerland: Palgrave Macmillan.

Oruka, Odera H. 1975. The Fundamental Principles in the Question of 'African Philosophy'. *Second Order: An African Journal of Philosophy* 4 (1): 44–55. https://philarchive.org/archive/ODUOOI.

Oruka, Odera H. 1983. Sagacity in African Philosophy. *The International Philosophical Quarterly* 23 (4): 383–393. http://doi.org/10.5840/ipq198323448.

Oruka, Odera H. 1990a. *Sage Philosophy: Indigenous Thinkers and Modern Debate on African Philosophy*. Nairobi: African Centre for Technological Studies.

Oruka, Odera H. 1990b. *Trends in Contemporary African Philosophy*. Nairobi: Shirikon.

Osha, S. 2011. *Postethnophilosophy*. Value Inquiry Book Series, 227. Amsterdam, the Netherlands: Editions Rodopi.

Owakah, Francis E. A. 2012. Race Ideology and the Conceptualization of Philosophy: The Story of Philosophy in African from Placide Tempels to Odera Oruka. *Thought and Practice: A Journal of the Philosophical Association of Kenya* 4 (2): 147–168.

Oyowe, Oritsegbubemi Anthony. 2013. Personhood and Social Power in African Thought. *Alternation* 20: 203–228.

Oyowe, Oritsegbubemi Anthony. 2014. An African Conception of Human Rights? Comments on the Challenges of Relativism. *Human Rights Review* 15 (3): 329–347. http://doi.org/10.1007/s12142-013-0302-2.

BIBLIOGRAPHY 231

Oyowe, Oritsegbubemi Anthony. 2022. *Menkiti's Moral Man*. Lanham, MD: Rowman & Littlefield.

Oyowe, Oritsegbubemi, and Yurkivska, Olga. 2014. Can a Communitarian Concept of African Personhood Be Both Relational and Gender-Neutral? *South African Journal of Philosophy* 33: 85–99. http://doi.org/10.1080/02580136.2014.892682.

Parfit, Derek. 1986. *Reasons and Persons*. Oxford: Oxford University Press.

Paris, Peter J. 1995. *The Spirituality of African Peoples: The Search for a Common Moral Discourse*. Minneopolis: Augsburg Fortress.

Penner, Myron A. 2015. Personal Anti-Theism and the Meaningful Life Argument. *Faith and Philosophy* 32: 325–337. http://doi.org/10.5840/faithphil201563039.

Popper, Karl. 2002. *The Logic of Scientific Discovery*. New York: Routledge.

Postow, B. C. 1978. Ethical Relativism and the Ideal Observer. *Philosophy and Phenomenological Research* 39 (1): 120–121. http://doi.org/10.2307/2107034.

Price, Richard. 1758. A Review of the Principle Questions in Morals. In *The British Moralists 1650–1800, II*, ed. D. D. Raphael, 131–198. Oxford: Clarendon Press, 1969.

Putnam, Hilary. 1992. *Renewing Philosophy*. Cambridge, MA: Harvard University Press.

p'Bitek, Okot. 1971. *African Religions in Western Scholarship*. Nairobi: Kenya Literature Bureau.

Quinn, Philip L. 1978. *Divine Commands and Moral Requirements*. Oxford: Clarendon Press.

Quinn, Philip L. 1979. Divine Command Ethics: A Causal Theory. In *Divine Command Morality: Historical and Contemporary Readings*, ed. Janine Idziak, 305–325. New York: Edwin Mellen Press.

Quinn, Philip L. 1992. The Primacy of God's Will in Christian Ethics. *Philosophical Perspectives* 6: 493–513. http://doi.org/10.2307/2214258.

Rakotsoane, Francis, and Anton van Niekerk. 2017. Human Life Invaluableness: An Emerging African Bioethical Principle. *South African Journal of Philosophy* 36: 252–262. http://doi.org/10.1080/02580136.2016.1223983.

Ramose, Mogobe B. 1999. *African Philosophy through Ubuntu*. Harare, Zimbabwe: Mond Books.

Ramose, Mogobe B. 2001. An African Perspective on Justice and Race. *Polylog* 3. http://them.polylog.org/3/frm-en.htm.

Ramose, Mogobe B. 2003a. The Philosophy of Ubuntu and Ubuntu as a Philosophy. In *Philosophy from Africa: A Text with Readings*, 2nd Edition, eds. P. H. Coetzee and A. P. J. Roux, 230–237. London, UK: Oxford University Press.

Ramose, Mogobe B. 2003b. The Ethics of Ubuntu. In *The African Philosophy Reader,* 2nd edn., eds. P. H. Coetzee and A. P. Roux, 379–387. New York: Routledge.

Ramose, Mogobe B. 2007. But Hans Kelsen Was Not Born in Africa. *South African Journal of Philosophy* 26: 347–355.

Ramose, Mogobe B. 2015. Ecology through Ubuntu. In *Environmental Values,* ed. Roman Meinhold, 69–76. Bangkok: Konrad-Adenauer-Stiftunge. V. & Guna Chakra Research Center.

Ramose, Mogobe B. 2020. The Philosophy of Ubuntu and Ubuntu as a Philosophy. In *Philosophy from Africa*, 2nd edn., eds. P. H. Coetzee and A. P. J. Roux, 230–238. Oxford: Oxford University Press.

Rosa, Frederico Delgado. 2023. Edward Tylor's Animism and Its Intellectual Aftermath. In *Animism and Philosophy of Religion,* ed. Tiddy Smith, 63–93 Cham, Switzerland: Palgrave Macmillan.

Ross, W. D. 1927. The Basis of Objective Judgements in Ethics. *International Journal of Ethics* 37: 113–127.

Ross, W. D. 1930. *The Right and the Good*, ed. P. Stratton-Lake. Oxford: Clarendon Press, 2002.

Ross, W. D. 1939. *The Foundations of Ethics*. Oxford: Clarendon Press.

Rountree, Kathryn. 2012. Neo-Paganism, Animism and Kinship with Nature. *Journal of Contemporary Religion* 27 (2): 305–320. https://doi.org/10.1080/13537903.2012.675746.

Rountree, Kathryn. 2023. Towards a Cosmopolitan Animism. In *Animism and Philosophy of Religion,* ed. Tiddy Smith, 341–364. Cham, Switzerland: Palgrave Macmillan.

232 BIBLIOGRAPHY

Samuel, Olusegun and Ademola Fayemi. 2020. A Critique of Thaddeus Metz's Modal Relational Account of Moral Status. *Theoria* 67: 28–44.

Seepe, Sipho, ed. 1998. *Black Perspective(s) on Tertiary Institutional Transformation*. Florida Hills, South Africa: Vivlia Publishers and the University of Venda.

Sen, Amartya. 1985. *Commodities and Capabilities*. Amsterdam: Elsevier Science Publishers.

Sidgwick, Henry. 1874. *The Methods of Ethics*, 7th ed. London: Palgrave Macmillan, 1967.

Singer, Peter. 1972. Famine, Affluence, and Morality. *Philosophy and Public Affairs* 1 (3): 229–243. http://www.jstor.org/stable/2265052?origin=JSTOR-pdf.

Sindima, Henry. 1989. Community of Life. *The Ecumenical Review* 41: 537–551. http://doi.org/10.1111/j.1758-6623.1989.tb02610.x.

Sogolo, G. S. 1993. *Foundations of African Philosophy: A Definitive Analysis of Conceptual Issues in African Thought*. Ibadan, Nigeria: Ibadan University Press.

Steinhart, Eric. 2023. Scientific Animism. In *Animism and Philosophy of Religion*, ed. Tiddy Smith, 227–255. Cham, Switzerland: Palgrave Macmillan.

Storm, Willem. 1993. Bantoe-Filosofie vs. Bantu Philosophy. *Quest* 7 (2): 67–75.

Stratton-Lake, Philip. 2020. Intuitionism in Ethics. In *The Stanford Encyclopedia of Philosophy*, ed. Edward N. Zalta. Stanford, CA: The Metaphysics Research Lab.

Sussman, David. 2009. On the Supposed Duty of Truthfulness: Kant on Lying in Self-Defense. In *The Philosophy of Deception*, ed. Clancy W. Martin, 225–243. Oxford: Oxford University Press.

Sumner, L. W. 1996. *Welfare, Happiness and Ethics*. Oxford: Oxford University Press.

Taiwo, Olufemi. 2016. Against African Communalism. *Journal of French and Francophone Philosophy* 24 (1): 81–100. http://doi.org/10.5195/jffp.2016.759.

Taliaferro, Charles. 1988. Relativisng the Ideal Observer. *Philosophy and Phenomenological Research* 49 (1): 123–138. http://doi.org/10.2307/2107995.

Tangwa, Godfrey. 2010. *Elements of African Bioethics in a Western Frame*. Bameda, Cameroon: Langaa Research and Publishing CIG.

Tempels, Placide. 1959. *Bantu Philosophy*, 2nd edn. Trans. Colin King. Paris: Présence Africaine.

Towa, Marcien. 1971a. *Leopold Sedar Senghor: négritude ou servitude*. Lyon, France: Clé.

Towa, Marcien. 1971b. *Essai sur la problématique philosophique dans l'Afrique actuelle*. Lyon, France: Clé.

Tutu, Desmond. 1999. *No Future without Forgiveness*. New York: Random House.

Tylor, Edward B. 1871. *Primitive Culture: Researches into the Development of Mythology, Philosophy, Religion, Art, and Custom*, 1. London: John Murray.

Tylor, Edward B. 1873. *Primitive Culture: Researches into the Development of Mythology, Philosophy, Religion, Language, Art, and Custom*, 2. London: John Murray.

Ubah, C. N. 1982. The Supreme Being, Divinities and Ancestors in Igbo Traditional Religion: Evidence from Otanchara and Otanzu. *Africa* 52 (2): 90–105. http://doi.org/10.2307/1159143.

Uchendu, V. C. 1965. *The Igbo of Southern Nigeria*. New York and London: Holt, Rinehart and Winston.

Uduma, Uduma Oji, and Victor Nweke. 2018. Ndubuisi: An Igbo-African Understanding of the Value of Human Life and Its Implications for the Death Penalty Question. In *The Death Penalty from an African Perspective*, eds. Fainos Mangena and Jonathan Okeke Chimakonam, 29–60. Wilmington, DE: Vernon Press.

Ukagba, George. 2005. Afroxiology: Ethical Study of African Values. In *Kpim of Morality Ethics*, eds. Pantaleon Iroegbu and Anthony Echekwube, 179–189. Ibadan, Nigeria: Heinemann Educational Books.

Unah, Jim I. 2014. Finding Common Grounds for a Dialogue between African and Chinese Ethics. In *Ontologized Ethics: New Essays in African Meta-Ethics*, eds. Elvis Imafidon and John Ayotunde Bewaji, 107–120. Lanham, MD: Lexington Books.

BIBLIOGRAPHY 233

Uzukwu, E. Elochukwu. 1982. Igbo World and Ultimate Reality and Meaning. *Ultimate Reality and Meaning* 5: 188–209. https://doi.org/10.3138/uram.5.3.188.

Vicente, Mercedes. 2020. A River with Standing: Personhood in Te Ao Māori. *PARSE* 12: 1–12. https://parsejournal.com/article/a-river-with-standing-personhood-in-te-ao-maori/.

Wainright, William J. 2005. *Religion and Morality*. Burlington, VT: Ashgate.

Wallace, Mark I. 2019. *When God Was a Bird: Christianity, Animism, and the Re-enchantment of the World*. New York: Fordham University Press.

Weidtmann, Niels. 2019. The Philosophy of Ubuntu and the Notion of Vital Force. In *Ubuntu and the Reconstitution of Community*, ed. James Ogude, 98–113. Bloomington, Indiana: Indiana University Press.

White, Ethan Doyle. 2022. *Wicca: History, Belief and Community in Modern Pagan Witchcraft*. Eastbourne, UK: Sussex Academic Press.

Wielenberg, Eirk J. 2005. *Value and Virtue in a Godless Universe*. Cambridge: Cambridge University Press.

Wielenberg, Eirk J. 2014. *Robust Ethics: Metaphysics and Epistemology of Godless Normative Realism*. Oxford: Oxford University Press.

Wielenberg, Eirk J. 2021. Three Sources of Human Dignity. In *The Inherence of Human Dignity, Volume I: Foundations of Human Dignity*, eds. B. Bussey and A. Menuge, 243–246. New York: Anthem Press.

Wijsen, Frans. 2022. Placide Tempels: An Introduction. In *Beyond Bantu Philosophy: Contextualizing Placide Tempels's Initiative in African Thought*, eds. Frans Dokman and Evaristi Magoti Cornelli, 1–4. New York: Routledge.

Willerslev, Rane. 2007. *Soul Hunters: Hunting, Animism, and Personhood among the Siberian Yukaghirs*. Berkley: University of California Press.

Williamson, Timothy. 1998. Conditionalizing on Knowledge. *British Journal for the Philosophy of Science* 49: 89–121. http://doi.org/10.1093/bjps/49.1.89.

Wiredu, Kwasi. 1980. *Philosophy and an African Culture*. Cambridge: Cambridge University Press.

Wiredu, Kwasi. 1983. The Akan Concept of Mind. *Ibadan Journal of Humanistic Studies* 3: 113–134.

Wiredu, Kwasi. 1992. Moral Foundations of an African Culture. In *Person and Community: Ghanaian Philosophical Studies*, 1, eds. K. Wiredu and K. Gyekye, 192–206. Washington, DC: The Council for Research in Values and Philosophy.

Wiredu, Kwasi. 1996. *Cultural Universals and Particulars: An African Perspective*. Bloomington and Indianapolis: Indiana University Press.

Wiredu, Kwasi. 1998. Toward Decolonizing African Philosophy and Religion. *African Studies Quarterly* 1 (4): 17–46.

Wiredu, Kwasi. 2004. Prolegomena to an African Philosophy of Education. *South African Journal of Higher Education* 18: 17–26. http://doi.org/10.4314/sajhe.v18i3.25477.

Woodard, Christopher. 2008. *Reasons, Patterns, and Cooperation*. New York: Routledge.

Woodard, Christopher. 2019. *Taking Utilitarianism Seriously*. Oxford: Oxford University Press.

Woodard, Christopher. forthcoming. Metz on the Common Good and the Relational Theory. *Social Theory & Practice*.

Index

For the benefit of digital users, indexed terms that span two pages (e.g., 52–53) may, on occasion, appear on only one of those pages.

abortion, 122, 195
Abraham's Dilemma, xiv, xvi, 170, 179–83
Adams, R., xvi, 169, 170–74, 176–77, 178, 179–84, 188–89
'African communitarianism' (also 'African Communitarian ethics'), 7–8, 13–14, 74, 90, 113–14, 201–2
African moral philosophy, xi, 8, 13–14, 61, 71–72, 116–17, 166, 220
African Traditional Religion (also ATR), 1, 6, 7–8, 9, 13–14, 43–44, 71–72, 89, 169–70, 171–72, 173, 174, 179, 183
Agada, A., 22–25, 30–31, 66–68
ancestor, 18, 38–40, 41, 44, 45–46, 84, 139, 141, 173, 174, 179
Anglo-American philosophy (also Anglo-American philosophical tradition), ix, xi, xiv, xvi, xvii, 1, 31, 100–1, 203
animism (also 'new animism', 'old animism', theory of animation) xii, 54–56, 219
anti-realism, 191, 201–2, 218
Anyanwu K.C., 37, 38–39, 40, 41, 42–44, 45, 205
Asante, M.K., 154–55

Bantu Philosophy, 17–35, 36–37
Brandt, R., 185–86, 187
Bujo, B., 1, 7–8, 37–38, 39–40, 41–45, 46, 47, 48, 49, 79, 80, 154–55, 205–6

Christianity (also Christian), 23, 25–26, 27–28, 54, 63, 64, 109–10, 171–74
consequentialism (also consequentialist), 1, 11, 64–65, 83, 93–94, 99, 104, 106, 107–8, 128–29, 220
cosmopsychism, 65–66

Darwin, C., 207–8
deception (see also lying), 21, 87–88, 91–92, 108, 109
deontological liveliness, 72–73, 76–79, 80, 82–83, 84, 85, 86, 87–88, 90, 91–92, 93, 97, 100, 104–6, 107–9, 115, 116, 135, 136, 137, 138, 145, 147, 150, 153, 156–57, 159–61, 217
dignity, 8, 22–23, 49, 50, 51, 52, 66–67, 76, 77, 78, 81, 82–83, 84, 85, 86, 87–88, 90, 91–92, 93, 100–6, 107, 109–10, 114, 116, 123, 124, 125–26, 145–47, 150–51, 153, 155–56, 158, 159–60, 211, 217
disagreement(s), 153, 171–72, 187, 197–98, 220
disharmony, 8, 144, 156, 160, 201–2
Divine Command Theory (also DCT), 11, 165, 167–77, 178–83, 185, 188–89, 200, 202–3, 217–18
duties (duty), 49, 51, 52, 74, 77–78, 91, 94, 112, 114, 115–16, 124, 131, 135–36, 156–58, 167, 168
Dzobo, N., 41, 48, 49, 205, 211

Einstein, A., 208, 209
ethnophilosophy, 32
Etieyibo, E., xi, 32, 33–34, 35, 113
Euthyphro Dilemma, xvi, 165, 174–78, 179, 180, 182–83, 217–18
excavationist philosophy, 32, 33

Firth, R., 185–88
Friedman, J., 214
friendliness, xv, 102, 141, 145–47, 149–50, 152, 154, 156–58, 159–60, 189

Goff, P., 65–67
guilty (also guilt), 82, 95, 98, 105–6
Gyekye, K., 3–4, 64–65, 67–68, 121–22, 125–29, 130–31, 137, 142, 166–67, 169

Hamminga, B., 37–38, 39, 41, 42–43, 45–46, 179, 205–6
harmony (also teleological harmony), 8, 13–14, 138–39, 140–41, 142–43, 144–46, 160, 174, 201–2, 216, 217
Horsthemke, K., 113–14
Huemer, M., xvi, 185, 190–94, 195–99, 202–3

236 INDEX

human rights, 88–89, 100, 102–4, 107, 123, 126, 128–29, 138, 144, 149–50, 160, 217
hybrid theory (also hybrid theory of liveliness), 106–10, 115–16

ideal observer theory (also ideal observer), 185–89, 202–3
identity (also personal identity), 21, 32, 122, 126, 127, 142–43, 145–46, 148, 154, 200–1
Igbo (also Igbo people, Igbo peoples, Igbo universe), 37, 38–39, 40, 43–44, 45, 48
injustice, 18, 205–6, 208
intuitionism (also ethical intuitionism), 64, 183–84, 185, 188–90, 191–93, 195–96, 197–98, 199, 200, 202–3, 217–18
Iroegbu, P., 37–38, 47, 49, 51, 142, 205–6

justice, xiii, 12, 81, 83, 91–92, 93–94, 123–24, 140, 171, 220

Kant, I. (also Kantianism, Kantians), 11, 22–23, 26, 100–1, 109–10, 116–17, 159, 180–81, 182
Kasenene, P., 1, 38, 41, 43–44, 47, 48, 49, 205–6
Kawall, J., 188–89

liveliness theory of meaning in life (also liveliness theory of meaning) xvii, 204–5, 206, 209–10, 211, 213–14, 215
living dead, 19–20, 40, 42, 44, 84, 139, 173, 174

Magesa, L., 1, 38–39, 40, 41, 48, 205–6
Maraganedzha, M., 50–52
Menkiti, I., 1, 121–26, 127–29, 130–31, 137
metaphysics (also metaphysics of life force), 3–4, 6, 37, 38–39, 61, 62, 63, 69–70, 124, 166–67, 171–72, 183, 189
Metz, T., 1, 2–4, 5, 8, 9–12, 13–14, 61–62, 64, 65, 69–70, 72, 73–74, 75, 76–83, 84, 85, 86, 87–88, 89, 91–92, 101, 104–5, 106, 113, 115, 127, 138–39, 141–49, 150–55, 156–57, 158–61, 166–70, 183, 185, 189–91, 201–2, 204–15, 217
Miller, S. C., 94
moderate communitarianism, 125–26, 166–67
Molefe, M., x, xiv, 1, 50–52, 64–65, 74–75, 101, 127, 128, 129–31, 132–33, 137, 169–70, 175–77
mood, 65–69
moral relational theory, 104–5, 138, 145–48, 150, 154, 155, 156, 158–61, 217
moral status, 47, 49–50, 52–53, 56–57, 63, 72–73, 76–77, 85, 115, 122, 145–46, 158–60
Mosima, P., 22–23, 24, 26–27, 29, 30, 31
Mungwini, P., 27, 30, 31

naturalism (also metaphysical naturalism), 1, 62, 68, 69–70, 166–67, 185, 199, 201, 202–3
Nkrumah, K., 26, 29
Nussbaum, M., 100–1, 102

Owo, 66–67

panexperientialism, 65
panprotopsychism, 65–66
panpsychism (also proto-panpsychism, panpsychist, panpsychist theory), 68–70, 216
Paris, P. J., 138–39, 140–41
paternalism, 25–26, 89, 143
perfectionist normative theory (also perfectionist theory), 29, 50, 51, 52, 112–13, 129–30
Principle of Phenomenal Conservatism (also Phenomenal Conservatism), 193, 196
Punishment, 82–83

radical communitarianism (also extreme communitarianism), 123, 127, 171–72
Ramose, M. B., 138–39, 140, 141
realism (also moral realism), 12–14, 165, 185, 196, 201–2, 218

self-regarding, 74, 131, 135–36
solidarity, 8, 39, 50, 142–43, 145–46, 148–49, 150, 151, 154, 158
Storm, W., 24, 25

Taliaferro, C., 186–87
teleological liveliness, 73, 74, 75–77, 78–79, 82, 87–88, 91, 93, 97, 98–99, 104, 105, 108–9, 112, 135–36, 147, 149–50, 152–53, 155–56
Tempels, P., 17–24, 25–31, 32, 34, 35, 36–37, 71

Ubuntu, 90, 140, 141, 142
unfriendliness, 146–47, 152, 157–58
utilitarianism (also utilitarian, Act-Utilitarianism, Rule-Utilitarianism, Motive Utilitarianism, Institutional Utilitarianism), 11, 91–92, 93–97, 98, 99, 116, 149–50, 159, 170
Uzukwu, E. E., 38, 41, 48, 205–6

welfarism, 83–84, 91–92, 93–94, 99, 104–6, 110–13, 116
Wielenberg, E. J., 115, 200–1
Wijsen, F., 23, 25–26
Woodard, C., 93–94, 104–6, 111